Modern
Educational
myths

Modern
Educational
myths

The future of democratic comprehensive education

Edited by Bob O'Hagan

**KOGAN
PAGE**

<u>YOURS TO HAVE AND TO HOLD</u>
BUT NOT TO COPY

First published in 1999

Apart from any fair dealing for the purposes of research or private study, or criticism or review, as permitted under the Copyright, Designs and Patents Act 1988, this publication may only be reproduced, stored or transmitted, in any form or by any means, with the prior permission in writing of the publishers, or in the case of reprographic reproduction in accordance with the terms and licences issued by the CLA. Enquiries concerning reproduction outside these terms should be sent to the publishers at the undermentioned address:

Kogan Page Limited
120 Pentonville Road
London N1 9JN

© Bob O'Hagan and named contributors, 1999

The right of Bob O'Hagan and named contributors to be identified as the authors of this work has been asserted by them in accordance with the Copyright, Designs and Patents Act 1988.

British Library Cataloguing in Publication Data

A CIP record for this book is available from the British Library.

ISBN 0 7494 2932 1

Typeset by Kogan Page Limited
Printed and bound in Great Britian by Biddles Ltd, Guildford and King's Lynn

Contents

v

Contributors

Michael Armstrong is Headteacher at Harwell Community Primary School, Oxford. He taught in London and then at the pioneering Countesthorpe College in Leicestershire. He is the author of *Closely Observed Children: The Diary of a Primary Classroom*, and the joint editor of *Tolstoy on Education*. He has been a member of the editorial board of *Forum: For Promoting 3-19 Comprehensive Education* since 1965 and is currently its chairperson. He is currently working on a study of children's narrative thinking.

Stephen J Ball is Professor of Sociology of Education and Director of the Centre for Public Policy Research at King's College, London. He is the managing editor of *The Journal of Education Policy* and the author of several books on education, including *Beachside Comprehensive* (1981), *Politics and Policy Making in Education* (1990), *Education Reform* (1994) and, with Hilary Radnor, *Local Authorities: Accountability and Control* (1996). He is currently researching choice of Post-16 and Higher Education and the consumption behaviours of young children.

Caroline Benn has worked in further education for 30 years, specializing in the development of access courses for mature students. A founder member of the national comprehensive campaign, she was for 25 years editor of its journal, *Comprehensive Education*, as well as being a comprehensive school parent and governor. With Professor Brian Simon, she published *Half Way There*, the first national survey of comprehensive secondary education. In 1996 with Clyde Chitty, she published *Thirty Years On*, a second survey of comprehensive education. She was a member of the Education Section of the UK's UNESCO Education Commission for several years, and is currently president of the Socialist Educational Association, the Labour Party's affiliated educational body.

Tim Brighouse is Chief Education Officer for Birmingham City Council and Joint Vice-Chair of the government's Standards Task Force. He taught in Grammar and Secondary Modern schools and spent some time in adult education before moving into administration. He worked for Monmouthshire, Buckinghamshire, the Association of County Councils, the Inner London Education Authority and, from 1978, as Chief Education Officer for Oxfordshire. Between 1989 and 1993 he was Professor of Education at Keele University. He has written and broadcast for press, radio and television and has published several books.

Clyde Chitty is Professor of Educational Studies and Head of the School of Education at Goldsmith's College, London. Having taught in London comprehensives, he was appointed Senior Vice-Principal and subsequently Principal at Earl Shilton, one of Leicestershire's newly established integrated community colleges. From 1985 he taught at the London Institute of Education before becoming Reader at the University of Birmingham. He is joint editor of the journal *Forum: For Promoting 3–19 Comprehensive Education* and has published several books on education, including *Redefining the Comprehensive Experience* (1987), *The National Curriculum: Is It Working?* (1993) and, with Caroline Benn, *Thirty Years On* (1996). His principal interests centre on the history and politics of the school curriculum and issues concerned with the implementation of whole-school curriculum policies.

Michael Fielding is a Lecturer at the University of Cambridge School of Education. His teaching career in schools included posts in two pioneer comprehensive schools – Thomas Bennett Community School, Crawley and Stantonbury Campus, Milton Keynes. After brief spells at the University of Sussex and as a Senior Adviser in Bedfordshire, he moved to Cambridge where he is a member of the Improving the Quality of Education for All (IQEA) international school improvement project. He has published articles in a range of books and journals. His present research and development work with schools includes (school) students as researchers and the development of educational alternatives to school effectiveness and school improvement.

Colin Fletcher was inaugural Professor of Educational Research at the University of Wolverhampton for five years until his semi-retirement in 1997. Before that, he was a Reader at the Cranfield Institute of Technology developing practitioner research particularly for professionals in education and the public services. He spent five years as a Senior Research Officer for Nottingham University based at the pioneering Sutton Centre, culminating in *The Challenge of Community Education* (1982) and was later Chair of Community College at the Stantonbury Campus. Other books have included *Schools On Trial* (1985) co-authored with Maxine Caron and the late Wyn Williams. In recent years, he has been closely involved in many community education initiatives. He remains engaged in adult learning and community development from the base of his Shropshire smallholding and as a partner in Catalyst Research.

Valerie Hannon has been Chief Education Officer in Derbyshire since 1994 and is a member of the National Advisory Committee on Creative and Cultural Education. She started teaching in a London comprehensive school, moving north to work for Rochdale LEA, the Equal Opportunities Commission and as a Senior Research Fellow at Sheffield University in the field of educational policy and accountability. In particular, she explored the concept of parental rights in education and the increasing use parents were making of courts and tribunals to claim their rights. She subsequently held several posts including Deputy Director of Education with Sheffield City Council. As a UK Harkness Fellow, she studied education policy and reform in the United States.

Maurice Kogan is Professor Emeritus of Government and Director of the Centre for the Evaluation of Public Policy and Practice at Brunel University where he was Dean of the Faculty of Social Sciences and Acting Vice-Chancellor. His first career was as an administrator in the Department of Education and Science where he was Secretary to the Plowden Committee. He is the author of many books and articles on education, higher education, local government, health and science policy. He edits *Higher Education Management* and is currently engaged on an international study of the impact of higher education reforms on academic values and an evaluative study of the impact of Ofsted on schools.

Bob Moon has been Professor of Education at the Open University School of Education in Milton Keynes since 1988. His prior career included teaching in Lambeth and Headships at the Stantonbury Campus and Peers School, Oxford. He has written extensively on curriculum, schooling and teacher education with particular reference to international developments in these fields and has been an adviser to the OECD, UNESCO and *World Book*. Most recently, he has directed a number of experimental programmes on the role of interactive technologies in the pre-service and in-service education and training of teachers. His most recent book, *Openings to Learning: New Models for Teacher Education*, is to be published by Routledge shortly.

Bob O'Hagan has been the inaugural Head Teacher at the innovative Hasland Hall Community School in Chesterfield since 1990, having previously developed imaginative approaches to community education at schools in Solihull, Rochdale and Leicestershire. He has contributed articles to various books and journals, and compiled *The Charnwood Papers: Fallacies In Community Education* which was published in 1991.

Ken Spours is currently a Lecturer and Research Officer at the Post-16 Education Centre, London University Institute of Education, and was previously an Inspector in Tower Hamlets. He specializes in research and development work on the reform of post-14 qualifications. In 1997, he co-edited *Dearing And Beyond*, and is soon to publish a co-authored book on New Labour's approach to post-14 education and training. His current research, for QCA, is in models for overarching advanced level certification and he hopes to be involved soon in developing a new qualifications structure to replace A levels.

Tom Wylie is Chief Executive of the National Youth Agency. He was born and educated in Belfast where he worked as a teacher and youth worker before moving to England in 1970 to work for the Scout Association and later as one of Her Majesty's Inspectors. He managed the Inspectorate's teams for youth and community work, for educational disadvantage and for school curriculum, and was responsible for the HMI Inspection that led to *Access and Achievement in Urban Education* (1993). Since joining the new National Youth Agency in 1996 he has played a major part in creating an *Agenda for a Generation: Building Effective Youth Work* (1996).

Preface

Modern Educational Myths began as a series of lectures held in 13 comprehensive schools in north-east Derbyshire during the Autumn Term 1997 and the Spring Term 1998. Planning took place in the months preceding the election of a new Labour government, or rather as we later discovered, a New Labour government. The Heads of these local authority schools, myself included, felt that the focus on school effectiveness and school improvement had tended to exclude genuine consideration of other broader educational issues. With the psychologically symbolic millennium approaching, we felt that all those concerned with and committed to comprehensive education yearned for a change from the policies of the past decade. We felt most would be hopeful that change may come soon, but that few would be confident of what direction the comprehensive movement would, or even should take.

We invited contributions from contemporary thinkers and practitioners in the field of education generally and schooling in particular to present an original paper at one of the schools. We chose speakers who we believed shared a commitment to comprehensive education and asked that their papers dissect a widely held fallacy and thereby shine a light on the renewal and future direction of comprehensive education.

Within Derbyshire, those who work in the north-east are proud of the collaborative stance their schools have steadfastly maintained in recent years despite the pressures to compete and conflict. It provided an ideal location, close to several major cities, for a target audience of school managers, teachers, student teachers, governors, officers and advisers while recognising the papers might also be of interest to parents and students (pupils).

The lectures were advertised under the umbrella title *The Chesterfield Papers: Modern Educational Fallacies*. The audiences grew as the series progressed, and feedback indicated a demand for the papers to be collected and published. Of course, a transcript of a talk is not appropriate as a chapter of a book, so in most cases, the papers collected here have been substantially revised for publication. Moreover, translating a series of separate lectures, albeit with a common theme, into a book requires substantial re-ordering in order to achieve a sense of a developing argument, and the papers have been updated, and in some cases extended for this volume.

Two of the original papers, given by Professor Carol Fitz-Gibbon of Durham University and Bernard Clarke, Headteacher of Peers Campus, Oxford (and now of King Alfred's School, Wantage) are not included in this collection for various reasons. In order to further integrate the collection, I have added both an Introduction and a Conclusion.

Acknowledgements

There would have been no papers to collect without the fulsome encouragement and financial sponsorship of the North Derbyshire Training and Enterprise Council and Derbyshire County Council, especially the help of Tony Howell, Sue James and Gill Howland. Carol Fitz-Gibbon's early acceptance gave the project status, and her continuing support provided sustenance. I am grateful to all of the contributors for their patience with my impertinent editorial intrusions and their generosity of time and spirit through the re-drafting stages. I am particularly indebted to my conscripted mentor, Colin Fletcher, who provided comments on my own contributions and who, together with Clyde Chitty and Valerie Hannon, gave invaluable advice in the selection of contributors to *The Chesterfield Papers*.

The Governors of all of the schools involved have been resolute, committed and reliable throughout, as have the Heads, all of whom I count among my friends. Almost all of the schools are designated as Community Schools and they include Bolsover, Brookfield, Dronfield, Eckington, Frederick Gent, Heritage, Meadows, Newbold, Parkside, Shirebrook, Springwell, Tibshelf, and my own school, Hasland Hall. At Hasland Hall, Heather Boulton, Gerry Richardson and John Sutcliffe have provided much help, guidance and moral support, and Margaret Heaver's financial and general administration of the project has brought order from time to time to the spectre of chaos that loomed over my anarchic organization.

The biggest sacrifices have undoubtedly been made by my wife Gill, and daughters Siân and Katie, whose abiding compassion, patience and forbearance have carried me through the rigours of co-ordinating first the lecture series, and then this volume. I dedicate this book to them and to their future.

Bob O'Hagan,
Chesterfield

Introduction

Bob O'Hagan

Myths and fallacies

A myth is a fictitious – or at least unproven – person, thing or belief. For this volume, the term myth is used in the more specific sense of a fallacy that is widely held to be true. According to *Collins English Dictionary*, a fallacy is 'an incorrect or misleading notion or opinion based on inaccurate facts or invalid reasoning'. The contributors to this book seek to expose a range of such falsehoods that have dominated educational policy-making for more than a decade. Few of them are entirely new, as we shall see. Very similar, and equally false, ideas have been popular in the past, either continuously or recurrently, which helps to give them the stature of what we might call great educational myths. Others, though exposed as fallacious in the distant past, have mutated and re-emerged in a variant form in recent years to enjoy a new lease of life. Still others are entirely new – and therefore perhaps cannot yet claim the status of full-blown myth, even though they have already basked in the glory of articles of faith among policy-makers from both Conservative and New Labour administrations.

Our contributors do not settle for exposing these myths, however. Iconoclasm alone is unsatisfactory. It is not sufficient simply to uproot the weeds; other, truer flora must be planted to variegate a barren landscape. Within each of the chapters that follow, as each myth is exposed, an alternative, truer formulation is offered. As the argument develops, we catch a glimpse of a fresh, more harmoniously balanced landscape stretching to a horizon depicting alternative policies for the future.

There has been no shortage of modern myths and fallacies, crowding the field of educational policy, outliving the Thatcher and Major governments and probably that of Blair too, unless there is an imminent change. The difficulty has been to select a manageable number from the host that jostle for attention. How can it be that at the close of the twentieth century so many myths still dominate and circumscribe the way many people perceive the process of education?

First, it is because neither pedagogy (the methodology of teaching and learning) nor epistemology (what counts as knowledge) is a science or even capable of a single, accepted and dominant interpretation. The sums of money spent in the United Kingdom every year on educational research are considerable, in contrast to the more modest sums spent on, say, research into economics. Despite this, three educationalists are no more likely to agree about policy direction than three economists.

Second, while education is undoubtedly a private possession, it is also a public investment. Eliminating ignorance not only benefits the individual but also the whole society. So whether we like it or not – and most of us probably do not – education is and will remain a political issue, and educational provision an instrument of government. The sustaining of old myths, along with the creation of new ones, has always been a useful weapon of politicians, for personal and party promotion as well as for social control. Consequently, public education has always offered a stage for the dramatization of myths.

The setting: comprehensive education

In this book, the discussions and conclusions take place against the background of comprehensive education. All of the contributors share a commitment to comprehensive education, and Part I sets the scene for their forays.

In Chapter 1, Caroline Benn and Clyde Chitty show that the myth of fixed potential – that any individual's future potential is a fixed quantity – has dogged educational debate throughout much of the nineteenth and twentieth centuries. Moreover, the widespread adoption of a comprehensive system first for primary schools and then the secondary sector, has failed to nail that myth.

In its early years, mainstream secondary comprehensive schooling in the United Kingdom bore the traces of its selective predecessor. Neither teachers nor Heads could eliminate the imprint of the fallacy of fixed potential. So streaming according to ability became commonplace within the early comprehensives and few teachers adapted without difficulty to the new styles, methods and resources needed to make mixed-ability teaching work effectively. The uneasy co-existence of GCE and CSE examinations added to the continuing divisiveness (Ball, 1981).

The change to a largely comprehensive system coincided with the arrival of the 'baby boom' generation and the new schools were frequently enormous in comparison with their predecessors (Benn and Simon, 1970). It became easier for the needs of the individual to be lost in establishments that were giving their attention to promoting equality rather than individual difference.

The rapid proliferation of examinations and syllabuses, especially the Mode 3 GCE and CSE syllabuses which were designed and assessed primarily by staff within the schools, was meant to address the needs of the new comprehensive clientele. Giving up to a quarter of a million teachers the opportunity to devise tests and other forms of assessment including coursework, produced many outstanding examples of innovative schemes of work and forms of assessment. The best were often in the vanguard, charting the way for mainstream assessment in the subject to follow some years later. Inevitably, however, courses of more dubious quality also slipped through, including those that emphasized student choice and 'relevance' at the expense of rigour. Consequently, a thousand projects were spawned amounting to little more than scrapbooks of fleeting fashion. Too often they contained the trivia of favourite football clubs, pop stars, cars and motorcycles. Copying out at length from magazines and annuals now masqueraded as genuine research from secondary sources.

The contributors to this book have no sentimental attachment to an imagined 'golden age' of comprehensive education: there was never any such period. They do not advocate a return to past structures and methods. In any case, only the future, not the past, can replace the present. They investigate the development of comprehensive education and the impact on it of the turbulent years of the Thatcher, Major and Blair administrations through the great myths of this period. In doing so, they are critical of many of the assumptions that have dominated the educational agenda, and apparently still do.

Myth and ideology

At the heart of the policy-making agenda for education has been an ideology. From the point of view of the contributors to this book, this ideology has comprised a sequence of myths. Elements of this fallacious core ideology recur at various points in the book. It runs like this:

1. It is in the nature of children that they acquire important knowledge predominantly, if not exclusively, by (a) being deliberately taught (b) by teachers (c) in schools and colleges.

2. Children know much less important knowledge nowadays than they used to and less than children in other comparable countries.

3. This can be remedied by (a) defining the important knowledge, and by increasing (b) the quantity and (c) the quality of teaching of the important things by teachers in schools.

4. Important knowledge can be specified by a National Curriculum.

5. Quantity can be increased by setting minimum amounts of time children must spend in front of teachers and on homework.

6. Quality can be increased by specifying national standards for pedagogic skills and methods, and ensuring new and old teachers are trained in them.

7. The success of these three remedies can be measured accurately through national tests every few years throughout children's schooling.

8. As they acquire more important knowledge, the economic success of the country will improve.

9. Since guaranteeing the future economic success of the country is a key responsibility of government, the government has a duty to intervene directly to ensure that each of these remedies is brought about and is effective.

While they are explored in more detail later on, let us look briefly at each of these in turn:

1. *It is in the nature of children that they acquire important knowledge predominantly, if not exclusively, by (a) being deliberately taught (b) by teachers (c) in schools and colleges.*

Few would gainsay the power of the well-trained, well-motivated and well-resourced teacher over the well-intentioned amateur in promoting effective learning. But it would be preposterous to deny the power of other modes of education: (a) books, cinema, the Internet and a world of experimental and discovery-based learning; (b) teaching by parents, family, friends and neighbours and those we invest with 'authority' for example; and (c) organized learning which takes place at home, in the community, in the playground and in the workplace. Not only are all of these important to us as alternative or at least additional sources of learning, but they are also capable of being promoted by government, for example. The exclusive concern with formal teaching in schools is therefore ideological, as well as fallacious.

2. *Children know much less important knowledge nowadays than they used to and less than children in other comparable countries.*

Among those who have attempted to compare the level of knowledge of children across time and space, almost all have commented on the difficulties of reaching any firm conclusions. Even the well-funded and respected International Maths and Science Studies have been unable to reach a single overall conclusion about standards of achievement in the United Kingdom in comparison with other nations, noting instead both strengths and weaknesses among British pupils (Keys, Harris and Fernandez, 1996). There is at least the *prima facie* evidence that overall achievements at GCE/CSE/GCSE, at A level and even at degree level have all risen very substantially during the second half of the twentieth century. To base a whole strategy for upheaval in schools and colleges on an entirely unproven and quite possibly false assumption is at least hazardous, though cynics would argue this is the norm among politicians and governments![1]

3. *This can be remedied by (a) defining the important knowledge, and by increasing (b) the quantity and (c) the quality of teaching of the important things by teachers in schools.*

Even if it were true that standards have in fact declined in recent decades, it does not follow that the cause lies in either epistemological disputes or inadequate teaching. For example, Galton (1998), having repeated his landmark *Oracle* study of reading results achieved by primary school pupils of 20 years earlier, concluded that standards probably had declined. However, his evidence indicated the decline had taking place during the ten years following the introduction of the National Curriculum which was therefore at least as likely to have been a cause as a response to declining reading standards. Of course, it will always be convenient for governments to heap blame onto their predecessors, onto the hapless teaching profession or onto both in equal measure.

4. *Important knowledge can be specified by a National Curriculum.*

The degree to which the National Curriculum has changed at regular intervals during its first ten years of existence is evidence enough that successive ministers within a single administration are incapable of agreeing priorities for what counts as important knowledge. Even more disagreement is evident among the 'experts' – educators themselves.

5. *Quantity can be increased by setting minimum amounts of time children must spend in front of teachers and on homework.*

Despite several attempts to demonstrate a difference which is statistically significant, no research has yet been able to show a causal relationship between examination performance and length of time spent either in class or on homework.

6. *Quality can be increased by specifying national standards for pedagogic skills and methods, and ensuring new and old teachers are trained in them.*

While there is a certain 'common-sense' appeal to the notion that specific training in the best teaching methods will lead to better teaching, a National Pedagogy is likely to prove even more contentious than the National Curriculum. Galton's research (1998), for example, also concluded that the recent emphasis on whole-class interactive teaching might also be a factor in declining reading standards.

7. *The success of these three remedies can be measured accurately through national tests every few years throughout children's schooling.*

At first, Kenneth Baker's intention was that the whole National Curriculum would be tested and re-tested throughout each child's school life. This proved completely impractical and ruinously expensive. Instead, national tests are now restricted to reading, writing and arithmetic (but not speaking, listening or using maths) at Key Stage 1, and to the three core subjects of English, Maths and Science at Key Stages 2 and 3. National Curriculum grading has been quite impractical since Professor Paul Black's TGAT Working Party decided that levels of achievement should be comparable across all stages. Thus, Level 4 should mean the same thing if achieved by a 5-year-old or a 16-year-old. In practice, a small proportion of 7-year-olds are awarded Level 4 each year, as well as a sizeable proportion of 14-year-olds. Yet in the case of English, the knowledge (of Shakespeare), skill (writing for different audiences) and application (over a sustained examination) required of a 14-year-old for the award of Level 4 are not at all comparable with those for a high-achieving 7-year-old. The problems are even starker in the cases of Maths and Science where the breadth of knowledge required by the national programmes of study make comparisons quite impossible even between 11-year-olds and 14-year-olds. While the QCA has encountered little criticism either of its tests or of the marking process at Key Stages 2 and 3 in the case of Maths, the same cannot be said of Science. As for the English tests, they have provoked so much disquiet every year that the QCA has found itself perpetually on the defensive.

It is true that teachers are required to produce National Curriculum assessments for every National Curriculum subject, at least at Key Stage 3, and that these are aggregated to produce national statistics. However, the government, QCA and Ofsted have all failed to establish systems for standardization, moderation, inspection or review which would offer comparability between teachers within a single school, let alone between schools or from one year to the next. No doubt the establishment of standards of reliability for teacher assessments would be extremely costly.

8. *As they acquire more important knowledge, the economic success of the country will improve.*

Of all fallacies, this is perhaps the most self-evidently absurd. The vagaries of the economic cycle, the buoyancy of international markets, levels of investment, fiscal and monetary policy and other purely economic factors all play a part in determining a country's economic performance. The idea that standards of National Curriculum knowledge have a direct effect on a country's industrial competitiveness is patently fanciful. Since none of the current workforce was taught the National Curriculum from the age of 5, and hardly any were taught the National Curriculum for even as much as one year, no correlation can be determined.

Even if we compare the performance of different countries' pupils in the International Maths and Science studies, no direct link with countries displaying notable subsequent economic success is discernible.

9. *Since guaranteeing the future economic success of the country is a key responsibility of government, the government has a duty to intervene directly to ensure that each of these remedies is brought about and is effective.*

As I have pointed out earlier, schooling is a public investment and represents a legitimate concern of governments. Successive governments have used this as an excuse to intervene in an unprecedented way in the proper business of schools and teachers. The same governments that have deregulated areas of public sector activity as a precursor to privatization, market testing and the establishment of independent agencies have sought to accumulate for themselves vast powers of ministerial regulation. The same governments which have eschewed directing operational decisions by policemen, probation officers, doctors and RAF pilots have determinedly set about laying down the who, the what, the where, the when and the how of teaching. Hardly anything appears too small a detail to warrant a government directive; almost nothing, it seems, can be trusted to professional judgement or delegated to local politicians, however large their democratic mandate.

In Part II, Valerie Hannon and Maurice Kogan disentangle the shifting roles of national and local government, schools, teachers, governors and quangos in controlling what happens in schools. They consider successive governments' apparent displays of virility to be naïve and superficial. They go on to sketch out a future for schools and teachers that does not replicate past relationships, but places them at the centre of a wider network of professional freedom, rights and obligations, and of democratic accountability.

The democratic alternative

The contributions to this volume spell out the myths of the Thatcher and Major years. This period witnessed a shift in perspective on education from national structures and local systems to individual institutions – schools and colleges – and pupil performance. Part III focuses on the institutions. In the wake of these upheavals, what has happened to the relationships between the groups that make up the school community? How is it that giving power (through local management of schools), responsibility (through attention to outcomes rather than processes) and accountability (through annual reports, inspections and league tables) to institutions has occasioned fragmentation and disintegration within those institutions? Nothing less than a mini-exodus from teaching has left the Labour Government facing an acute recruitment crisis. Michael Fielding explores the meaning of the term community and the reasons for teachers' alienation within schools while Stephen Ball examines the implications of the more impersonal and technocratic approach to school management evident in schools today.

The contributors to this volume examine the relationship of the New Labour government to its Conservative predecessor, not with pessimistic intent but with an eye to the future. They recognize there can be no going back. So where are the signs of fresh growth? Where are the pointers to the authentic education of the future, where myths and fallacies no longer undermine its very existence?

The first requirement is a fresh vision for *comprehensive education*, one which treasures the entitlement to equity but not in the drab, uninspiring sameness that characterized the limited horizons of some of the earlier comprehensive schools. This fresh vision links the concept of equality to that of personal freedom and social solidarity, seeking reconciliation between the archetypes of socialism and individualism.

The Thatcher–Major years saw central government wrest control of the curriculum – what counts as education – by specifying the framework and content of the curriculum, the range of accreditation and the limits of assessment. In doing so, it set up tensions and contradictions that have yet to be resolved. Part IV directs the spotlight onto curriculum and assessment. Michael Armstrong draws on one case study to question the jealous determinism of the National Curriculum and Bob Moon exposes the poverty of its associated testing and assessment. What forms of curriculum and assessment will be required for the new millennium? Ken Spours analyses the shortcomings of the peculiarly English approach to qualifications for 16–19 year olds.

The second requirement is a fresh vision for *community education*, one that recognizes the importance of education beyond schooling and has an ambition to create a wider educational franchise. But out must go the ever-widening conception of the legitimate role of the teacher, in which teachers are expected to become social workers, community activists and even legal advisers. Instead, community education must embrace the necessity for accountability in education, and seize the initiative as a means to promote local democracy not only outside the school but also within it.

Schools do not and cannot exist within a social vacuum. Steadily over the last 20 years, secondary schools have followed their primary counterparts in seeking out instead of resisting partnerships with parents, employers and wider community networks. These trends have been countered by modern myths concerning the relationship between schools (the 'service providers') and parents and the community, particularly employers (the 'consumers'). Tim Brighouse, Colin Fletcher and Tom Wylie explore the wider setting of the comprehensive school and provide an opportunity to relate the school back to the central purposes of community education.

At heart, comprehensive education and community education have both been movements promoting greater democracy in education. Along the way, too many instances of comprehensive and community schools have undermined this core feature, creating caricatures of their ideals. Over the years, these tendencies made it all too easy for the opponents of both comprehensive and community education to impose a new agenda, dominated by modern educational myths.

Finally, the Conclusion reasserts the place of the comprehensive school within a political milieu. It dissects the elements of democratic education and draws together the themes of the book: freedom, fairness and friendship; power, accountability and partnership. In doing so, some of the key features of the comprehensive community school of the future are identified.

Note

1. For a description of the way the electoral strategies of parties and presidents influenced government and media interpretations of the Third International Maths and Science Study (TIMSS), see Brown (1998).

References

Ball, SJ (1981) *Beachside Comprehensive*, Cambridge University Press, Cambridge

Benn, C and Simon, B (1970) *Half Way There: Report on the British Comprehensive School Reform*, Penguin, Harmondsworth

Brown, M (1998) The tyranny of the international horse race, in R Slee, G Weiner and S Tomlinson (eds) *School Effectiveness for Whom? Challenges to the School Effectiveness and School Improvement Movements,* Falmer, London, pp. 33–48

Galton, M (1998) Back to consulting the ORACLE, reporting on his as yet unpublished research, *Times Educational Supplement*, 3 July 1998

Keys, W, Harris, S and Fernandez, C (1996) *Third International Maths & Science Study: First National Report, Part 1*, NFER, Slough

PART I
The Context

1

Comprehensive Education

Myth: Educational Potential is a Fixed Quantity

Caroline Benn and Clyde Chitty

Drawing on data from their large 1994 survey of comprehensive schools and colleges in Britain, Benn and Chitty show that 30 years after the famous Department of Education Circular 10/65 heralded comprehensive reform, the myth of fixed potential has not disappeared. Setting the scene with a broad historical sweep, they conclude that the struggle for comprehensive education that began in the nineteenth century with primary schools, and was fought in the twentieth over secondaries, will in future extend to the comprehensive reform of the college sector.

Comprehensive education challenges the fallacy of fixed potential in education. It dismantles structures rooted in this fallacy that act as barriers to learning while fashioning practices that enable everyone to enjoy a full education. It is not concerned to offer *opportunities* to learn. It recognizes the *right* to the full range of learning that is available for each age group in the compulsory period, and a full choice of learning at the other stages of life.

Comprehensive education is immensely popular. People of all ages in all areas support their local non-selective schools and further education colleges because they support a system where educational institutions aim to provide good mainstream education that is accessible to everyone in the community. Those who choose not to participate in one of its many and varied forms are often unaware of its widespread support among ordinary people.

When public opinion polls ask whether elite institutions that eat up public resources and hand-pick a few winners should be 'abolished' or 'destroyed', the results are naturally inconclusive. But when the question is: do you want a system of education that follows the comprehensive principle or the principle of selection, the result is almost invariably a large majority in favour of the comprehensive.[1]

This does not mean that every example of that principle in practice will find favour – only that in making improvements, the majority would prefer that selection were not part of local or national educational structures.

The main spur to our research in the United Kingdom in the mid-1990s, published in *Thirty Years On* (Benn and Chitty, 1996), was the fact that no national examination of the comprehensive secondary system in the United Kingdom had taken place since 1972. This was hard to justify in view of the fact that argument about comprehensive education has never ceased. As recently as 1993, while the government declared its intention to provide a grammar school in every town, another of its publications noted with satisfaction that 90 per cent of state secondary pupils in Britain were in comprehensive schools (HMSO, 1993). Since 1979, a succession of education acts had given local authorities the right to reintroduce the 11+ examination. When no local area willingly chose to do so, City Technology Colleges and Grant Maintained Schools were tried instead, the latter announced at a press conference where Prime Minister Margaret Thatcher made clear that the 'opting out' policy was a new attempt to return selection to the system.[2] Although these two grand devices did not succeed as intended, they reinforced the contradictory policies operating at the heart of Britain's education system: one supporting comprehensive education, the other undermining it. This contradictory approach remains despite a change of government in 1997 and is one of the most serious problems facing the education system as we approach the twenty-first century.

A lethal legacy

The fallacy of fixed educational potential is much more deeply rooted than we like to believe, always justifying itself by the fact that people are different. Historically, this has manifested itself through different types of education for different social and economic groups. In the nineteenth century, working-class children did not need a proper education, just enough to equip them for their 'station' in life. Middle-class children needed a longer and more specialist education, while the upper class continued as before to have access to the best education without argument, no matter what their apparent 'educational potential'.

By the twentieth century more people were able to take part in education for longer periods of time and the grammar schools provided a lucky few of the working class with the chance to climb the social ladder. However, undiminished stood the need for division into 'gold, silver and iron' – the metaphor so often used to represent the British class-divided education system.

If anything the twentieth century saw the fallacy of fixed potential consolidated by building in an individual's intelligence at birth. Originally, measuring 'intelligence' was to be a 'modern', 'scientific' means for deciding people's access to education and it was supposed to transcend notions of social class. Inevitably, however, it ended up reinforcing class divisions.

Cyril Burt, foremost advocate of the new science of mind measurement or psychometrics, advised the Ministry of Education officially for much of the first half of the twentieth century, culminating in the 1944 Act. He set the educational establishment's structural aims for the system, summarized in these terms: 'our aim should be to discover what ration of intelligence nature has given to each individual child at birth, then to provide him [sic] with the appropriate education, and finally to guide him into the career for which he seems to have been marked out' (Burt, 1950).

'Fortunately,' he had claimed in 1933, intelligence 'can be measured with accuracy and ease' (quoted in Simon, 1974, p. 175). This was by means of an IQ Test, later adapted by the public education system to form the 11+ test that would decide which children would get the silver education in the grammar school and which the iron one elsewhere.

Read history's lips

In 1997 there was an electoral landslide sweeping Labour to power and an immediate White Paper, *Excellence in Schools*. In 1945, the last time there was such a convincing Labour victory, the government also produced its own instant White Paper, *The Nation's Schools* (MoE, 1945). It promised secondary education for all, not just for some, just as the 1997 White Paper spoke of excellence for the many, not just for the few.

The 1945 White Paper introduced the 11+ examination and the new tripartite system of grammar schools, technical schools and secondary modern schools. The end of the Second World War may have inaugurated a brave new Labour era in social and welfare policies but when it came to education, the White Paper showed society's sights were still set very low. For a start, despite the subsequent raising of the school leaving age to 15 in 1947, there was to be no change in the principle that only a minority of the working class could receive a full secondary education.

Both *The Nation's Schools* and the *Norwood Report* (Norwood, 1943) which formed the basis of the new government's policy, proposed secondary modern schools specifically for the working-class majority. These schools would offer no qualifications to any of their students. The short-sighted reason given was that their 'future employment will not demand any measure of technical skill or knowledge'. The White Paper raised a storm of protest at both Labour Party and TUC Conferences as well as from those MPs who hoped to see comprehensive schools introduced instead of a tripartite system. Half a century later, the speeches of those MPs who queried the 11+ at the time read a great deal better than do the speeches of their ministerial colleagues trying to defend the idea that the majority needed no qualifications.

In 1945, the world was about to enter an era where every aspect of culture, production and work would be internationalized, and competition would increase. Sensing this, other advanced industrial countries began introducing or consolidating systems that would provide qualifications for the majority. By 1970, when Britain was just beginning to develop a localized patchwork of comprehensive schooling, many of its competitors already had comprehensive structures firmly in place and in many, staying on to 18 had become the norm. Britain took two decades more to reach the conclusion that everyone should stay in full-time education up to 18.

If we look at what held Britain back for a crucial two generations, we find that all those who had power and influence were still dedicated to the fallacy of fixed potential. People of working-class origins did not need qualifications, unless they were 'clever' and were lucky enough to gain entry to a grammar school. Certainly, few after 15 years took part in continuing education, confined to the small minority who went to a university or to a trade college or enrolled in an improving course. On the other hand, the majority of the children of the middle classes would obtain qualifications and many would have the chance of a university education. Should they fail the 11+ they had the security of a well-worn route through fee-paying, which for some meant the most golden of opportunities, at the socially selective 'public' schools.

Despite the fact that selection offered a ladder for a minority, the system still reflected the belief that different groups had different social and academic potential and thus needed different forms of education. The latter always seems so very reasonable until we read the small print. Norwood (1943), for example, said young people's minds could be divided into three types which justified the three types of school Labour later duly introduced. It told the public what a 'grammar' mind was like, and then a 'technical' mind, when today such attempts to separate the two seem laughably contrived. But what really shocks is the characterization of the third type of mind, the one that the majority of young people possessed: it did not 'like ideas' and was 'generally slow' (ibid., pp. 2–3)

The bigger shock is that a majority within the educated world accepted such statements without question. Nor is there any reason to think that in today's world of education there are not statements being made that will be disowned by future generations just as thoroughly.

Establishing the comprehensive school

The comprehensive movement became inevitable as soon as the artificially divided school system came under public scrutiny. This started once the government launched the new General Certificate of Education (GCE) examinations in 1951 and teachers in the secondary modern schools were allowed to use them. Amazingly, they began reporting pupils rejected by the 11+ tests – some with IQs apparently as low as 85 – passing at the same level as grammar school pupils (Chitty, 1997, p. 47). In time, national reports like Crowther (1959) began showing how many older students and adults had been misjudged by the mechanisms of the selective educational structure, their potential never developed.

Supporters of selection in the 1950s began to argue about whether the problem was that educational potential was not fixed at birth in the way so long assumed, or whether the 11+ examination was just not very reliable at measuring it. Accordingly, some tried to develop 'better' 11+ tests, while others modified their views to agree that 'environmental' factors must have some effect on intelligence, even if it was not decisive. Confidence in the IQ test began to dissipate.

Meanwhile, another group of educators interpreted the accumulation of facts and research before them more radically. They concluded that education itself made a difference, that education held the key to unlock human development, not some mythical fixed potential existing before the start of schooling. This socially based view spread and by 1963 a major national report, *Half Our Future* was able to say 'Intellectual talent is not a fixed quantity with which we have to work, but a variable that can be modified by social policy and educational approaches' (Newsom, 1963, p. 6).

This more optimistic view of human potential still holds to the extent that we still believe schooling makes a difference. Indeed, the 1998 School Standards and Framework Act represented the idea that standards could continue to rise whatever the social setting. Wider social policy was accorded only a minor role. This narrower view of what makes for educational success discounts the interrelationship between standards and the structure of the education system, leading to the deceptively appealing call for 'Standards Not Structures'. In consequence, the task of removing barriers has all but stopped and the fallacy of fixed potential is seen to be extending its influence again.

The fallacy remains: grouping policy

The removal of the 11+ to enable secondary comprehensive education to be developed began unofficially in the late 1940s when isolated communities began approving local plans for comprehensive schools. The Labour Party leadership reversed its policy in the 1950s, aligning itself at last with the trades unions and the Party Conference which overwhelmingly backed comprehensive schooling. Reform gathered pace with the official support of the new Labour Government elected in 1964.

Public enthusiasm for comprehensive education was high in the mid-1960s but government policies sought only to encourage institutional change gradually, area by area. Little effort went into preparing for the likely consequences in terms of wider educational changes, like a new curriculum and assessment system or new pedagogical principles that would develop teaching and learning compatible with the new comprehensive principle. The structure of education changed outside but in the learning and teaching going on inside schools, the fallacy remained largely unchallenged.

One result was that many of the new schools divided their wide range of pupils, as before, into a 'grammar' side and a 'secondary modern' side, effectively perpetuating the old divisions under one roof. They still claimed the popular comprehensive title because, they argued, it was now easy to switch wrongly placed pupils from one section of the school to the other. Where the division operated through streaming, administrators claimed pupils could move from bottom to top and back again at last. In essence, there remained no substantive challenge to the grouping of children by prior 'ability' for teaching purposes.

This argument ignored one enduring feature of all systems of selection: mistakes are rarely if ever discovered. Transfers are hardly ever made, either from secondary modern to grammar schools or the other way round, or from lower streams to upper or vice versa. From the point at which so-called potential is measured and recorded, the frame freezes.

While administrators remained timid in their attitude towards more radical change, practitioners in certain comprehensive schools began a more robust challenge in their everyday teaching and learning. This included their grouping policy, which means that today we no longer have large academic divisions inside schools or even much strict streaming. Instead, we often have streaming by subject, known as setting. Widely developed over the last 20 years or so, this is another way of making decisions based on the fallacy of fixed potential. In most schools, pupils initially allocated to top sets rarely find themselves put down to lower ones. Once sorted, pupils tend to stay put. Lower sets are assumed to have less potential, although the justification is that pupils get to work at a pace which 'suits' them.

These were the arguments of the new Labour Government in 1997, laid down in *Excellence in Schools* that setting is a good thing because students' capacities differ. Mixed ability teaching is discouraged unless taught by those who are exceptionally good at it. It is essentially the same argument used to justify no secondary education, then a secondary modern one only, then strict streaming of all subjects and now streaming by subject. Comprehensive schools must include selection based on fixed potential, it is implied, for to do otherwise will inevitably compromise 'standards'.

Respect the evidence

All this might be persuasive were there any proof that setting is better than mixed ability teaching when it comes to achieving high rates of examination passes. There is not, just as before there was no proof that streaming was better than mixed ability grouping, or that selective school systems out-performed comprehensive ones. The selective versus non-selective issue has been researched rigorously both nationally and internationally for decades. Yet no one has ever produced conclusive evidence either way, except possibly individual countries like Sweden that took care to research the standards issue before committing themselves to comprehensive change, the results found to point in favour of non-selection (Husen and Boalt, 1968).

The grouping issue has also been looked at many times, including a well-known project conducted on streaming versus mixed ability in Oxfordshire comprehensive schools in the 1970s which found no difference in attainment at GCE O Level between the two systems (Postlethwaite and Denton, 1978). In our 1994 survey we looked again. Comparing those comprehensive schools which had mostly mixed ability grouping for academic subjects with schools that used setting, we found there was no difference at all in average 5+ GCSE A–C grades and A level points scores between the two groups.

When a difference has been visible, it often favours more open grouping. Recently a researcher from King's College in London decided to look at mathematics at the secondary stage, comparing two comprehensive schools with very similar intakes. One used setting for maths classes and the other used a variety of flexibly grouped classes, changed in composition at different stages of the course to respond to the working methods of the teachers and the individual wishes of pupils. In terms of results at GCSE A–C, the flexibly grouped school did better, with more maths passes overall for pupils at every level, including both those with learning difficulties and those with high initial attainment (Boaler, 1997a).

Conservative governments discouraged research on comprehensive education throughout the 1980s and 1990s. Had they not done so, the New Labour government might not have been so caught out in assuming that comprehensive schools are all held back by practising mixed ability teaching. In *Excellence in Schools,* the New Labour government advised schools to switch to setting, apparently oblivious of its widespread use. Mandelson and Liddle (1996) made the same error.

In fact, no more than a small minority of comprehensive schools has ever experimented with completely mixed ability grouping. In our 1994 survey, we found that by Year 9, only just over 6 per cent of comprehensive schools were using it for all subjects (Benn and Chitty, 1996: Table 6.4, p. 258). The most widespread use of mixed ability grouping appears in the first year of entry (Year 7). Here, comprehensives are evidently keen to give all new arrivals an equal start before allocating pupils to sets in Year 8.

The new government's advocacy of setting came at a time when many schools, anxious to improve performance, were reviewing their use of setting. They were beginning to explore other methods more compatible with promoting learning in a comprehensive context, including a few who were anxious to extend and update mixed ability teaching.

At least we know enough not to expect changes in grouping practice to be government-led. Practitioners lead change, particularly in a system where the attitude of governments to comprehensive education has been so ambiguous. The new flexible mixed ability grouping used in the school which scored so well in the King's College research quoted above (Boaler, 1997a) is one alternative. It involves regular changes to group composition throughout the year, depending on what the topics are and how comfortable individual pupils feel with them. Regular revisions take account of interest and pace, with pupils given full encouragement to work individually. As Boaler (1997b, p. 593) explained: 'Grouping students according to ability and then teaching towards an imaginary model pupil... will almost certainly disadvantage pupils who deviate from the ideal model.'

Comprehensive-compatible curriculum and assessment

Inside schools, curriculum changes have also been practitioner-led. Had ministers sought out precise information about comprehensive school practice during the 1980s, the expensive, carelessly conceived and thoughtlessly overloaded National Curriculum exercise might not have needed such frequent adjustment and readjustment. The original conception barely exists any longer, and its broad and balanced nature – its one good feature – is now being usurped at least in the Junior years (3–6) by over-concentration on the mechanics of literacy and numeracy. Many secondaries, meanwhile, have dropped the wide curriculum at Key Stage 4 (Years 10 and 11) in favour of the narrower one of work-related education. As in earlier epochs, such proposals for a narrower curriculum are justified as education 'suited' to the minds and lifestyles of particular groups, invariably those at the less advantaged end of society. The new Education Action Zones, which can suspend the National Curriculum entirely, pose a further threat. Luckily the supporters of a broad and balanced curriculum are very numerous and will fight for this advantage to remain for all pupils up to 16 years (see for example Searle, 1996).

Another structural change that made a difference was the introduction of the GCSE in 1986. This was an examination intended for the whole of the 14–16 age group. Other than the 11+ itself, there never had been a whole-cohort external examination in the UK before. GCE O level, which preceded it, was designed for only the top 20 per cent and the CSE which had been introduced in the 1960s, had been intended for only the next 40 per cent.

This means that throughout the first twenty years of comprehensive reorganization, teachers continued to wrestle with the 'problem of the bottom 40 per cent'. This group had no qualification goals because the assessment structure reflected the supposedly fixed nature of their potential. The same structure also forced comprehensive schools to select ahead of time which students would take the top-tier route to GCE and which the second best route to CSE – a division that became increasingly problematic for all schools and parents. Teachers particularly grew increasingly dissatisfied with the daunting responsibility of having to make this division work.

Change was again made possible by almost two decades of practitioners' preparatory action on the ground, as one by one comprehensive schools refused to accept the idea of a 'bottom 40 per cent', no matter how official. They began simply entering all of their pupils for one or other of the two examinations, just as a generation earlier, secondary modern schools had demonstrated success at GCE with students who were not supposed to have any academic capability.

Throughout the latter half of the 1970s, deputation after deputation of teachers and parents met Labour ministers in an attempt to explain how this divided assessment system, based firmly on the fallacy of fixed potential, undermined any comprehensive purpose. Year after year, a government supposedly attuned to the needs of comprehensive reform rejected a unified assessment system. It clung doggedly to a divided system of assessment, as today's Labour Government clings still to the academic/vocational divide (see Ken Spours, Chapter 8). There would be no change of mind once Prime Minister Jim Callaghan made his 1976 Ruskin College speech undermining comprehensive developments just when they needed support. With mass unemployment looming, government policy concentrated increasingly on basic skills for the perceived short-term needs of employers.

After ten years of training programmes that promoted 'transferable skills' and successive attempts to get employers to accept CSE as a respectable qualification, even the right-wing Conservative Education Secretary Keith Joseph had to face facts. In international comparisons, Britain failed to match the standards of most competitor countries because far lower percentages in Britain had meaningful qualifications or stayed in education until they were 18. Once again, expectations were seen to be painfully low. As much as ever, the system rested upon a notion of fixed potential rather than upon one where diverse intelligences and a range of talents and attainment could develop among individuals learning alongside each other.

New danger: selection driven by the market

As statistics show, qualifying and staying on in schools after 16 years took a quick turn upward with the introduction of the unified GCSE qualification (DfE, 1994: Fig. 1). Yet, the myth of fixed potential remained essentially unchallenged. One barrier disappeared, but almost at once, league tables emerged, presenting a new hurdle to success. League tables used a simplistic criterion of five GCSE passes at grades A–C in one type of examination in one type of education. For most of the 1990s, this single percentage has decided where schools and individual students stand in terms of educational success or failure. At a stroke, the 5-pass matriculation examination for university entrance of the nineteenth century has returned to haunt the late twentieth century.

The exercise of league tabling was ostensibly about standards but its purpose was also to support the reintroduction of selection and it has had some unfortunate results. To begin with, vocational attainment implicitly has received less respect, paradoxically at a time when the government has been trying to promote vocational courses within schools – a strategy that needed equal status to be a success. Furthermore, many schools now spend less time encouraging those expected to get scores below the magic five higher grades. They will not improve the position the school occupies in the tables, no matter how excellent their achievements may be in their own terms. A third consequence has probably been the great rise in the numbers excluded from schools – by 1997, it had reached some 13,000 annually. Part of this rise is accounted for by pupils' poor behaviour or attainment which means that retaining them is also likely to harm a school's league table position.

Perhaps the largest effect league tables have had within an education structure deliberately being left to the market was to encourage selection to take many new forms and thus accelerate the polarization of the system into 'good' and 'bad' schools. This development was inadvertently fuelled by government policies designed to improve all schools: the technique known as 'naming and shaming', the designation and public acknowledgement of both 'poor' and 'successful' schools and other similar initiatives. Superimposed on the open enrolment policies of the late 1980s that directed funds towards schools with high league-table positions, these designations became self-fulfilling prophecies. Inducements for schools to grasp higher funding available with City Technology College (CTC) or Grant Maintained (GM) status intensified these trends. Pursuing naked self-interest, a minority of schools 'opted out' of a co-operative, locally accountable public education service, and 'opted into' control by self-perpetuating oligarchies instead.

Although the Blair administration claims to be ending selection for admission by interview except among schools with religious denominations, opportunities for covert selection remain. So great is the neglect of equitable arrangements in a system left almost entirely to the market that it is unsurprising to discover disreputable selection practices in use. For example, some schools may canvass for new pupils only in private housing areas, denying information or invitations to visit the school to families on council estates.

Hidden selection also emerges where LEAs persuade schools to 'specialize' informally in dealing with pupils with learning difficulties, possibly induced by the extra funding that follows such pupils. Our survey brought in many reports from comprehensives that claimed they were the schools that the LEA had 'designated' to be used for slow learners or those with difficulties. This may raise few eyebrows when such pupils form but 10 per cent to 20 per cent of the intake of a comprehensive school. When they reach 40 per cent or even 50 per cent, discerning parents choose the school further down the road where their child will work alongside only 10 per cent of pupils with special needs. The virtuous or vicious cycle of 'success' and 'failure' moves on another turn. In this case though, the polarization takes place *within* the neighbourhood rather than *between* neighbourhoods.

Most parents simply want a good comprehensive, properly balanced in intake, neither selecting nor selected against, aiming and able to teach all major subject areas equally well rather than specializing in one, and available to all those who live locally. A local education service could oversee such a system. While equitable admissions arrangements will encourage diversity of provision and will honour parental preferences wherever possible, they should also acknowledge the objective of a balanced entry to each school. This may involve priority admission on grounds of feeder school or 'nearness', to ensure that there are enough places locally for all neighbourhood children. That none of this is possible any longer in so many areas, and in particular in so many cities, is a major cause for concern.

Many observers hoped the 1998 School Standards and Framework Act would establish such an equitable structure of education by giving all schools the same legal status and the same rights and responsibilities within the system, but were disappointed. Instead, it deepened the polarization problem by adding partial selection to the system, including 'specialist' schools that can select up to 10 per cent of their pupils on grounds of their 'aptitude'. Such schools are not obliged to select by attainment, but it is unrealistic to expect them not to do so over time, especially with selectivity increased by automatic access for siblings. Education Action Zones, where specialization is also being encouraged, may further compound the problem. Most serious of all though, City Technology Colleges, Grant Maintained and certain voluntary schools continue to act as separate admissions authorities, able to hand-pick entrants if they choose to do so.

Selection is growing in kind and in number

Luckily, most areas of the country operate within a clear public commitment to education as a service for everyone, where policies designed to help one school inch its way forward at the expense of its neighbours, are discouraged. However, in areas containing a lot of GM, CTC, voluntary or 'specialist' schools, the task of forging a system that is fair to all parents alike is becoming increasingly difficult. In part, this is because governments have systematically curtailed the capacity of local authorities to undertake this role.

Of course, there is nothing to prevent such schools deciding to co-operate with neighbours, seeking the same link to their local authorities and accepting equal responsibility to serve the local community. In fairness, a number of comprehensives which could begin selecting, including those which are oversubscribed and a few which have been GM, agree instead to operate within the rules agreed by all local schools. But without legal support for such initiatives, in other areas it is hard to maintain commitment to an equitable structure and a fair and transparent admissions system that applies to all schools equally.

On top of all this, Britain still operates overt grammar-school selection in dozens of local authorities, including 30 in England. There are over 225 grammar schools and over a thousand primary schools where pupils still face the verdict of the old 11+, fixing their potential for ever, certainly in their own eyes. Almost all of the grammar schools are in England and Northern Ireland since Scotland and Wales have set their backs against them.

In recent years, grammar school advocates have tried to convince opinion formers that they protect 'excellence' while not harming other local schools. Yet, this is not so when the other local schools are comprehensive, as most of them now are, for this denies them the chance to be fully comprehensive. In our research, we compared the GCSE results of comprehensive schools in areas with, and without, local grammar schools. Using the 5+ A–C criterion, the comprehensives facing local grammar school selection averaged only 29 per cent, while those without any grammar selection, where all schools were comprehensive, averaged 48 per cent. This is a significant difference (Benn and Chitty, 1996: Table 4.4, p. 182).[3]

We also found several schools, nominally comprehensive, where hidden selection operated in their favour, enabling them to have intakes where 80 per cent of pupils were in the top 20 per cent of the attainment range nationally. At the other end, a far greater number of comprehensive schools had much lower proportions from the top 20 per cent than they would have had if all schools in their area had operated the same admissions rules. It is discouraging for those comprehensives that refuse to select for their own advantage to find themselves occupying lower rungs on the league table ladder than their neighbours practising overt or hidden selection. In effect, they are penalized for trying to protect the common good.

Some of these comprehensive schools eventually give in and even against their better judgement, try to commandeer as many middle-class and high attaining pupils as they can. Then they start to avoid those who are entitled to free meals, who come from 'underclass' areas, who have special educational needs, or whose command of English is not yet perfect. Our survey showed clearly that GM comprehensives and a good proportion of Church of England schools were starting to diverge significantly in respect of all these characteristics from LEA comprehensive schools. No doubt in time 'specializing' schools with partial selection could do the same.

Those who are black, Asian or from other minority ethnic groups suspect that the mechanism of hidden selection also brings skin colour into the frame. Our research did not find fewer such pupils in GM or voluntary aided comprehensive schools. However, it did find that pupils admitted to such schools were more likely to be those with a good command of English and far less likely to have English as a second or other language. Others who monitor racial issues, like the Commission for Racial Equality, have found that GM schools' interview and admissions procedures can be prejudicial to black, Asian and other minority ethnic groups (CRE, 1992). Many observers have no doubt that the most insidious fallacy of all regarding academic potential – that black pupils have less of it – still pervades schooling.

For this reason alone, the whole process of admissions needs overhauling and the structure of selection needs examining. For the hidden selection which successive Education Acts have encouraged within state supported education involves a far broader application of the fallacy of fixed potential than the old 11+. This is because it brings into judgement every aspect and condition of pupils' lives. In the nineteenth century it was just their social or economic status, for most of the twentieth it has also involved their 'intelligence'. As we head for the twenty-first century, it now includes their command of the language and their cultural and behavioural status as well.

Selection leads to polarization

The play of these forces unhampered within the structure of education risks a slow, poisonous polarization of schools in an ever-growing number of areas, divided between those deemed 'acceptable' by the majority of local opinion and those deemed unacceptable. The ostensible reason is 'standards' or neighbourhood differences, but it is just as likely to be the degree of selection some schools can practise as against the degree to which others are being manifestly 'selected against' within the local structure.

Yet governments and governmental organizations appear unwilling to challenge, or even recognize, the problem of escalating selection. Neither the Government nor the Office for Standards in Education (Ofsted) have investigated it or taken it into account in any policy-making or judgements upon schools and teachers; and many local authorities, while privately acknowledging it, are powerless to do much about it. Ironically, in all too many areas the very policies that were designed to allow parents to have a say in choosing schools have re-created a system that encourages schools to choose, and to polarize, parents instead.

A new Labour government could have grasped the chance to put this right. For example, it could have ensured that all schools receiving public funds enjoyed equal legal rights and status, no matter how different in terms of ethos or approach. It could have required all to take part within the same equitable admissions system that everyone understood. It could have strengthened the operation of local democratic accountability. A major study by the Organization for Economic Co-operation and Development has shown that strict avoidance of social and academic selection is the only way for choice and diversity to flourish (OECD, 1994). Sadly, none of this has happened. Under the 1998 Act, grant maintained status is largely unchanged in the new foundation status while local authority schools are to be re-titled 'community schools'. Other types of schools including CTC and the voluntary aided sector will still enjoy a different, preferential status which will allow some of them to be as selective in their admissions arrangements as any GM school has been.

Selection has not been ignored altogether. The White Paper *Excellence in Schools* condemns it in a generalized way and some measures within the

1998 School Standards & Framework Act address it directly. These include a requirement for schools to confer locally on admissions (whatever that turns out to mean), an adjudicator to receive complaints about local admissions policies and provision for local parental ballots to decide whether grammar schools should remain. Taken together though, these fall short of a policy to end selection or a fair admissions system. There is no assurance that the adjudicator will be able to hear objections from parents, students and teachers as well as local education authorities, and no assurance that ballots will be fair. In some cases, it is expected that the parents of pupils at grammar schools may be entitled to vote while those in local comprehensive schools will not.

None of these policies will tackle the myth of fixed educational potential that still operates within the structure of the system. In the 1980s most people laughed at Margaret Thatcher's assertion that 'there is no such thing as society' but a decade later, a Labour government's statement is just as absurd, that in education 'only standards matter' and structures are unimportant. This mantra, oft-repeated in ministerial statements, seems to mean: do not bother about structural divisions which strengthen selection between schools (differential rights, duties, privileges, funding and control over admissions); simply concentrate on improving individual teachers and their classroom practice.

Undoubtedly, good teaching and effective classroom management matter; no one has ever said otherwise. But so does the achievement of a fair and equitable public system in which all parents and teachers have faith. For however any individual or group defines 'good practice' or 'high standards' – and definitions differ a great deal more than is commonly acknowledged – school success is primarily related to structures. Sometimes we could even say this literally, for example, in the classroom with a leaking roof, standards might be harder to raise than in a classroom where pupils and equipment are dry.

The structure of society matters too. Common sense tells us that school experience has to be seen in relation to adverse home circumstances, unemployment, poverty, instability of family relationships and poor housing. All these make an imprint on a pupil's ability to attend school or to undertake homework, and on their educational aspirations. Such factors should not give us the right to lower our expectations, but can we discount these experiences, which bear so directly on the attainment we hope to promote? What prevents us from linking educational policy to social analysis and social action in the way that earlier generations found to be so necessary?

Behind the damage that present inequitable educational structures are inflicting, as perceived by ever more young people, their parents, teachers and local communities, lies an even deeper issue: the assumption buried in our beings that those who are middle class, rich or white, or who have achieved high SAT scores or five or more GCSEs, have more potential than others, and that this fixed potential, should condition what people expect – and get – from education as pupils, students or later as adults.

Without proper legislative protection against the way the market operates to reinforce these negative assumptions, misusing concepts like 'choice', 'diversity', 'aptitude' and 'standards', progress in education is going to be much harder to achieve than it need be. Driven by market competition for funds within a hierarchical structure, even those schools most anxious to uphold the comprehensive principle will, in sheer self-defence, turn to practices which they know will be at the expense of neighbouring schools. Our education system fuels social polarization. Unrecognized and unchecked, this mechanism always threatens to bring down the system in the end.

Build on the co-operation, not competition

There is still time to change direction and to build on the success comprehensive education has achieved. The comprehensive principle remains strong: a wide coalition of people still supports the idea of a democratically responsible comprehensive system of public education. This coalition, which includes the majority of schools and staff in Britain and those locally elected, as well as a few in government, is dedicated to serving everyone alike and making sure all local communities get the best there is. Many local authorities strive to achieve an equitable service and refuse to play one institution off against others until one has to go to the wall and the remainder form a new hierarchy of competing legal entities.

All institutions have to co-operate in a single system. Only this will meet one of the key demands of comprehensive education: that at every age it should be possible for all students to have access to the full range of education available for the age group as a whole. At the age of eleven, it can be in one school. After 16, it can come only by pressing on with structural reform of the system itself. For after 16, market competition denies the full choice of courses to millions of young people. Instead, each institution claims its own students and limits their choice to what it alone can provide. The issue is particularly crucial for those 40 per cent of all comprehensive schools that possess no sixth form of their own. For them, the various alternative post-16 providers must work closely together, pooling their efforts and moving towards a coherent, unified structure of public provision.

A straight split among 16–19 education providers along grammar/secondary modern lines has not yet emerged because, on the one hand, sixth forms and sixth form colleges have introduced vocational courses and, on the other hand, further education colleges have developed A level work. However, as our survey discovered, the social and academic differences between different educational venues at 16–19 remain dangerously wide, as well as grossly inefficient in terms of costs. Only tertiary colleges come anywhere near being comprehensive in operation.

Still, the present structure affords opportunities for improvement. After 16, nothing prevents post-16 providers of all kinds from co-operating rather than competing, and in a few areas, there are attempts to encourage such developments. The 1998 Act gives special help for Welsh schools and colleges in this respect though authorities in England have no legal support to harmonize or rationalize educational provision in this way.

Even if they did, it would not be enough. For after 16, and increasingly from the age of 14, the 'fixed potential' barrier is just as likely to be curricular as institutional. In particular, the academic/vocational split forces decisions about which type of education is suitable for which type of student instead of allowing students to combine courses to suit their needs and aspirations (see Ken Spours, Chapter 8). Vocational education struggles to achieve equal status and rigour, and academic education narrows its own development.

Integration of the curriculum allowing vocational and academic courses to develop within a single system of accreditation is the only common-sense course, but it involves structural change. This means that as well as increasing the funds made available, they should be redistributed so that more is concentrated on those who have always had less than their fair share of education. Schools that deal with an accumulation of distinct educational problems should receive proportionately more and it should be easier for young people who are unemployed or who have not yet been awarded five higher grade GCSE passes to gain qualifications.

The nineteenth century saw the introduction of universal comprehensive primary education and the struggle to make universal secondary education comprehensive has dominated the twentieth. The twenty-first century will surely see the battle for universal education for adults, or lifelong learning. This means a system that is there to help adults learn what and when they want to learn, organized so that it is easy to get the help they need to promote their learning. It also means having education available on terms they can afford.

Far from the historical drive for comprehensive education being over, it is very much in mid-struggle. For the fallacy of fixed potential is far stronger in respect of adults than children. We are always willing to say children have the world before them but with adults, we tend to demand their CVs and look askance where prior learning is minimal. Many adults have been convinced they are incapable of advanced study and society will continue, as it always has, to tell them this is the case by not providing education for them. The hidden message of our current post-18 system is that certain people are worth educating after 18 to a very high degree, but most are not. This is what comprehensive education has to challenge in the coming century.

The challenge will come from below, as it always has. In the last 30 years, while comprehensive secondary education has been developing, comprehensive education for adults has also moved steadily ahead. To take but one example, hundreds of access courses around the country have helped thousands of adults previously failed by the system to qualify for university entrance. Indeed, nearly half of all entrants to some universities are no longer 18-year-olds coming straight from sixth forms, but mature students who have played a major new part in proving the notion of fixed educational potential to be a myth. In fact, the mature student who once failed in school and is now succeeding on a university course (as most of them do) is the greatest proof of all that potential for education is always there. It can grow, provided we as a society build a comprehensive and publicly accountable education service of high standards and equitable structures designed for the entire society.

Notes

1. See, for example, ICM poll, reported 7 March 1997 in *The Guardian* where 65 per cent favoured a comprehensive system, 27 per cent grammar schools and 8 per cent were undecided. See also recent poll of parental opinion on admission to secondary schools conducted by Hertfordshire County Council. Over 25,000 parents replied; less than 20 per cent favoured selective entry tests to schools, reported on BBC *First Sight*, January 1998.
2. Conservative Party Press Conference, 22 May 1987, reported in *The Guardian*, 23 May.
3. Our survey, reported in *Thirty Years On* (Benn and Chitty 1996), gives evidence of the differences found between Roman Catholic and Church of England comprehensive schools, some of the latter more likely to share some of the characteristics of GM schools.

References

Benn, C and Chitty, C (1996) *Thirty Years On: Is Comprehensive Education Alive and Well or Struggling to Survive?*, David Fulton, London

Boaler, J (1997a) *Experiencing School Mathematics: Teaching Styles, Sex and Setting*, Open University Press, Buckingham

Boaler, J (1997b) Setting, social class and survival of the quickest, *British Educational Research Journal*, **23**, 5, pp. 575–95

Burt, C (1950) Article in *The Listener*, 16 November 1950

Chitty, C (1997) The school effectiveness movement: origins, shortcomings and future possibilities, *The Curriculum Journal*, **8**, 1, pp. 45–62

CR E (1992) *Secondary School Admissions: Hertfordshire County Council Formal Investigation*, report for the Commission for Racial Equality, CRE, London

Crowther (1959) *Fifteen To Eighteen*, Report for the Ministry of Education (the *Crowther Report*), HMSO, London

Department for Education and Employment (1997) *Excellence in Schools*, White Paper, HMSO, London

DfE (1994) *Department for Education: Statistical Bulletin 10/94*, HMSO, London

HMSO (1993) *Education Statistics for the United Kingdom*, HMSO, London

Husen, T and Boalt, G (1968) *Educational Research and Educational Change: The Case of Sweden*, John Wiley, New York

Mandelson, P and Liddle, R (1996) *The Blair Revolution*, Faber, London

MoE (1945) *The Nation's Schools*, Ministry of Education White Paper, HMSO, London

Newsom (1963) *Half Our Future*, Report for the Ministry of Education (the *Newsom Report*), HMSO, London

Norwood (1943) *Curriculum and Examinations in Secondary Schools*, Report for the Secondary Schools Examinations Council (the Norwood Report), HMSO, London

OECD (1994) *School: A Matter of Choice*, HMSO, London

Postlethwaite, K and Denton, C (1978) *Streams for the Future? The Long Term Effects of Early Streaming and Non-Streaming*, Final Report of the Banbury Enquiry, Pubansco Publications, Banbury

Searle, C (1996) A different achievement: excellence in the inner city, *Forum*, **38**, 1, pp. 17–20

Simon, B (1974) *The Politics of Educational Reform 1920-1940*, Lawrence and Wishart, London

PART II

The Balance of Power

2

Local Government and Schools

Myth: Local Government as a Serious Educational Force is Finished

Valerie Hannon

Hannon asserts that providers of education must be accountable, though there are different methods through which accountability could be secured. Though it may have come close to death in recent years, a revitalized if chastened local government has a vital role to perform in the provision of education. Certain essential functions cannot be fulfilled effectively either by schools alone or by central government through its quangos.

I have to begin with the necessary disclaimer of the public servant: what follows is entirely my personal view. Even so, I am by no means as utterly certain in my views as a would-be demolisher of myths probably should be. Is it possible there's life left in the creature so regularly buried by commentators and writers in the last ten years? And if so, is the 'life' just a form of permanent vegetative state – or is something more animated capable of emerging?

The first point I would want to make is that I have deliberately elected to write about 'local government' and not specifically about LEAs. In short, my argument will be exploring the serious educational contribution to be made by a re-invented local government – not the same thing as a face-lifted LEA. And I am thinking of a timescale not exceeding a generation. Social forms are evolving faster than ever before in history. Who can say what institutions, if any, will support learning in an environment of unimaginable information and communications technology? The history of universal education in this country has been, in the overall scale of things, brief: and local government's central position in relation to it even briefer. Some see this as a brief interlude that is more or less over. I should like to consider what the options are.

The scale of the contribution thus far, however, should not be underestimated. Since their creation in 1902, and especially after 1944, LEAs were the engines of development and innovation in education. As John Tomlinson (1986, 1993) has reminded us, it was local government at full throttle of Victorian confidence which threw itself into extending universal education, and then to modernizing it to meet new needs – far outstripping the parliamentarians. LEAs were locally elected and yet were a handy means by which general policy could be adapted to local conditions and aspirations. They were agents of central policy: yet avoiding the tiresome detail that would fall upon ministers and civil servants if power were centralized. LEAs were at the heart of the major educational advances – and sought so many ways to pursue progress, from improving designs for learning environments, to establishing in-service training for teachers; from creating education psychological services to self-evaluation by schools. In any catalogue of significant educational innovations in this country this century, LEA involvement is to be found – frequently LEA initiative. Interestingly, the innovations that have particularly excited central government in recent years have also originated in LEAs. The establishment of meaningful school governing bodies, the introduction of local management of schools, the application of school improvement techniques and the first family literacy schemes – these were innovations by LEAs, not at the behest of central government. It was the LEAs, moreover, that attended to the structural pre-conditions to support learning, so unfashionable now that 'standards' matter, not structures.

Commentators tend to dwell on the size of the 'empire' which has been lost, rather than on the scale of the contribution previously made. The asset-stripping has certainly been awesome: polytechnics, further education colleges, careers services, GM schools. Perhaps more significant though, has been the erosion of capacity for influence. The major methods through which LEAs exerted influence were:

- structural design and change: school reorganizations, bringing in comprehensives, middle schools, community colleges etc
- curricular influence: innumerable curriculum development projects, subsequently co-ordinated via the Schools Curriculum Council but now largely centralized into the hands of the Qualifications and Curriculum Authority
- quality assurance: a function now almost wholly transferred to Ofsted, and

■ determining resources: funding flexibility being severely limited now by government-imposed Standard Spending Assessments and capping.

If, to all intents and purposes, LEAs are dead, who killed them? Rounding up the usual suspects will not take much time. Natural causes can be immediately eliminated. Local government in general and LEAs in particular have been vigorously assaulted. This has been no case of an institution outliving its usefulness and fading quietly away, as the parish councils or guild assemblies did. Though Margaret Thatcher is frequently cited as the major assailant, as Andrew Marr (1995) shows, neither did she set out to 'smash' local government, nor were her initial actions in seeking to control local government spending entirely novel. Previous Labour administrations had had a go, after announcing that 'the party was over'. Not only was the Tory Party strong in local government, but Thatcher's advisers on the right of the party had evolved a powerful critique of oppressive centralism. Neither individual nor collective ideological malevolence was the primary cause. Rather, a set of powerful forces came together, some of them irreversible.

These forces are still at work. They are partly, but not wholly, connected to global changes in markets and technology which require re-thinking the role of the state in general, the welfare state in particular and therefore, in due course, the role of local government. The decline of central bureaucracies; the blurring of public–private boundaries; contracting out; the rise to supremacy of managerialism over professionalism (see Stephen Ball, Chapter 5); efficiency-based forms of audit; league tables; charters, and customer 'empowerment'. All of these have characterized the changes in public life over the last decade. Many studies have analysed their pervasive spread and the early, if not long-term effects.

LEAs were seen by their critics as summing up much of what was deemed to be wrong with the education service as a whole: it was producer-dominated, inefficient, monopolistic. It was administered not managed, and it was party-political. Radicals put their faith in the market: parental choice and the elimination of producer-supremacy. Sir Keith Joseph, in a much-quoted, characteristically elegant aphorism, wrote:

> The blind, unplanned, uncoordinated wisdom of the market... is overwhelmingly superior to the well researched, rational, systematic, well-meaning, co-operative, science-based, forward looking, statistically respectable plans of government.

(Joseph, 1976)

Some of the radical right (the Centre for Policy Studies, the Institute of Economic Affairs) would have had none of the centralization (of, for example, the National Curriculum) which accompanied the devolution of power to schools and, allegedly, to parents. Others (eg the Hillgate group) accepted that the market as a mechanism for reform should be tempered by national controls to safeguard academic traditions and cultural values. But, fundamentally, the shift in control and accountability in education were part of the latest stage in the history of central government restructuring local–central relations. Nigel Lawson in his autobiography (1992) wrote:

> [The Education Reform Act] would kill two birds with one stone... Not only could we make possible the improvement in standards of education the country so badly needed, but we could also solve the linked problem of the relationship between central and local government, and the lack of local government accountability.

In this post-mortem on LEAs in their previous manifestation, though we can rule out suicide as a cause of death, it is certainly possible to argue that LEAs contributed to their own demise, or perhaps more accurately that some did. Individual instances of inefficiency or incompetence were readily generalized. Some LEAs were guilty of a loss of focus, and arrogance, especially in relation to the competence of some of their own staff. Whilst many local authorities invested heavily in education, well in excess of what the SSA system, after its introduction, suggested they should; others used their discretion to resource other projects to the detriment of education. Birmingham provides a key example of this, preferring to fund high profile municipal building programmes, as the Wragg Commission pointed out. Peter Housden (1995) put it succinctly:

> whatever larger factors were at work, and however small-minded central government might have been, local government contributed to its own decline. It could not free itself from the municipalism of earlier times. This municipalism was the product of isolated, closed and self-seeking cultures in local government politics and the professionalism of its officers. In the post-war period, allied to an increasingly strong trade union organisation, municipalism could be constructed as a 'producer culture' where the interests of the organisation and staff came first; and, at the extremes, as a home for corruption and thuggery. This blank cheque has been cashed a thousand times by our enemies.

To stay with the assault metaphor a little longer, the battering LEAs received resulted in survival techniques that led to interesting adaptations. In the research literature, one will find a whole range of typologies from field-workers observing LEAs in action in the 1990s. Kathryn Riley (1995) described a continuum of LEA styles as ranging through responsive to interventionist. Radnor and Ball (1996) basing their findings on more recent field-work found that different forms of partnership with schools was the key operating style being adopted. In some areas, new partnerships have extended in other directions. Local government has started to recognize what its distinctive contribution might be. It will need to enter into new forms of relationship with other agencies and it will have to work closely with the full spectrum from both public and private sectors. But more of this later.

Of the many consequences deriving from the attempt to kill off LEAs, that which is attracting increasing concern is the resulting lack of accountability – 'the democratic deficit'. The scale of it really needs to be underlined. Since 1979 there have been more than 150 Acts of Parliament diminishing the powers of local authorities, whilst some £24 billion of spending has been shifted to quangos. Government-appointed and self-governing bodies are now responsible for overseeing nearly £50 billion of public funds (Stoker, 1997). In 1994, there were an estimated 63,120 non-elected 'new magistrates' on these bodies – as against just over 25,000 elected local councillors. A high proportion of this is in education. Does this matter? Is it not efficiency and – to coin a phrase – standards which really count?

There are some very powerful reasons for believing it does matter. Will Hutton in his highly influential book *The State We're In* (1995) made the general case that, for Britain to progress economically or socially, the constitutional malaise had to be addressed, because they are intimately inter-connected. The 'malaise' Hutton identified is that of unaccountable, undemocratic institutions; and a semi-autocratic system of central government. The effects are felt at all levels, including that of individuals. The House of Commons Select Committee on Education (1993) observed that:

> The problem that faces us is that it is impossible to know which authority to hold accountable for any shortcoming in educational provision or use of resources. Should a parent aggrieved because the roof of his child's classroom leaks blame the governing body of the school for spending too much on (say) teachers' salaries and too little on repairs and maintenance? Or should he blame the LEA (Local Education Authority) for spending money on town halls and public relations rather than on the school's budget? Or is it the fault of the Secretary of State for the Environment in allocating insufficient revenue support grant or preventing the authority from levying the community charge or the council tax at the necessary level? Or the Secretary of State for Education for refusing to let the LEA borrow for capital spending?

But perhaps (it may be objected) accountability need not be of the political variety as long as someone can be held to account – or to 'blame' as the Select Committee put it. 'Education no more needs political control than does the provision of groceries' argued Norman Tebbit (1993). So some clarity about the forms of *accountability* available is crucial. Peter Scott (1995) suggests there are three basic forms:

1. *Market accountability* reduces the matter to a series of individual private choices. Schools, hospitals – any institutions – work when people choose them: markets promote autonomy, offering people what they want. Choice, combined with consumers empowered with information, in turn drives up standards.

2. Alternatively, *audit accountability* is a limited affair, where the focus is on ensuring that public money is spent with probity and efficiency. Parliament determines both the direction and purposes in advance. Thus, accountability is secured through processes such as those undertaken by the Audit Commission, the Funding Agency for Schools and, to some extent, the FEFC. One might argue that Ofsted provides a form of audit accountability. The trouble is, in practice no such process can be entirely value-free: and who is to say what the values should be?

3. *Democratic accountability* is, in contrast, open to public scrutiny, and judgements are made at the ballot box, not just by immediate users of the service or provision, but by all citizens. There are strong arguments to suggest it is particularly vital in relation to education which is fundamentally a public project touching, as Scott puts it, the very nerves of our society. It is, or should be, concerned with our values, our direction and our purposes as a society. Neither equality nor justice can be pursued, let alone achieved, using market or audit mechanisms alone. Moreover, it concerns the whole of the community because all have an interest in what education produces.

I do not see that the three forms of accountability outlined are mutually exclusive: we probably need all three. Currently, I think, matters are badly out of balance. But to be certain, you need a settled answer about the nature of the activity. Is the education service more like refuse collection or more like environmental planning? Can shopping replace voting? In quoting Scott above, my view is clear. The outcomes are a mix of private gain and public good, to be sure: but the public good is paramount.

If that is accepted then, it may be argued, it points to central government assuming full responsibility for education with the authority of its democratic mandate to back it. Both France and Germany consider a sound education system to be of broad public interest, so the National and *Land* (State) governments largely run the system respectively. Interestingly, though, both have been recently engaged in decentralizing. Maurice Kogan develops the specific role of central government in more depth in the next chapter. Central to my argument, though, are the contentions that democracy and accountability, in a range of forms, are vital to an education system; that this is beginning once more to be recognized, and that central government cannot of itself fulfil these functions.

If the argument for democracy and accountability is accepted, two questions follow: is a *local* dimension really necessary; and is local *government* up to the job? Some commentators argue that social mobility, along with the demand for uniform standards of service, pre-empt the need for local choice, quoting the changes in society touched on at the beginning of this chapter to support their case. Conversely, writers like John Stewart (1997) suggest that far from societal convergence, there is an increasing awareness of differentiation in society. Multi-cultural, multi-ethnic, Britain is now a place where there are growing differences in the experience of work or lack of it. People are more concerned with their local environment (especially as more begin to work at home) and seek a distinctiveness of place. Rather than a uniform standard of service, it is probably the case that people want a *satisfactory* level of service which takes account of their needs and local conditions – subject to a certain standard of acceptability. It does not take much effort of the imagination to contrast the diverse educational challenges – arising from their unique social and economic mix – of, say, Tower Hamlets, Buckinghamshire, and Barnsley. Increasingly, elected councillors believe that 'the most important role of local government is to represent the interests of people in their area'. Different people or circumstances demand different choices and ideas. This results in innovation.

To recap thus far, there is an increasing recognition that the thrust of recent changes may have put at risk some of the vital ingredients for an education system fit for a modern democratic society. These are:

- local democracy
- public accountability, in addition to market and audit forms
- innovation arising from local choice.

Before examining whether local government can be sufficiently re-shaped to take up the challenge of providing these, we may pause to consider what the options are. The first is that central government, emphasising its mandate, becomes ever more *dirigiste* and assumes ever-increasing penetration of the education service. There are some signs that that is the direction in which the Labour Government elected in 1997 is moving. National targets may be within the national government's proper domain, but is national instruction on classroom organization (DfEE, 1997) and national directives on pedagogy (cf., National Literacy Strategy)? How far are we prepared to see central control extend?

The second is that, notwithstanding mounting public disquiet, the rise of the quangos will stealthily continue. This is a seductive option for any government that is impatient of dissent and anxious for demonstrable 'results'. It satisfies the desire to control but avoids swamping Ministers with decisions and their being directly answerable. In effect, it is the scenario that Chris Woodhead (1997) recommended to the government ('any government') in his Annual Lecture in February 1997:

> the greatest conundrum any reforming politician has to face [is] how to reform when the agents for reform are necessarily part of those that are to be reformed?... The answer is... to define what schools are expected to do, to devolve real freedom to them to meet these requirements, and then to audit their performance... This must be the best tactic for any government, irrespective of its political persuasion, that wants to give parents the education they believe their children deserve.

It must be observed that the 'real freedom' for schools is increasingly difficult to discern in a context of Ofsted-sanctioned orthodoxies.

Post-16 or lifelong learning is the arena most comprehensively occupied by quangos and causing the greatest concerns about public accountability. This is not simply the matter of a few scandals involving college governors and principals, or even of locally insensitive policies being pursued wholly out of self-interest. These can, after all, be found at all levels to differing degrees, witness Jonathan Aitken, cash-for-questions, Westminster Council, Doncaster, etc. A more fundamental problem in the FE sector is the democratic deficit – the basic lack of legitimacy of governance in the FEFC sector. Whom do governors represent? To whom are they accountable? This is now widely acknowledged within the sector itself. The government has made a number of proposals for addressing this issue.

So can local government shape up to this challenge? Again, I use the term 'local government' and not LEAs. The success of the project depends upon an overall reinvention of local government, not a single element within it. And we should be clear that the LEAs of yesteryear are not to be resurrected, any more than are the styles of operation within which they worked. Too much of local government is still characterized by outmoded bureaucratic structures, outdated technology and hierarchical styles. The pre-conditions for reinvention though may be favourable. First, the Nolan and Hunt Committees have set out a clear agenda both for re-making legitimacy in democracy and the local form of it. Hunt (the House of Lords Select Committee, 1996) is a major statement, which concludes that the central–local balance needs to be re-set and makes several recommendations for action to improve relations between central and local government. The new government has already acted on some of them, ratifying the Council of Europe's Charter on Local Self-Government and undertaking to replace compulsory competitive tendering with a system of 'Best Value'. The European connection is important, since for the most part in Europe local government is seen in positive terms, treated as responsible, and not as a problem (Hirsch, 1994).

A major question is whether reform is achievable without recourse to the entrenchment of local authorities in a new constitution (which is the position in Europe and which Charter 88 advocates for Britain). Consensus appears to be growing around identifying the key functions for local government:

- the representation and advocacy of local interests
- the securing of delivery for specific services
- the regulation of specific activities.

What are the implications for the role, function and effectiveness of newly styled LEAs?

There is no shortage of models. Cordingley and Kogan (1993), after examining several forms of educational governance, concluded that an elected, multi-purpose authority, using the power to purchase whilst eschewing provision and management, could revivify local government. They conceived of this new entity as being underpinned by values of social cohesion and equality; and they saw it as brokering the market to ensure that needs were met and that there were no unfilled gaps. Similarly, the National Commission on Education (NCE, 1993) proposed a system of Education and Training Boards with a majority of members drawn from among elected local councillors but with other community interests such as TECs and Churches also represented. Analogous to the Cordingley/Kogan model, they would not be service providers but, operating at arm's length, would secure them; and they would be responsible for strategic planning, quality assurance and – interestingly – fostering innovation. Tim Brighouse's model (1996) building upon the above, proposes a *local education council*, a term designed to draw a symbolic line to mark the end of an era and signal there is no going back. His LECs would have a threefold role:

- to promote school improvement
- to act as an honest broker (answerable to the local democracy) for securing equity, and
- to be the body responsible for securing the provision of various services.

Ranson (1994), in arguing powerfully that education would benefit from stronger local government, also emphasizes a break with the past. His concept of the primary function of the local government of education is 'to enable the unfolding of the learning society within an LEA's area of responsibility'. In contrast to some of the other architects' designs, Ranson emphasizes the *structural* responsibilities to be assumed at the local democratic level: 'the functions of the strategic authority would be to establish the infrastructure, the foundations for more participation within the community'.

The Audit Commission revisited the territory it covered in *Losing an Empire, Finding a Role* (1989) with *Changing Partners* (1998). And, for this parliamentary term at least, the government has formalized its intentions with respect to LEAs in the Schools Standards and Framework Act (1998). This gives legislative expression to the new 'job description' for LEAs set out in the preceding White Paper (DfEE, 1997):

- to work in partnership with all schools in their area and with other 'key stakeholders' (eg churches)
- to develop plans for the education service and oversee their implementation
- to challenge and support schools to improve
- to have some new powers of intervention.

Many regard this as a positive new start, and perhaps it is. It is hardly radical though. It scarcely addresses the underlying problems of accountability and democracy; these are considered elsewhere in the context of local government as a whole. It is a partial view, with no account yet taken of the formidable issues in respect of lifelong learning – especially, in my view, the need to stimulate and sustain wider participation at the local level. Realistically, local government has yet to transform and reinvent itself to a much greater degree if it is to be proffered any more than the limited role under licence, policed by Ofsted inspection of LEAs.

So we return to the broader project of local government reinvention. In July 1998 the government published a White Paper *Modern Local Government: In Touch with the People* which outlined the greatest reform agenda for local government in 20 years. Key proposals include:

- new duty on councils 'to promote the economic, social and environmental well being' of their areas
- reformed electoral processes – more frequent elections, more accessible processes
- reviewed decision-making processes – options of elected mayors, cabinets etc
- scrapping of crude, universal capping, and access to business rates, and
- duty to provide Best Value in the provision of services, replacing compulsory competitive tendering.

As a result, lively debates are being held in council chambers about the agenda for local government. The government's initiative will provide a powerful incentive to accelerate this process. I believe this will create conditions in which councillors, previously committed to providing services directly, will be able to focus outward on the needs of the locality and the best ways to meet them. This outward focus is the first step in recapturing the opportunity held out in the Bains Report on local government of 1972:

> Local government is not in our view limited to the narrow provision of services to the local community... It has in its purview the overall economic, cultural and physical well-being of that community.

This represents a fundamental shift in what has been the basic outlook of the majority of local councils. Without it, it is improbable that local government, through the isolated efforts of its education committee and department, can be a *serious force* in education in the future, though it could continue to fulfil a number of roles.

Representing the interests of localities, by first identifying needs and subsequently striving to secure they are met, can be defined specifically with reference to education. Cordingley and Harrington (1996) in their study of 'Communities, Schools and LEAs' investigate a range of needs that schools cannot meet individually. They include ensuring equitable access; monitoring standards; balancing long-term and short-term requirements; appeals and complaints, and so on. However, the most powerful impact will be achieved by developing an understanding of needs in the broader social context of a locality. These are likely to include issues such as economic regeneration or development. This will play out very differently in Kent, looking toward the impact of European integration, as opposed to South Yorkshire, recovering from the closure of the mines. Similarly, concerns over environmental sustainability and community safety will have distinctive local features. The role of the education service in responding to these needs, *in real partnership with other services and agencies,* is only beginning to be explored.

A new role

Time to offer my own blueprint. I emphasize again that the role I propose only makes sense if it is part of a new approach in local government as a whole. It will be through developing the following roles that the new style LEAs will seriously take education forward.

Developing an educational vision for the locality

Lest there be any confusion, I am *not* talking here about more of the dreaded target-setting. Rather I am referring to conducting that wider debate which gives meaning to the whole process of learning. It is just no use endlessly to exhort 'raising standards' if the nagging question remains unanswered: 'what's it all for?' Neil Postman (1997) suggests we have two sets of problems with schooling. One is technical – 'the means by which the young become learned – the how to do it'. The other is to construct a *reason* for schooling. This is not the same as motivation, which is a temporary psychological event. What is our idea of its purpose? He shows that the answer is reinvented over time: it has to be as the environment changes, for 'there is no surer way to bring an end to schooling than for it to have no end'. In the USA, Postman suggests that the great 'narratives' which have underpinned education have been, in turn:

- *the Great Project of Democracy*: creating the model society from 'the huddled masses'
- *the Protestant Work Ethic:* hard work and deferred gratification bring their own rewards
- *the God of Economic Utility:* in which the purpose of learning is to prepare for entry into economic life.

He proposes a new narrative – that of *Spaceship Earth*. In this, human beings are stewards of the vulnerable space capsule Earth. It is a vision of interdependence, which, when fully developed, can evoke in the young a sense of responsibility and commitment. In his book, he develops a few other narratives. We are, of course, back to values again, but these will only have resonance if they connect with 'how it is'. More mundanely, this can be described as reflecting needs and interests, but not just in the sense of advocacy. This entails leadership which, as Howard Gardner (1995) shows in his insightful study of the nature of leadership, is often about telling a story. The power of the 'story' to be told will relate to how far it connects with the experience of individuals and communities. The very language and metaphors adopted can make a difference.

Promoting a learning community and raising achievement

I have not dubbed this function 'school improvement' because I believe it goes much deeper than that. A cultural shift – towards a learning community – is a pre-condition for raising achievement across the board. Hence energetic promotion of lifelong learning – for teachers and education officers as well as unemployed parents and pre-schoolers – must be a high priority and it must take place at the *level of communities*. For example, the

Kennedy Report (1997) on Widening Participation proposes to create a national network of strategic partnerships to 'identify local need, stimulate demand, respond creatively and promote learning'. In the fractured, still-competitive world of post-16 and higher education, this is surely right. Local government should have placed upon it the duty to convene and support such partnerships – in much the same way as they have been with respect to the Early Years sector. The partnership should do the following:

- share an analysis of local need
- commit themselves to shared goals
- set out explicit targets for participation, and
- show evidence of multi-agency partnerships.

This is the kind of approach adopted in some 'Learning City' initiatives. It has relevance for all areas. So too does the under-developed potential of the Youth Service in re-engaging in learning those whom the compulsory system has not reached.

Supporting continuous improvement amongst schools is, of course, central and the particular contribution LEAs can make is taking shape. The key elements are as follows:

- knowing about levels of achievement, through data analysis and interpretation
- communicating these analyses
- planning for improvement
- implementing change, and
- monitoring progress.

Classically, the old LEAs were much better at implementation and weaker on the other aspects. That is changing very fast, and the government's agenda will accelerate it. Since Ofsted's recognition (1997) that 'most schools in [these] disadvantaged areas do not have within themselves the capacity for sustainable renewal', LEAs have ceased to be cast as the rescue-and-retrieval service for failing schools alone. The model is emphatically *not* one in which the LEA promotes a given orthodoxy. Rather it is one that creates a learning community of schools, informed by evidence and research, and supported both in modifying practice and in evaluating the results. Currently the main measures of achievement are test and exam results. If they can develop some self-confidence, LEAs and schools will want to monitor improvement in other aspects of learning also. They should both promote and monitor aspects of achievement in personal and social education, for example, the degree to which both self-esteem and citizenship are developed. This will come as no surprise given what I have said about the intimate relationship between education and democracy and the importance of the *ends* of education. Interestingly, support for this view comes from an unexpected source, in the shape of the Chief Executive of the QCA, Nick Tate. He recently observed (1997):

> We are almost unique in the world in not having education for citizenship as part of our formal curriculum. ... there is a key role for local authorities here: in helping schools prepare children to be citizens of local communities and in bringing together the different agencies with an interest in young people's development.

I see this as a vitally important aspect of raising achievement, and one that is in some danger of being marginalized or worse in the target-driven, determined focus on the 'basics.'

I do not wish to detail further the role of the LEA in school improvement here. In any case, there is now widespread recognition of the need for an intermediate tier, at least at the professional level. One aspect that requires thought though, is how innovation is to be fostered. Of course, the 'implementing change' phase of the cycle I have described should enable schools to select a method or approach on which there is evidence to show its effectiveness. Where, though, is the safe space for innovation to be created? It is a high-risk strategy for a single school to embark upon. New orthodoxies are in danger of taking a rigid hold. LEAs should be capable of sponsoring innovative initiatives from schools, ensuring they are rigorously evaluated and creating the intellectual climate where ideas can emerge and not just be received.

Deciding upon and planning the infrastructure

Debate and decision about which structure is best suited to promoting the learning community and securing equity at the local level should take place where public accountability is strongest. No quangos, no individual schools can properly fulfil the function. If it is left to the market, equity will be the casualty.

Ensuring equity and fairness

Protecting the interests of the disadvantaged, the excluded and the disengaged will be in the best interests of the whole community in the long run. Again, the specific forms of this will differ widely between localities. So promoting inclusive education is properly a function for the local authority, to be achieved through structural means, through its values, and by making practical support available.

Securing services of best value

This means ensuring that the services provided to schools by whatever supplier are of high quality and value for money, including any directly provided services, from the Youth Service to Education Social Work. It extends also to identifying where new needs arise, and reacting responsively, but not alone, to them. I am thinking here of examples such as new forms of social exclusion; and the learning, leisure and social as well as care needs of an ever-ageing population, living longer and longer.

Conclusion

What, then, are the immediate prospects? I'd say 50/50. The government, in their proposals so far, have been cautious. They have, as far as education goes, been distrustful of local democracy – although quite willing to use LEAs as their agents. The 'settlement' they propose (between central government, local government, schools and quangos) will, I suspect, prove to be unstable and they or their successors will need to look at it again. Some have pointed, rather than at the modest rehabilitation cautiously offered in the 1998 Act, to the new power it provides for the centre to assume the education functions of an LEA where it is judged to be 'failing'. At the time of writing, two authorities (Hackney and Calderdale) face this threat. LEAs must retain the approval from the centre if they are to 'retain their licence'. Here is a further acknowledgement that an education service does need effective strategic management at the local level. But, of course, it sweeps aside the Elected Member dimension.

Curiously, in another part of the forest the Tories, under the leadership of William Hague, are re-discovering the importance of local government, particularly for the revival of a party now virtually bereft of local roots or activism. A curious left–right–communitarian reappraisal of local government could be in prospect. The right can call upon the most respected of their gurus in support:

> While it has always been characteristic of those favouring an increase in governmental powers to support maximum concentration of these powers, those mainly concerned with individual liberty have generally advocated decentralisation. There are strong reasons why action by local authorities generally offers the next-best solution where private initiative cannot be relied upon to provide certain services and where some sort of collective action is therefore needed; for it has many of the advantages of private enterprise and fewer of the dangers of the coercive action of government. Competition between local authorities or between larger units within an area where there is freedom of movement provides in a large measure that opportunity for

experimentation with alternative methods which will secure most of the advantages of free growth.

(Hayek, 1960)

Sir Norman Fowler announced on 31 October 1997 the Conservative Party's 'commitment to a fresh approach to local government'. One task confronting any government in this field will be to sort out the appalling mess made of local government reorganization initiated by Sir John Banham, the legacy of which now lacks any rationale.

I am not really in the business of making predictions though. What ought to be is not necessarily what will be. However, I do believe that the 'unfolding of the learning society' depends upon an active, participative local democracy with a direct investment in education. It also serves to create and sustain that democracy.

References

Audit Commission (1989) *Losing an Empire, Finding a Role,* Audit Publications, Abingdon, Oxon

Audit Commission (1998) *Changing Partners,* Audit Publications, Abingdon, Oxon

Brighouse, T (1996) *A Question of Standards,* Politeia, London

Cordingley, P and Kogan, M (1993) *In Support of Education,* Jessica Kingsley, London

Cordingley, P and Harrington, T (1996) *Communities, Schools and LEAs: Learning to Meet Needs,* AMA, London

Department for Education and Employment (1997) *Excellence in Schools,* White Paper, HMSO, London

Department for the Environment, Transport and the Regions (1998) *Modern Local Government: In Touch with the People,* White Paper, HMSO, London

Department of the Environment (1972) *New Local Authorities: Management and Structure,* the Bains Report, HMSO, London

Gardner, H (1995) *Leading Minds: An Anatomy of Leadership,* HarperCollins, New York

Hayek, FA (1960) *The Constitution of Liberty,* Routledge and Kegan Paul, London

Hirsch, D (1994) *A Positive Role for Local Government: Lessons for Britain from Other Countries,* Joseph Rowntree Foundation, London

Housden, P (1995) A rough guide to local government, unpublished presentation to ALG Annual Conference at Institute of Contemporary Arts, London

House of Commons Select Committee on Education (1993) *First Report Session 1992–93,* HMSO, London

House of Lords Select Committee (1996) *Rebuilding Trust: Report of the Select Committee on Relations between Central and Local Government,* HMSO, London

Hutton, W (1995) *The State We're In,* Random House, London

Joseph, Sir K (1976) *Stranded on the Middle Ground*, Centre for Policy Studies, London

Kennedy, H (1997) *Learning Works: Widening Participation in Further Education*, FEFC, London

Lawson, N (1992) *The View from Number 11*, Bantam Press, London

Marr, A (1995) *Ruling Britannia: The Failure and Future of British Democracy*, Penguin, London

NCE (1993) *Learning to Succeed: Final Report of the National Commission on Education*, Heinemann, London

Ofsted (1997) *Access and Achievement in Urban Education*, HMSO, London

Postman, N (1997) *The End of Education: Redefining the Value of School*, Methuen, New York

Radnor, H A and Ball, S (1996) *Local Education Authorities: Accountability and Control*, Trentham Books, London

Ranson, S (1994) *Towards the Learning Society*, Cassell, London

Riley, K (1995) *Managing for Quality in an Uncertain Climate*, LGMB, London

Scott, P S (1995) Why public accountability matters in the governance of education, unpublished presentation to CLEA Annual Conference, Brighton

Stewart, J (1997) The government of difference, in M Chisholm, R Hale and D Thomas (eds) *A Fresh Start for Local Government*, CIPFA, London

Stoker, G (1997) The new forms of local governance, in M Chisholm, R Hale and D Thomas (eds), *A Fresh Start for Local Government*, CIPFA, London

Tate, N (1997) Innovation and excellence, speech to CLEA Annual Conference, Bristol

Tebbit, N (1993) *Unfinished Business*, Weidenfeld and Nicolson, London

Tomlinson, J (1986) Public education, public good, *Oxford Review of Education*, **12**, (3)

Tomlinson, J (1993) *The Control of Education*, Cassell, London

Woodhead, C (1997) Do we have the schools we deserve?, Annual Lecture of HMCI, Ofsted, London

3

National and Local Government

Myth: Good Education Requires Strong Central Direction

Maurice Kogan

Kogan dissects the way the Thatcher administration reversed the long-standing theory of government, rupturing the previous delicate consensual balance of power. Using the concept of a 'corporatist bargain', he argues for a new relationship between central government and local government, and the professionals who have the 'hottest' on-the-spot knowledge. We must allow schools and teachers more professional autonomy and authority, to counterbalance the overwhelming degree of public accountability they now have to endure.

National and local policy is an area in which red herrings ride hobbyhorses up blind alleys in abundance. In exposing myths, we can easily build up equally fallacious opposite propositions. Strong ministries do not necessarily make for good education, but neither do weak ones. Undoubtedly, the national authority has a right to create frameworks within which public services work. My point is that there has to be a carefully worked out balance and interaction between national policies and the factors that actually bring about quality in education. These are not statements from ministers or their courtiers. They include the knowledge, values and immediate working contexts within which teachers and other practitioners work. A system that sucks power to the centre but fails to clarify the mandate within which teachers work, will fail. I hope this chapter will stimulate thinking about that mandate.

In this chapter, I will explore different patterns of national policy-making, the ways in which they might relate to local policy making, and how both of these frame the work of the schools. I will try to test both efficacy and the legitimacy of the national authorities and I will then relate them to what might be the professional identity of the teacher.

I will begin by briefly outlining the two historic models of the national role in education, if only to remind us that what we now have is not was has always been, or needs to be.

The post–1945 model

From the early 1900s, the British educational system became increasingly decentralized. In the early 1900s, there were still powerful prescriptions from the centre about the curriculum, and these were promoted by the activities of Her Majesty's Inspectors of Schools, who were putatively autonomous, but, in fact, part of central government.

In so many ways, the British had kept themselves free from the power of the central state. Unlike every other European country, we had not made our teachers or academics into civil servants. As Britain moved towards universal public services, it put its weight behind local rather than central governance of public services. John Stuart Mill (1859) had put the argument for local government much earlier: 'The very object of having local representation is in order that those who have an interest in common which they do not share with the general body of their countrymen may manage that joint interest by themselves.'

Support for local government derived from both positive and negative considerations:

- dislike of the clutter of private and privileged groups that hitherto had performed essential functions
- fear of an over-centralized state apparatus
- a belief that local groups should be able to re-interpret national interests
- proximity of control to those affected by services
- effectiveness of delivery
- the encouragement of democratic ways of working and thinking, and
- an emphasis on the needs of local society.

In Europe, only perhaps the Netherlands had traditionally sustained the argument for governmental pluralism. When, in the late 1980s, some countries (for example, Norway and Sweden) moved from somewhat oppressive centralization to radical decentralization, they displayed ambivalence about the need for the central government department to exercise strategic powers. This seems essential if education is to contribute usefully to general social and economic policy.

In 1950, Education Minister George Tomlinson and Permanent Secretary Sir John Maud wrote that the Ministry had aimed 'to build a single, but not a uniform, system out of many diverse elements'. The release from central control had been in train since the early years of the century and was enshrined in the 1944 Education Act. This gave local education authorities the power over curriculum and conduct of schools, a power that they effectively delegated to schools. The strategic powers included:

- certification to the department responsible for local government finance (now the Department of the Environment) on the resources that should flow for education to local authorities
- the supply and structure of teacher training
- approval of major building projects
- approval of the creation of or change in status of schools, and
- secondary school examination policy

The central department could pass legislation which affected the structure of education, for example, the ages and stages of pre-school, primary and secondary education. From the mid-1960s national legislation determined how far secondary education should be organized on selective lines, a choice which government had not decided to exercise in 1944. (It is, incidentally, a fallacy to assume that the 1944 Act *required* LEAs to organize secondary education in a selective tripartite system.) Only the central government could decide to raise the school-leaving age to 15 and then 16 or that trainee teachers should receive a three-year rather than a two-year course. Social policy determined some of these while others were decided on educational grounds.

National policies were essentially frames within which local authorities and schools were relatively free to develop their own styles and thereby add to the stock of practical knowledge. They could determine much of the 'what' as well as the 'how' of education.

It was explicitly the duty of publicly elected local authorities to run education. Lord Hailsham, in the course of his brief tenure of the education Ministry, was clear about the limitations on national power. As he put it:

> In the Admiralty, you are a person having authority. You say to one person 'Come' and he cometh, and another 'Go' and he goeth. It is not so in the Ministry of Education. You suggest rather than direct. You say to one man 'Come' and he cometh not and to another 'Go' and he stays where he is.

(Kogan, 1971)

It is a pity that he did not go into the reasons for the differences. We do not want admirals deciding whom to attack. We do want teachers acting out of individual professional strength.

Local education authorities owned the schools, employed the teachers, inspected schools (in parallel with Her Majesty's Inspectors at the centre), set admissions policies and were, in general, a real level of authority as experienced by the schools. For a long time, ministers were loath to interfere in what local authorities did even when they thought some of their decisions wrong or unfair. The central departments had the power to declare an action either in default of duty or unreasonable, although those powers, too, became increasingly restricted under the scrutiny of the courts.

Legally LEAs had power over the curriculum in the schools, but invariably delegated that power to the schools. Schools mainly determined their curriculum and conduct for themselves. I am puzzled by more recent ministerial statements to the effect that the LEAs held the schools in a bureaucratic stranglehold – the excuse for taking away many of their powers. This assumption continues to colour the actions and words of the most recently elected government. Certainly there were some powerful Chief Education Officers – Morris of Cambridgeshire, Clegg of the West Riding, Newsam of Hertfordshire, Longland of Derbyshire, Chorlton of Oxfordshire, Mason of Leicestershire. They influenced the work of the schools profoundly through the advisory services they offered and through their links with heads whose appointments they also influenced. It is also true that in the 1970s and 1980s, when ideology entered education policies and politics more sharply, some local authorities became more prescriptive than hitherto. By world comparison, however, the schools were the freest anywhere to make their curricula, within the broadest of policy steers, and the resources made available by the LEAs.

If the attacks on LEAs were largely misdirected, from the late 1950s there were several better-founded criticisms of local government in general. Many considered the system inadequate to cope with the growing demands made on it as the state continued to extend the range of public services. There were concerns about the quality of the democratic process and its formal and unresponsive nature. In the 1970s and 1980s there were strong criticisms of the way in which local government handled local taxes and of the behaviour of some local councillors and officials (Redcliffe-Maud and Wood, 1974; Widdicombe, 1986).

Within, then, this relatively relaxed regime of central and LEA control, the schools, under mainly ineffective boards of governors, had *de facto* control over the curriculum that they offered. Secondary schools were constrained by the requirements of the public examination system. Although a quango (the Secondary School Examinations Council) supervised the examination boards, they were largely independent of government, and school and university teachers determined the syllabuses. The secondary schools could choose which examination board they used. The primary schools no longer deferred to the requirements of 11+ selection once most LEAs had abandoned these tests in the 1970s. In effect, the headteacher and governors appointed teachers, although usually with the advice of the local authority in the case of senior appointments. They were free to create their own style and their own relationship with client groups. Although barely recognized as such, there was an implicit negotiation between social and economic norms and the norms of individual child development.

There were two linked theories underlying these arrangements, one educational and the other political. The first derived from assumptions about the nature of learning and teaching, and the second from consequent assumptions about the relationships between professionalism and democracy.

A long while ago now, Julia Evetts (1973) made the distinction between the idealist and the progressive theory of education. The idealist theory of education assumes that learning can and should depend upon a world of knowledge, skills and values which is built up and can be handed on to successive generations of teachers and learners. In the progressive theory, the teacher has to introduce knowledge, skills and values but pupils then acquire them more firmly because they have 'discovered' them for themselves. This does not mean that all is to be play and freedom, but rather that pupils' readiness, interest and involvement mediate the acquisition of mathematical concepts and mastery of the spoken or written language powerfully.

By the late 1960s, American authors influenced by John Dewey were celebrating the progressive nature of English primary schools. In fact, however, the Plowden Report on primary education (1967) showed that about 40 per cent of primary schools worked in the progressive mode. At secondary level, it never really took hold. Indeed, it is difficult to see how some of the knowledge required to master foreign languages, calculus, trigonometry or organic chemistry, which does not contain self-evident propositions, could be acquired in that way.

That theory of learning went along with assumptions about the nature of educational government. It assumed that the professionals (teachers) should negotiate the curriculum in the light of what they perceive to be the needs of their groups of pupils. In this theory, notions of hierarchy and of control come under challenge and schools are collegial rather than hierarchical in managerial style. The curriculum and methods for its transmission are to some extent a matter of choice, or, as Denis Lawton (1980) put it, they are a selection from the culture. Professionals in interaction with their pupils should make this selection. It follows that schools should not have to accept the particular selection made for a national curriculum or by the standards and criteria implied in HMI judgements. The local education authority and HMIs acted more in an advisory role, although both had powers of inspection.

The schools acted within such external frames as the public examinations, biting particularly into the later stages of secondary school curriculum, the expectations of employers and those of higher education with its selective entry. The complaints of successive governments from the mid-1970s were that schools neglected social and economic in favour of permissive ideologies. These were fuelled by employer organizations who complained of having weaker candidates to choose from (as more stayed on into sixth forms, colleges and universities with the expansion of higher education following the Robbins Report), and by high profile moral panics such as those at Risinghill and William Tyndale.

Anxiety came to the surface in the Green Paper published in 1977 by a Labour government (Green Paper, 1977). Pressure for change built up mainly in the period of the Thatcher and post-Thatcher governments (from 1979), although Conservative anxieties about standards were being expressed as long ago as in the 1950s (Knight, 1990). By 1986, the Conservatives had reached the point where they felt able to turn on their head previous understandings of local government and decentralization.

The post–1986 model

The new dispensations assume the idealist universe of knowledge, skills and values of which the school curriculum is to be a derivative. Teachers must abide by these common reference points and standards, and 'deliver' (a word that has all but replaced the word 'teach' in official parlance) a centrally ordained curriculum. This will not only be sound knowledge but also the knowledge which society needs to meet common social, economic and cultural objectives. In the idealist theory, there is also a national culture. Dr Nicholas Tate, Chief Executive to the Qualifications and Curriculum Authority, emphasizes that it is sacrosanct, and schools should induct their pupils into it. With knowledge and skills firmly circumscribed by the Secretary of State and mirrored in examination boards syllabuses, the publication of assessment and inspection results will provide parents with information equivalent to that available to the customer in the free market. Ofsted becomes a kind of Consumers' Association. Schools will be 'freed' from the local authority who retain a much-weakened monitoring and support role. At the same time, central government has taken control of the curriculum from the teaching profession, the schools and local authorities.

In this set of transactions, knowledge is not negotiable, in principle. The school with its individual teachers is not the site where knowledge grows through a pedagogical relationship, but a kind of sub-station for handing over the knowledge generated elsewhere by great minds. This is the model underlying many continental systems, most famously the French, though it underpins the Swedish Läroplan and the Norwegian Mønsterplan as well.

From this theory of educational development springs a model of governance that places power in the hands of central entities. This is now taken to the point where a National Literacy Strategy specifies a Literacy Hour for every primary school and dictates the methods to be used, and asserts for secondary schools that grouping by ability should be the norm. The British welfare state entailed the assumption that professionals would mediate altruistic objectives through public institutions. The 'public' element in this would be the elective principle, as represented by the LEA. Both recent governments have substituted for the public institutional model something far more ambiguous. Central control over content and powerful evaluation of inspection of standards and performance go alongside quasi-market philosophies and mechanisms. Pupils are free to enter the school of their own choice, within certain limits, and schools must now compete for pupils. 'Special measures' apply to those that fail and closure will follow continued failure. Government measures and publishes performance results. More than ever, central government dictates the size of school through its Standard Spending Assessment and rate capping. Yet, headteachers and governors have more freedom to dispense their budgets. They must become entrepreneurs both by exploiting their resources and by marketing their schools. In the past, LEAs held schools together in an educational community, providing leadership based on consensus and connection between different parts of the education system within an area. Now the LEAs, too, find themselves part of the market. They retain some providing and monitoring functions from their own funds, but have no resources to provide their own support to schools, such as in-service training, curriculum advice and the like. The schools now choose whether to 'buy' services from the LEA or elsewhere. However, the leaner and streamlined 'service' is often too weak to be coherent or effective.

Thus, we see a radical shift in concepts of governance and democracy. Negotiation is not the order of the day. Local authorities are largely crowded out of the political arena. Getting good representation at the national level for teachers as professionals has never been easy but the proposed GTC looks like a weak version of 1930s' corporatism. The only democratic inputs come from the elected central government and the somewhat uncertain inputs of parents on governing bodies. National government is democratic in a somewhat remote sense. We have little encounter with, let alone control over, David Blunkett, Estelle Morris, Chris Woodhead or Michael Barber.

Should educational policy and practice be decided solely by central government and its quangos in response to national needs, or also by those elected to analyse and respond to local needs and wants, as Valerie Hannon has argued (Chapter 2). If the national authorities, the local community, professional teachers and their client groups all have a part to play in setting educational values and content, then we have to look to a negotiated, not an imposed order.

The constituents of power

Where should this leave us? In thinking about what ought to be, we need to pull out the whole range of social preferences or value positions that reasonable people might wish to advance. Both the New Labour government and its predecessor have adopted a coercive social engineering model, deaf to the complaints, feelings and subtleties of the other prime actors.

Central government should lay down the broad structure and purposes of the education system. It cannot evade its role in guaranteeing the proper monitoring of educational content and structure. The relationship between professionals and the state in determining the shape and quality of public policies is an issue that goes well beyond education. In the health service, medical and clinical audit, as well as disciplinary codes, have become more stringent. In the legal sphere, judges and lawyers are subject to rigorous forms of review and appeal. However, none of them undergoes unremitting external inspection in order to weed out incompetence. At the same time, there is not much satisfaction with the redress available to complainants. For the most part, the state has depended upon a 'corporatist' bargain (Cawson, 1986) in which it develops a trustful relationship with the professions and other interest groups and incorporates them into its policy-making and supervision of standards. This has never fully developed in education, because politicians, and perhaps the public at large, do not consider teachers to be well enough qualified to be in control of their own standards. However, as central government's mistrust of its professional teachers grows, so those teachers become less capable of making their own professional judgements.

If there is indeed a real problem of standards, and I am not competent to judge, external monitoring is certain to be required. But if, at the same time, the teaching profession is to move into a position where it is both trusted and trustworthy, they have to be incorporated more closely into that monitoring process. Criteria by which they are judged will also need to take account of the individual creative potential of teachers and of schools.

These are some of the factors that will circumscribe the power exercised by government. Others are the extent of the knowledge that it can bring to bear, and the identity and power conceded to other actors in the scene.

Knowledge limitations

Knowledge first, then. What can government know? There are two sources of its knowledge. First, it has the knowledge of standards offered to it by Ofsted and by the battery of standardized tests which schools are required to undergo. Second, it receives advice from savants, chosen by itself, on quangos, or within the walls of the central department.

A third source is missing – what Martin Rein (1973) calls 'hot knowledge'. It is the developing knowledge generated by professional practitioners who have to 'deliver' the curriculum, who face the client groups and whose vision of reality may be quite different from that of the central curriculum makers and inspectors. Hot knowledge grows cold when far away from its point of origin.

The preferred knowledge of officials and ministers is very cold indeed. Central administrators have to decontextualize if they are to make over-arching judgements. That, however, weakens the legitimacy of over-arching judgements in comparison with those of the field professionals. Performance indicators are prime examples of knowledge with no context – cold knowledge. Their use involves making judgements on outputs. These have the advantage of being easily comparable whereas everything we know suggests that the components of school performance include subtle and complex processes and contextual factors including the following:

- the 'stock' of buildings and staff with which a school is endowed
- the human capital – pupils and their families with which they work
- the expectations generated within the community, and
- the network of schools within which it acts.

Some of these factors are immovable, or affected only by careful work with individual pupils and their families over time scales beyond those of annual target setting. In operating on them the school has to rely on individual teachers within their basic units – the departments and the like. All difficult factors for national policy-makers to convert into aggregate national policies.

Change models must therefore start with individual practitioners and factors that affect them: school leadership, collaborative work, the support of friendly but rigorous critics. The use of data will help focus action, but it is not the action itself. Performance indicators should be used as can-openers rather than as dials.

The repertoire of change agents offered by the government uses knowledge of a particular type, determined by its susceptibility to central exploitation. There is an enormous superstructure of monitoring and inspection, accompanied by such phrases as 'No hiding place', first used I think by the FBI and more latterly by US Presidents referring to terrorists. In two 1997 White Papers, the rhetoric was that schools have both the freedom and the responsibility to improve themselves, but that the penalties for not doing so will be severe. The frame will be set by targets which they may set themselves, but by reference to externally imposed standards, national averages, the criteria employed by Ofsted and the monitoring in which LEAs are now to have a part. The setting of targets on comparative performance may mean that schools may advance themselves but never get to average or above average performance.

Professional power and legitimacy

Central government has legitimacy but it is constrained by the remoteness of its democratic mandate and by the equally remote nature of its knowledge. Yet, recent governments focused their attention mainly at the school. We are told there will be unrelenting pressure on teachers, that they will be celebrated for their achievements, and they will have access to external expertise. The Standards and Effectiveness Unit and the task forces will formulate the changes and lead them. There will be scholarships for those thought outstanding (selected by whom?), and the Houghton formula of the senior teacher is to be resurrected under another name.

None of this meets with the notion of teaching as a profession. At its core, professionalism is individualistic. Professionals acquire legitimacy through their possession of specialized knowledge and skills created by the professionals themselves, and through their altruistic concern for their clients. Public and social concerns prescribe limits within their work, but within those limits, discretion and freedom on content and style of work are what distinguishes professionalism from routine skilled work and functions. Professionals conform to norms laid down by professionals, with their actions judged against those norms; even judges are subject to review and appeal. Nevertheless, the power of those exogenous forces merely balances the power, knowledge and values of the practitioner. Knowledge and external prescriptions need to be internalized if they are to contribute to good work.

If there is no living concept of the self-interrogating practitioner, education is a dead process, a collection of uncoordinated external inspection and curriculum frames. There has been no competent statement of what constitutes the teachers' role in terms of their knowledge and their free-doms to develop their styles and methods and knowledge. We need a state-ment of a teacher's mandate. The 1997 White Papers and the legislation built on them contain statements about what others will do to teachers. I cannot see why anybody would want to be a teacher under this life plan. It does not face up to the essential issue of what should be the relationship between professionals and the state.

Teacher identity

It is possible to view the same issues from a different perspective. A gifted colleague of mine, Mary Henkel (1996), has been working on the concept of academic identity. She has done so for the same purpose as underlies the composition of this chapter – to assess the impacts of reforms on, in this case, higher education. We have been asking what have been the effects on research agendas, curriculum, modes of teaching and learning and the pro-fessional heartland of epistemic identity.

In looking through the philosophical and social psychological literature on identity, Mary Henkel identified essential concepts that are as relevant to schoolteachers as to university academics. They depict the distinctive individual who has a unique history, who is located in a chosen moral and conceptual framework, and who is identified by the goods that she or he has achieved. These three elements of individual identity make a teacher an effective professional and a good person. The processes of professional education and experience adds strength and maturity.

The distinctive individual is nevertheless an embedded individual. He or she is a member of communities and institutions which have their own lan-guages, conceptual structures, histories, traditions, myths, values, prac-tices and achieved goods. The individual has roles that are strongly determined by the communities and institutions of which he or she is a member.

Thus, we need a notion of professional identity that is both individual and social. People are stronger because of their expertise and their own moral and conceptual frameworks but also because they are performing a range of roles required of them by their communities and institutions.

All of this is compatible both with professional freedom and with observ-ing social needs. Nowhere in recent official literature does one see an effec-tive statement of the role and identity of the individual teacher. Instead the teacher is someone who has things done to him or her. The constituents of professionality that I have just outlined sit at odds with the kind of behav-ioural steering and prescriptive frames laid down by recent govern-ment-inspired actions and policies.

The local authority

This chapter is not about the role of the local authority, but there is a wider polity than the school, most obviously incorporated in the local authority. Election is not a pure process, and it brings some funny coves to the surface or even the top of the power system, but we have no other way of legitimizing the exercise of subjective choices. There are issues that go beyond single schools, and beyond the education service. The need is patent for planning mechanisms that can, for example, sort out post-16 provision, or relations between teachers and social workers. And the role of the critical friend, which so many schools now buy back from LEAs, but which government regards as part of 'pressure and support', is also important. It becomes more so as schools have to face the whole burden of raising standards, setting targets, evaluating performance, developing staff, monitoring budgets and educating probationary teachers, not to mention providing education for their pupils. The strength of the local authority will depend on its capacity to both enhance professional co-operation across schools and relate education to the wider concerns of its area, providing for locally determined needs.

Conclusion

We need strong central government. Its strength will rest not only on the powers it has accumulated, but also on its ability to understand that it is dealing with a complex world. It is a world where knowledge is multi-faceted and conflicting, where the values, interests and knowledge sets of competing groups have to be reconciled. They are the central authorities, the local authorities, the schools, the teachers and the clients.

In the present scheme, central government assumes it knows best. It is astonishing that the leaders of local authorities have done nothing to bring them to book. That set of relationships is undemocratic and dysfunctional. We are not looking for uniform outputs produced by pre-set machines. Rather, we need a system in which young people learn habits of human interaction and creativity as well as basic knowledge and skills. They will acquire these from teachers who themselves feel fully mandated and not in deference to some inspector. This is inimical to hierarchy. Instead, it requires a negotiated order or a corporatist bargain.

References

Cawson, A (1986) *Corporatism and Political Theory*, Basil Blackwell, Oxford

Evetts, J (1973) *The Sociology of Educational Ideas*, Routledge and Kegan Paul, London

Department for Education and Employment (1997) *Excellence in Schools*, White Paper, HMSO, London

Henkel, M (1996) Academic identity, unpublished paper given to Higher Education Studies Group, London

Knight, C (1990) *The Making of Tory Education Policy in Post-War Britain 1950-1986*, Falmer Press, London

Kogan, M (1971) *The Politics of Education*, Penguin Books, Harmondsworth

Lawton, D (1980) *Politics of the School Curriculum*, Routledge and Kegan Paul, London

Mill, J S (1859) *On Liberty*, republished in 'On Liberty and Other Writing', *Cambridge Texts in the History of Thought*, (ed. Stefan Collini), Cambridge University Press, Cambridge

Ministry of Education (1963) *Report of the Committee on Higher Education*, the Robbins Report, HMSO, London

Plowden Report (1967) *Children and their Primary Schools*, Report of the Central Advisory Council for Education (England), HMSO, London

Lord Redcliffe-Maud and Wood, B (1974) *Local Government Reformed*, Oxford University Press, Oxford

Rein, M (1973) *From Policy to Practice*, Macmillan, Basingstoke

Widdicombe Report (1986) *The Conduct of Local Authority Business, Report of the Committee of Enquiry into Local Government Business*, Cmnd 9797, HMSO, London

PART III
The School Community

4

Communities of Learners

Myth: Schools are Communities

Michael Fielding

In this chapter, the focus moves to the institutional level. Most schools refer to themselves as communities, but what exactly does this mean? Fielding draws on the work of Scottish philosopher John Macmurray, interweaving the concepts of freedom and equality to show that learning communities have uniquely powerful characteristics. Empirically, they may be much harder to find than the looser associations of individuals cohabiting in school buildings for functional purposes. He shows how the myth of the school community has masked a fragmentation of community-type relations and a competitive ideology at work both outside and inside the school has undermined its true purpose.

Why community?

In the United Kingdom most of the current pressures on schools centre round the raising of attainment as measured in public tests or examinations, largely though not exclusively in order to improve industry's economic efficiency and national competitiveness. This is at once superficial, counter-productive, and profoundly ignorant. It is superficial in the sense that it fails to understand that technical solutions to problems that demand a more comprehensive engagement with meaning and purpose lead to an even greater frustration and a deeper sense of despair. It is counter-productive in the sense that overemphasis on an uninspiring, impoverished view of schooling will alienate teachers and students alike and thus turn out to be self-defeating. It is fundamentally ignorant in the sense that, as John Macmurray observed in a paper originally published in

1932: 'We have immense power, and immense resources; we worship efficiency and success; and *we do not know how to live finely*' (Macmurray, 1935, p. 76, [my italics]). Furthermore, even in its own terms of economic efficiency and competitiveness, recent work indicates that the connection between educational attainment and economic performance is far from unproblematic (Robinson 1998).

Of much greater importance than the bare facts of numeracy and literacy, is the wider context of meaning and significance that gives reading and numeracy their point. I am not, of course, suggesting that literacy and numeracy do not matter; I am, however, suggesting that we need to be not only clearer, but wiser, about the human contexts that make them matter. Clarity will help us to understand the components of the argument; wisdom will help us to weave them together in intelligent action. Only then will we be in a position to answer the question, 'What are literacy and numeracy for?'

For an increasing number of people, questions of this sort reaffirm the necessity of a larger framework of thinking. What is, perhaps, different from the past is that the coherence that is sought must not be at the expense of the particular, the complex or the dynamic aspects of ourselves and our world. What is needed is a framework which encourages and enables us to relate the parts and the whole in such a way that their interdependence is not merely respectful, but productive of an inclusive, changing individuality. John Gardner's suggestion that 'Wholeness incorporating diversity is the transcendent goal of our time, the task for our generation – close to home and world-wide' (Gardner, 1991, p. 15) captures both the hope and the challenge of community that face us. This, too, is both the hope and the challenge for education as we enter the twenty-first century. It applies, not just to the education service as a whole, but to schools individually. Yet there is little in our current thinking and increasingly less in our current practice that helps us to recognize its importance. Whilst schools are often not communities in anything other than a rather minimal, inconsequential sense, the intention of this chapter is to suggest they could and should aspire to flourish as communities, in ways which are maximally and demandingly so. Indeed, unless we are prepared to rethink our current organizationally obsessed approach to schooling, then despite our best intentions, we will drift further and further away from the very point and purpose of all our work, namely the education of persons in and through community.

I begin taking a radical look at the notion of community with the help of the centrally important work of John Macmurray, the most outstanding British philosopher of community this century. I go on to suggest three key issues raised by Macmurray's work which seem to me central to the current debate about the nature of education and schooling. I then look, on the one hand, at contemporary ideologies and practices undermining community in schools and, on the other, at forces creating community in schools. I conclude the chapter by arguing for the indissoluble unity of community and dialogic democracy,[1] an advocacy which returns to fundamental questions concerning the relationship between means and ends, between society and community, with which we began. It suggests that our contemporary obsession with what works is unsustainable, that ends and means must be interwoven, and that whilst schools are both functional organizations and communities, their life as communities is more important. Community is, in Macmurray's words, 'the first priority in education' (Macmurray 1958).

Rethinking community: being and becoming persons

In arguing for the importance of schools as communities, one of the biggest difficulties is to set out clearly what is meant by community and why it is important. After all, community is one of those words that goes in and out of fashion, invariably claimed by left and right as centrally important, and yet proves endlessly and irritatingly elusive.[2]

If the standpoint of community is to make any serious headway against the current managerialist myopia, we need an account of community that is clearly linked to an understanding of what it is to become a person. We also need an account of community that addresses issues of diversity and difference, acknowledging the capacity of community as a form of human association to be suffocating, inward and exclusive as much as to be life-giving, outward-looking and inclusive. Finally, we need an account of community which helps us to a more satisfactory understanding of the relationship between community and society, and, by implication between community and organization.

In attempting to give the briefest of sketches of what a radical account of community might look like, I draw heavily on the work of John Macmurray.[3] There are four main strands:

1. Persons in relation.
2. Two fundamental forms of human unity.
3. Community and society.
4. The necessity of freedom and equality.

Persons in relation

The first concerns his account of what it is to be a person. Macmurray argues that human being – becoming human – is essentially a relational rather than a solitary process. In other words, we become human in and through our relations with others. 'We need one another to be ourselves. This complete and unlimited dependence of each of us upon the others is the central and crucial fact of personal existence' (Macmurray 1961, p. 211). Furthermore, it is not just that we become persons in and through our personal relationships with others; certain kinds of relationships are more likely to enable personal becoming.

Two fundamental forms of human unity

Macmurray suggests that as human beings, we enter into two kinds of relationships. These are what he calls *functional* and *personal* relations. Both are necessary for our well-being, but the latter are much more important than the former. Functional relations are those relationships with other people that we enter into for particular purposes. For example, when we buy a ticket for a train journey or a concert, our relationship with the person from whom we purchase it is defined by our respective roles and intentions; we are not entering a more open, personal relation in which other aspects of our lives and hopes are revealed or asked for. Personal relations are quite different. We enter into them not for any particular reason, but just to be ourselves. Good examples of personal relations in this sense are friendship or family. A personal relationship is not instrumental: it has no purpose beyond itself; purposes are *expressive* of personal relations, not constitutive of them. In a functional relationship, if you change the purposes, you dissolve the unity. In a communal relationship of friendship on the other hand, the change of purposes both maintains and enriches the unity, rather than dissolving it. Personal relationships are at the heart of Macmurray's understanding of the nature and the possibility of the human condition. It is for personal relationships, relationships in which we can be and become most fully ourselves, that all else exists or matters.

Community and society

This distinction between functional and personal relations also forms the basis of Macmurray's differentiation between community and society. In a *society*, people co-operate in a range of ways to achieve common purposes. Their unity is a functional unity; people are members of society because of their functions, because of the jobs they do. Society is, in fact, an organization of functions. However, while we take part in society and belong to organizations, we do not do so as full persons. We do so with only part of ourselves.

In contrast to society, *community* is not about common purposes and the ways in which our roles, tasks and functions relate to each other, but rather about a shared way of life. Community is essentially about the quality of relations between persons as persons, not persons as employees or buyers of goods, or in any other kind of role or occupation. Community is a relationship in which we 'associate purely for the purpose of expressing our whole selves to one another in mutuality' (Macmurray, 1935, p. 98). It is a mutual relation which is chosen, not imposed; you cannot require, organize or create community in the way that an employer can and does impose or require certain things of their employees.

The two forms of human association – the functional and the personal – are both necessary to each other, but not of equal importance: 'the personal is primary and the functional is secondary ... The meaning of the functional lies in the personal and not the other way around ... The functional life is *for* the personal life' (Macmurray, 1941, p. 822). Community is prior to society in the double sense that it precedes it and it provides society with its purpose. Having said that, it is equally important to emphasise that the functional is absolutely necessary for the personal, or, as Macmurray puts it, 'the personal life is *through* the functional life' (ibid.). Community is not about some ethereal disengagement from the world or about sitting around feeling endlessly well disposed towards each other. If community is to be a lived reality rather than a pretence or an illusion, it must express itself in action.

The necessity of freedom and equality

Whilst Macmurray's account of the relationship between the functional and the personal, between community and society is hugely important, it is his insistence on certain philosophical principles which give it its distinctive, radical edge. In this fourth strand of his argument, Macmurray suggests that there are two fundamental philosophical principles of community; they are the principle of freedom and the principle of equality. He suggests not only that freedom and equality are central to any adequate understanding of community or fellowship, but that these two principles have a mutually reinforcing relation with one another. His view is that:

> equality and freedom, as constitutive principles of fellowship, condition one another reciprocally. Equality is a condition of freedom in human relations. For if we do not treat one another as equals, we exclude freedom from the relationship. Freedom, too, conditions equality. For if there is constraint between us there is fear; and to counter the fear we must seek control over its object, and attempt to subordinate the other person to our own power. Any attempt to achieve freedom without equality, or to achieve equality without freedom, must, therefore be self-defeating.

> (Macmurray 1950, p. 74)

Freedom for Macmurray is freedom to become ourselves, something we can only do in and through our relations with others, and only in certain kinds of relations. Friendship or community 'reveals the positive nature of freedom. It provides the only conditions which release the whole self into activity and so enable a man [*sic*] to be himself totally without constraint' (ibid., p. 73). Likewise, equality, understood in a personal rather than a functional sense, is enriching rather than diminishing: 'It is precisely the recognition of difference and variety amongst individuals that gives meaning to the assertion of equality' (Macmurray 1938, p. 74).

Of these four considerations, perhaps the most important is the last, and for two reasons. What Macmurray gives us is not only an understanding of community with an emancipatory edge, but a powerful philosophical tool that has the capacity to take us far beneath the surface of particular instances to the core of human association. Here, at last, we have an understanding of the *principle* of community. Macmurray gives us a means of interrogating actual examples of human unity. We can not only decide the degree to which they are, in reality, true to the principles of community, but also work together to enhance its further development. In the end, community is not fundamentally about a shared sense of place, common memory, or even the belonging and sense of significance found in close relationships. Rather, community is the reciprocal experience people have as persons in certain kinds of relationships. Community thus turns out to be adjectival, not substantival; it is not a group of people, nor is it the mere fact of a relationship. Community is a way of being, not a thing. Community is a process through which human beings regard each other in a certain way, for example through care, love and concern for the other,[4] and in which they relate to each other, acting together in mutuality as persons, not as role occupants. Furthermore, that mutuality is informed by the values of *freedom* - freedom to be and to become yourself – and *equality* – equal worth. These two values condition each other reciprocally.

Schooling, education and community

If we think about these distinctions between personal and functional relations, between community and society, in relation to a school, we become more aware of at least three things: firstly, the importance of sorting out what we think schools are for; second, the relationship between the purposes of schooling and their organizational form, and third, the nature of the relationships between teachers and students that are likely to be educative.[5]

What are schools for?

With regard to the first of these – *What are schools for?* – it is important to reclaim a truth that is no longer obvious or understood. This is that schools are primarily *educational* institutions. They do, of course, have important functional dimensions to their work, like socializing young people and ensuring the country is equipped to compete economically. However, it is the specifically educational character of schooling that should provide both the end and the means of its accomplishment: in Macmurray's terms, the *functional* (socialization/building economic capacity) is for the sake of the *personal* (education). To raise questions about the human purposes of our policy and our practices is especially important today, when the initial and substantial plausibility of ever-increasing pressure for attainment sweeps aside subtle questions and queries as if they were all regressive remnants of a self-serving educational establishment. The elevation of half-truths into unblinking national imperatives can blind us to the obverse, which remains hidden and unexamined.

If the prime purpose of education is to help us to be and become persons, not mere economic functionaries, then schools should aspire to be communities, not mere organizations. It is only in relationships of community that education in this broad sense can begin to become a reality. For good teachers, teaching has always been *more than* an occupation; if we deprive it of its wider human purposes, if personal encounters are reduced to functional exchanges, then teaching becomes a prisoner of what is of least value. It becomes a warder merely of what works, rather than a creator of who and what we might become together.

Organizational structures and the education of persons

If schools are first and fundamentally about the education of persons, and if the education of persons is best undertaken in and through community, what are some of the implications for the ways that schools are structured and managed?

Because there must be an indissoluble interconnectedness of ends and means, the organizational contexts of our daily work must enable teachers and students, students and students, teachers and teachers, teachers and parents, to know each other in and through their learning. The structures and cultures of our daily work must not merely allow, but actively encourage dialogue and encounter, informed by the central values of freedom and equality.

As I suggest later in this chapter, this has profound implications for how we conceive leadership. It exposes the emptiness of much empowerment rhetoric, and it reveals the unctuous irrelevance of 'ownership' as little more than the dull mantra of an increasingly dreary managerialism. More generally, it suggests we need to transform not only the organization of the curriculum together with its pedagogy and assessment, but also the social, physical and linguistic architecture of our work together. We need to create new ways, new occasions, new opportunities and new spaces to talk and work with each other, just as we need to reclaim some of the old ones suffocated by the pervasive intrusion of audit, and to fashion them anew in a more robust and realistic form.

Meantime, we can usefully look at each other's traditions and practices and ask simple but searching questions that rest on the principles of community offered in this chapter. For example, is this a school whose public spaces reveal barren expanses of corridor and concourse? Do they, through the absence of students' work or the omnipresence of the slick and the ready-made, testify to a narrowness of view and a poverty of feeling? Or is this a school whose public spaces delight in the creativity and courage of those whose work they display? Do they, through the simplicity of carpet or the thoughtfulness of design, provide contexts which invite deliberation and dialogue, rather than the din and damage of indifference?

Is this a school which relies on impersonal, formulaic communications, however bright and bold, which betray no specific knowledge or genuine care of those to whom they are addressed? Or is it a school which values personal encounter, often in contexts outside school, and always in ways which speak of personal knowledge and detailed concern?

Is this a school which distances students from staff through the language of address, the required conduct of automatic encounter, the spaces which are forbidden, the frequency of separate provision or innumerable other articulations of institutional living? Or do staff and students address each other in ways that invite engagement, relate to each other as persons as much as role occupants, and share the daily necessities of living?

Teaching as primarily a personal, not a technical activity

The third issue that the functional/personal distinction urges us to confront is, perhaps, the most fundamental of all, concerning the nature of the relationship between teacher and student. My own view is that teaching for education is primarily a personal, not a functional activity. This is not to say that it does not have functional elements to it. But in an educational context, teaching is more than functional. The functional exists for the sake of the personal, and it is the personal that is revealed through the functional.

What might this mean for teachers and students within the context of a school which conceives of itself, first and foremost, as a community? It means that as a teacher, I do not treat the student as a client, but rather as someone for whom I care as a person, someone for whom I have unconditional positive regard – not because they have earned it, but merely by virtue of their belonging to the school community of which I am a part. It means that, whilst our relationship is informed by my role as a teacher, it cannot be confined by it. My teaching of, say, mathematics or geography is only justifiable in so far as it contributes towards a student's development as a person. If it begins to undermine that larger purpose, then it is the mathematics or the geography that needs to change or disappear, not the student.

It also means that the now increasingly vaunted 'technologies of teaching' (Reynolds, 1998) that are likely to inform future research and development priorities need to be seen for what they are – technical means towards personal ends. Their significance lies solely in their connectedness to those educational purposes and intentions. We need to avoid what has been so tellingly described in the United States as 'the methods fetish' (Bartolome, 1994), the over-zealous and counter-productive preoccupation with the techniques of teaching. This marginalizes the personal context without which education cannot get underway, let alone continue and flourish with any strength or joy. The technical without the personal is either without meaning and therefore pointless, or its meaning is anti-personal and therefore manipulative.

Undermining community in schools

Given the analysis and advocacy of community offered in this chapter, which of our current practices seem to undermine schools as communities? In other words, what ways of relating to each other through our current structures and organizational cultures are likely to be corrosive of our capacity to transcend the role and rule orientation typical of schools as organizations? Whilst the list is substantial, I have chosen to illustrate my concerns by instancing only four examples: two are taken from the overarching context within which schools currently work, and the remaining two from internal arrangements and processes within schools.

External context

School effectiveness
One of the main reasons that schools have difficulty in creating community both internally and externally is that the dominant intellectual framework shaping our understanding of what we should be doing has virtually nothing to say about community (Grace, 1998). Indeed, not only does the school effectiveness movement have little to say about community, in its manner of thinking and its mode of operation it is largely antagonistic to it. School effectiveness and school improvement are moribund categories of a

frightened, unimaginative society that values control over creativity, a society whose priorities and dispositions lie in the stultifying language of audit[6] and the tyranny of targets.[7] This is at once a betrayal of our children's future and a corrosion of their teachers' commitment. It increases rates of truancy and exclusion and leads to the spiritually exhausted departure, either literally or metaphorically, of good quality staff. It says more than we may wish to hear about daily encounters which are increasingly seen as pointless or pernicious, or both. School effectiveness, and, indeed, most activity in commercial and public services is outcomes driven, both in the United Kingdom and elsewhere. The results of this are that, on the one hand, processes are given little consideration and, on the other, there is an almost oppressive desire to trumpet what works, ignoring the relation between what works and *why* it works, or, indeed, what *'it'* is.

Much of what passes as school effectiveness research is too often immodest, myopic and ideologically implicated (Elliott, 1996). Causes and correlations are too readily conflated; a thin, measurement-driven notion of schooling too easily marginalizes concerns for wider, more profound aspirations for the development of persons. And education itself is refashioned in a way that makes the call for community seem weak, undemanding and vague. As Stephen Ball has recently reminded us, 'Quality and effectiveness are not neutral mechanisms. They do not simply improve education; they change it. What education is, what it means to be educated are changed' (Ball, 1996). Perhaps most serious of all, there is a tendency in such outcomes driven thinking to ignore or marginalize discussion of the relationship between means and ends, between what it is we wish to achieve and how we set about achieving it (Tierney, 1993, pp. 69, 79).

The language and practice of the market
Part of the process of changing our view of what education and schooling are about has, of course, to do with the wider economic and political context of the market in which nations as well as individual organizations work. This, too, is corrosive of community. First, as Macmurray reminds us, 'an economic efficiency which is achieved at the expense of the personal is self-condemned, and in the end self-frustrating (Macmurray, 1961, p. 187). Second, the very language we now use to talk about our work in education has changed, making it difficult to grasp aspects of our experience and our aspiration unless they fit readily into the cash nexus or the outcome measure. Thus, reference to pre-school children as VBUs (voucher bearing units) is not simply a harmless piece of 'marketese'; to talk about 'delivering' the curriculum is not just a matter of linguistic fashion. These and other myriad examples of market-speak are not only symptomatic of 'language that celebrates system and denies doubt, that touts objectives and denies ambivalence, that confesses frustration, but withholds love' (Grumet, 1988,

p. 56). They are not just destructive of a way of understanding and legitimating a person-centred approach to education. They also lead us down paths we may neither recognize, nor approve of. If we think about children in a sustained way as VBUs, as products, as SAT results or as GCSE A–Cs, then we not only tend to see the world through a semantic lens which is distorting and dangerous. We are also likely to find ourselves behaving in surprising and unpleasant ways. If we really do come to think we can 'deliver' the curriculum as we constantly say we can, then we are likely to find ourselves instructing more than we intend to, and listening less than we should. We are also likely to become easy targets for those who suggest that teaching is unproblematic and that all teachers need are a couple of 'A' levels and the experience of bringing up children.

Internal arrangements

The call for strong leadership

In the United Kingdom, the demand for strong school leadership, particularly from those external to the profession, is reflected in the salary structure of headteachers and in the management discourse of current initiatives such as NPQH.[8] The concern here is twofold. First, the way leadership is conceived, reflected in the implied insistence on strength, reinforces an individualistic understanding of what leadership is about. Invoking the secular trinity of values, vision and mission does little to alleviate such concern. Crusading exhortations of this kind are more likely to reveal the particular predilections of the individuals making them than the aspirations of a local community. Second, the market context of contemporary schooling, with its attendant emphasis on measurable outcomes, promotes the street-wise, the canny and the managerial over the harder journey of principled leadership – the cultivation of a communally articulate, democratically self-aware and reciprocally responsible public.[9]

'Ownership' and 'empowerment'

What is particularly striking about many contemporary arrangements is the degree to which the dispersal of power, and the engagement of both external and internal participants in genuine dialogue, is more apparent than real. Interestingly, a closer look at the language of contemporary management practice reveals a quite different picture to the one that first meets the eye.

Paradoxically, 'ownership' and 'empowerment' turn out to be sophisticated forms of control. More often than not, ownership is really about ways in which a particular group or individual attempts to get those with whom they work to agree with their views or strategies with a significant degree of conviction. Ownership is about getting your ideas accepted by others to such a degree that the ideas become theirs by commitment (Fielding, 1994). Such a process is not in any proper sense about the emergence of genuinely shared meanings through the difficulties and uncertainties of dialogue, discussion and shared action – activities central to the processes of community.

Similarly, the arena or extent of empowerment is invariably small, and the boundaries firmly fixed, even if indistinctly drawn. Despite its promise, empowerment often disappoints. Once the pyramids have been flattened and the communication systems freed up in these organizations, power remains pretty much where it always was. Far from the culture of dependence being replaced by the vibrancy of initiative and previously untapped energy, the demands of work proliferate and are intensified, secured through the asymmetry that persists between those who 'empower' and those who – whether they like it or not – 'are empowered' (Fielding, 1996).

The importance of student data

A number of favoured management practices that promise greater community actually reduce it. In the same way, the promise held out by collection of data about and from students and the increase in targeted conversations about learning frequently turn out to be enervating rather than enabling of community.

There are two separate but related developments here. First, there is a huge increase in the collection of data about student performance and an attempt to bring it together in ways which are helpful to teachers and to students as part of an ongoing formative process of learning. Second, there is a preparedness in both primary and secondary schools to go beyond scrutiny of test results to include student views about the effectiveness or otherwise of units of work and even series of lessons.

Whilst both these developments seem to me to hold the potential for communal flourishing, in their current manifestations they are, ironically, often destructive and limiting of human aspiration. For example, take the target-setting and mentoring conversations which are an increasingly familiar part of school life. What is being described often turns out to be a controlling process, part of an instrumental agenda drawn up to serve short-term school goals whose real origins lie in the market place. Work in the field is now beginning to encounter students expressing doubts about the genuineness of their school's interest in their progress and well-being as persons, as distinct from their contribution to the school's league table position. The overriding instrumentality of conversations makes listening difficult: attentiveness is overdirected and clues for meaning are trodden underfoot in the scramble for performance; dialogue disappears as reciprocity retreats under the sheer weight of external expectation, and contracts replace community as the bond of human association.

The danger with the collection of student views about particular lessons or units of work is that a complex and potentially rich undertaking is reduced to a one-way process in which students are used merely as sources of data. Even in this reified form, the results of this kind of data collection can be of substantial benefit to all concerned. However, the objection remains that in the process students remain objects not subjects of enquiry. There is seldom any sustained or systematic commitment to dialogue. The opportunity for shared learning, for teachers to be seen as learners and learners teachers, is too often fitful or non-existent.

Creating community in schools

In my judgement, the current context in which we work is largely corrosive of community, that is to say, it marginalizes the personal in favour of the functional, it dissociates means from ends, and it uses a dissembling rhetoric of empowerment to neutralize freedom and equality. How, then, might we proceed? Are there alternative practices already in use? Do research findings suggest the kind of advocacy exemplified in this chapter has even a small foothold in reality as well as the world of our imagination? To what degree do schools exist whose arrangements express and encourage mutual, personal relationships, expressions of care and regard for others as persons of equal worth, and freedom and honesty of thoughts, feelings and actions?

External context

Transformative education
The school effectiveness movement has performed an important corrective function in challenging an overly pessimistic, even deterministic, view of the influence of social and political factors on the efficacy of schools. However, it seems to me that school effectiveness has now largely run its course. Similarly, school improvement, which in the United Kingdom is often too closely linked to its effectiveness counterpart, strikes many as uninspiring (Perrone, 1989), bland (Riddell *et al*, 1996), and strangely disconnected from the lived concerns of those for whom education matters more than schooling (Elliot, 1996). My own view is that we should move on from school improvement to what I have hesitantly called the standpoint of transformative education (Fielding, 1997a). First, such a standpoint is concerned with education, not just with the more limited and derivative notion of schooling. Second, its values are explicit, contestable and contested; it is about the development of people as persons in and through an emancipatory, inclusive community. Third, it argues for the importance of

processes as both means and ends and for the necessary interconnectedness of the two. Fourth, its discourse seeks both to reclaim and to develop a
language that rejects the reductionist commodification of education, which
has come to blight so much of the current national debate.

The language of learning

Language plays a key role in imagining how the world might be different,
why it ought to be, and how it might become so. The language of the market,
dominated by outcomes, must be challenged and the language of learning
reaffirmed. After all, learning is pre-eminently what schools are for.
Learning, not the 'delivery' of 'packages' or the mechanics of the ware-
house, must once again provide the texture and the substance of daily discourse. As Michael Ignatieff reminds us so beautifully and so profoundly:
'Our needs are made of words: they come to us in speech, and they can die
for lack of expression. Without a public language to help us find our own
words, our needs will dry up in silence' (Ignatieff, 1984, p. 142). We must go
beyond the bullet points and the terse inventory of the market to regain the
contested complexities of negotiation, dialogue and discussion. That is
where the learning will begin, and it will only be sustained if we articulate
and explore our sensibilities and emerging understandings with a language
that captures delight as well as definition; nuance as well as number. The
uncertainty of exploration and the grip of engagement and critical encounter – these are the stuff of learning that the language of 'delivery' has neither time nor capacity to comprehend.

Internal arrangements

Democratic leadership

The IQEA (Improving the Quality of Education for All) school improvement
project is based at the Universities of Cambridge and Nottingham. Some of
the most exciting, innovative work currently taking place under its aegis
demonstrates a commitment to more genuinely participatory forms of leadership, exemplified by a consistently powerful agent of involvement and cultural change known as the *school cadre group*. Typically consisting of
about nine people in a secondary school, the cadre group consists of a
cross-section of staff, including the headteacher and a least one teacher
with no paid post of responsibility. The cadre acts as a co-ordinating
nucleus for the school's improvement strategy.

Three things strike me as particularly interesting about the work of such
groups. First, they are not just involved in the usual range of supportive and
facilitative activities; they also become expert in particular areas as well as
developing process expertise. Second, they develop and deepen their professional understanding of what the process of school improvement is

about, and contribute towards the growth of a research culture within the school. Third, and most importantly, the coupling of the transformative remit of the cadre group with its diverse membership is its particular strength. As the headteacher of one of our IQEA schools put it:

> One of the things an IQEA cadre does is place staff at a variety of different status levels into an arena which is by definition about development – it's actually about research and development – and I think that is culturally changing.... It's not a working party, it is a structural energy core; it is capacity-building and that is what school improvement is about.

From ownership to authorship

What this kind of professional learning exposes, of course, is the redundancy of 'ownership' as a useful conceptual tool uncompromised by the agenda of those who wish others to adopt ideas and practices thought to be 'correct'. The commercial metaphor of ownership is, in any case, deeply at odds with what many teachers feel they are about as people and professionals. The creative metaphor of authorship would serve us better. Authorship brooks no deceit; you are either involved in the process of exploration and articulation of meaning which authorship involves, or you are not. Ownership is most often and most fittingly applied to things, and the attempt to transfer it to ideas and values is inappropriate. Things have no will, no agency, no voice; people should have, and ubiquitous talk of ownership puts these very characteristics at risk.

Students as researchers: from data source to significant voice

The final contrast with the freewheeling instrumentalism so corrosive of community concerns developments that transcend the now frequent use of students as mere sources of data in the drive to school improvement. Gathering pupil perspectives on teachers' work and, indeed, on their own work is only likely to become educative and conducive to learning in its more profound, sustainable senses if at least four things are in place. First, the gathering of information is rigorously transparent and part of a mutually agreed, negotiated process. Second, space and opportunity are provided to make sense of the information. Third, the process of making meaning is located within a wider framework of human concern than the data or test scores themselves provide. Finally, each of the parties involved is regarded with appropriate respect as agents of their own learning, not merely as sources of interesting data for some-one else to analyse for their own purposes.

These desiderata form the core aspirations of a current research project with a large Bedfordshire comprehensive school that moves beyond the notion of teacher-as-researcher to that of student-as-researcher. The initiative (Jackson *et al*, 1998; Fielding, 1998a; Weatherill, 1998), now in its third year, rests upon a twin commitment, first to student agency as central to the educative process and, second, to that agency being as legitimately located within the public realm as within the arena of individual learning. In other words, students-as-researchers is educative of those involved, but also educative of the student body and the school as a whole learning community. The research findings have been both insightful and challenging. The resulting recommendations have important, sometimes radical, implications for current practice in the three areas of research, namely student teachers, profiling and student involvement in the life of the school.

What is of particular interest in the context of this chapter is the way in which the values of partnership between students and staff became the explicit touchstone of the ensuing work. Equally important has been the interplay between the cultural and structural developments within the school as the project gathered momentum. As with teacher research and indeed with the current preoccupation with target setting and value-added, the key issues have less to do with the collection of data than the occasions and spaces in which meaning is made. Where are the dialogic spaces within schools enabling staff and students to make sense of data or recommendations that emerge? What cultures need to develop to make that process a meaningful one? What processes and means of decision-making exist to take account of developments such as these? These and other questions of a similar kind are enabling of the kind of dialogic learning community I am proposing. They touch on issues of organization, but they are not primarily organizational issues. Rather, they are issues whose origins and meaning lie in our efforts to enable both teachers and students to be 'the agents and instruments of their own change processes' (Lincoln, 1993, p. 43).

Community and the development of dialogic democracy

I have sought to contrast those daily practices that are corrosive of schools as communities with those that inform and express the process of community, through which we relate to each other as persons. Finally, I should like to suggest what we might do now. It seems to me that if we are to make the transition from our current circumstance to one of emancipatory community, then we have to take *dialogic democracy* seriously. The perspective of a *learning organization* asks how we might create a little bit more community within society. We must move beyond this to the perspective of a *learning community* which asks how we might ensure that society – the totality of functional day-to-day interactions – both expresses and supports an inclusive community. It is not about identifying dollops of community to increase economic competitiveness. Rather, it concerns how we ensure economic competitiveness is subservient to human purposes. Only by understanding *why* economic competitiveness is important can we set about achieving it in a way that is not just compatible with, but *expressive of* our well-being as persons in relation with one another, ie expressive of community.

All this requires a fundamental reversal in our thinking and in our practice. At the heart of that reversal is the primacy of community. The functional life is *for* the personal life, the life of community; the personal life, the life of community is *through* the functional life. Schools as expressive learning communities are utterly different to schools as effective functional organizations. Functional and exclusive in orientation, effective schools are bounded by the preoccupations, processes and products of schooling. Personal and inclusive in orientation, learning communities transform and transcend the instrumental and the functional in a wider, more generous expansion of our human being and becoming. Schools are, of course, both functional organizations and expressive communities, *but their life as communities is the point of their existence* and this conditions the functional relationships through which their daily activity is expressed. Ends and means are interwoven, but always in such a way that it is the ends that condition the means. In so doing, the means become part of the ends themselves.

Thus, for those Hampshire secondary school teachers with whom I worked recently, the struggle was to retain the rigours and positive demands of target setting within a broader commitment to the development of persons. For these teachers, the struggle was to understand the complex tensions within a system that seemed to work well in most respects, but for some students meant being set a target at the bottom of the GCSE scale, fully two years before the examination. In these circumstances, as indeed in most others, functional clarity is not enough. Still less convincing is easy talk of honesty when, despite our best efforts, the social and political context remains divisive and dispiriting for more people than many of us would care to acknowledge. The brute reality and sheer obduracy of these issues and the searching, strenuous quality of the teachers' dialogue affirm the absolute necessity of creating community together. To attempt anything less is not just to betray education. It is to invite profound and pervasive failure – not failure to be efficient, effective or even a leader in the economic field, but failure to understand the most basic and most enduring of human truths. This is what Macmurray calls the first priority in education:

> The first priority in education – if by education we mean learning to be human – is learning to live in personal relation to other people. Let us call it learning to live in community. I call this the first priority because failure in this is fundamental failure, which cannot be compensated for by success in other fields; because our ability to enter into fully personal relations with others is the measure of our humanity. For inhumanity is precisely the perversion of human relations.

> (Macmurray, 1958)

Notes

1. I use the term dialogic democracy in a general sense here to signal the central importance of interactive engagement with each other in the communities, organizations and, particularly importantly, the public spaces which form such an important part of our shared experience. There are important disputes within social and political philosophy which make firm distinctions between, on the one hand, consensus-based approaches linked to dialogic democracy and, on the other hand, approaches which argue for an 'agonistic pluralism' that rejects consensus in favour of 'democratic channels of expression for the forms of conflict considered as legitimate' (Mouffe, 1998:17). For a clearly written, short contribution to the current debate see Chantal Mouffe's 'The radical centre' (1998). Useful articulations of the two different perspectives can be found in Mouffe's *The Return of the Political* (1993) and Anthony Giddens's advocacy of dialogic democracy in his *Beyond Left and Right* (1994).

2. This is true even of outstanding writers in the field of educational management and leadership like Thomas Sergiovanni (1992, 1994a, 1994b, 1995 and 1996) who argues not only that the development of community is supremely important for our future well-being as a society, but that building community provides the most appropriate way forward for the development of schools in the twenty-first century. Whilst I agree with his suggestions that schools are much more like communities than they are like organizations and that 'Changing the metaphor for the school from organization to community changes what is true about how schools are run, about what motivates teachers and students, and about what leadership is, and how it should be practised' (Sergiovanni, 1994a, p. 217), despite its many virtues, Sergiovanni's work is also seriously flawed. (See Fielding, 1997b.)

3. For a recent brief account of Macmurray's work on community which engages with some of the current debates in social and political philosophy see Fielding (1998b). For a useful thematic selection of Macmurray's writing which gives a sense of the breadth and depth of his thinking see Conford (1996). Amongst Macmurray's best essays on community are 'The Personal Life' which appeared in his massively popular *Reason and Emotion* (Macmurray, 1935) and the less well known 'Freedom in the Personal Nexus' (Macmurray, 1942). His *Conditions of Freedom* (Macmurray, 1950) is the best single, short book on the subject. It is accessible, lucid and profound.

4. A fuller account of the psychological principles of community than space permits would say a great deal more about the importance of the dispositions of love and care and also make reference to Macmurray's

insistence that fear, as well as love, is present and necessary in relations of community. The key point is that fear must be subordinated to love (Macmurray, 1961, pp. 158ff).

5.   Whenever I use the term 'student' in this chapter I intend it to refer to school students or pupils, not student teachers.

6.   For a short, interesting corrective to the still current mania for audits see Michael Power's Demos pamphlet *The Audit Explosion* (Power, 1994). See also his book *The Audit Society: Rituals of Verification* (Power, 1997).

7.   Of course, targets are not always tyrannical: at their best they help us to clearly identify something of importance, keep our attention on manageable tasks, and hold us accountable for the completion of our intended course of action. In practice targets too often turn out to be tyrannical for at least three reasons. First, the very act of focusing on a specific set of tasks can sometimes blind us to important, unforeseeable contextual developments to which we would ordinarily respond: the firmness with which our attention is held weakens the subtlety and narrows the range of our professional awareness. Second, the values and purposes which informed our choice of target too often drift to the periphery of our concerns, rather than playing an integral role in how we go about doing our daily work. The achievement of targets thus becomes a merely technical operation, rather than a reflexive educational undertaking; connections are severed where they should in fact be strengthened. Third, this internal tyranny is too often compounded by a well-intentioned, if ill-judged external pressure: the unrelenting fervour with which new targets are prescribed leaves even those who wish to support them exhausted and demoralized. The sheer ubiquity of targets defeats the singleness of purpose from which the process derives its most compelling force.

8.   It is interesting that this is not the case in other European countries such as Holland.

9.   This is a complex area to explore in a short paragraph. The impetus behind my position owes much to Gerald Grace's excellent study of headship in England from the nineteenth century to the present day (Grace, 1995). See Chapters 11 and 12 in particular for a thoughtful consideration of some of the key issues and dilemmas we need to address in the new millennium. See also the interesting overview of headship by Hall and Southworth (1997) in which some of the tensions I am alluding to come through their data in ways which suggest there are grounds for a qualified and cautious optimism.

References

Ball, SJ (1996) Recreating policy through qualitative research: a trajectory analysis, paper presented at the American Educational Research Association Annual Conference, New York

Bartolome, L (1994) Beyond the methods fetish: toward a humanizing pedagogy, *Harvard Educational Review*, **64** (2), Summer, pp. 173–94

Conford, P (ed.) (1996) *The Personal World: John Macmurray on Self and Society*, Floris Books, Edinburgh

Elliott, J (1996) School effectiveness research and its critics: alternative visions of schooling, *Cambridge Journal of Education*, **26** (2), pp. 199–224

Fielding, M (1994) Delivery, packages and the denial of learning: reversing the language and practice of contemporary INSET in H Bradley, C Conner and G Southworth (eds), *Developing Teachers, Developing Schools*, pp. 18–33, Fulton, London

Fielding, M (1996) Empowerment: emancipation or enervation?, *Journal of Education Policy*, **11** (3) pp. 399–417

Fielding, M (1997a) Beyond school effectiveness and school improvement: lighting the slow fuse of possibility, *Curriculum Journal*, **8** (1), Spring, pp. 7–27

Fielding, M (1997b) Learning organization or learning community? Senge, Sergiovanni and the possibility of organizational transformation: a philosophical critique, paper presented at the Annual Meeting of the British Educational Research Association, University of York

Fielding, M (1998a) Students as researchers: from data source to significant voice, paper presented at the International Congress for School Effectiveness and Improvement, University of Manchester

Fielding, M (1998b) The point of politics: friendship and community in the work of John Macmurray, *Renewal*, **6** (1), Winter, pp. 55–64

Gardner, JW (1991) *Building Community*, Independent Sector, New York

Giddens, A (1994) *Beyond Left and Right*, Polity Press, Cambridge

Grace, G (1995) *School Leadership: Beyond Education Management*, Falmer Press, London

Grace, G (1998) Realising the mission: catholic approaches to school effectiveness, in R Slee, S Tomlinson and G Weiner (eds) *Effective For Whom? School Effectiveness and the School Improvement Movement*, pp. 117–27, Falmer Press, London

Grumet, M (1988) *Bitter Milk: Women and Teaching*, University of Massachusetts Press, Amhurst, MA

Hall, V and Southworth, G (1997) Headship, *School Leadership and Management*, **17** (2), pp. 151–70

Ignatieff, M (1984) *The Needs of Strangers*, Chatto & Windus, London

Jackson, D, Raymond, L, Weatherill, L and Fielding, M (1998) Students as researchers, paper presented at the International Congress for School Effectiveness and Improvement, University of Manchester

Lincoln, Y (1993) I and Thou: method, voice, and roles in research with the silenced, in D McLaughlin and WG Tierney (eds) *Naming Silenced Lives: Personal*

Narratives and Processes of Educational Change, pp. 29–47, Routledge, New York

Macmurray, J (1935) *Reason and Emotion*, Faber, London

Macmurray, J (1938) *The Clue to History*, Student Christian Movement Press, London

Macmurray, J (1941) Two lives in one, *The Listener*, **36** (674), p. 822

Macmurray, J (1942) Freedom in the personal nexus, in R Anshen (ed.) *Freedom: Its Meaning*, pp. 176–93, Allen & Unwin, London

Macmurray, J (1950) *Conditions of Freedom*, Faber, London

Macmurray, J (1958) Learning to be human, Moray House Annual Public Lecture, 5 May, unpublished

Macmurray, J (1961) *Persons in Relation*, Faber, London

Mouffe, C (1993) *The Return of the Political,* Verso, London

Mouffe, C (1998) The radical centre, *Soundings*, Issue 9, Summer, pp. 11–23

Perrone, V (1989) *Working Papers: Reflections on Teachers, Schools and Community*, Teachers College Press, New York

Power, M (1994) *The Audit Explosion*, Demos, London

Power, M (1997) *The Audit Society: Rituals of Verification*, Oxford University Press, Oxford

Reynolds, D (1998) *Teacher Effectiveness*, TTA Annual Lecture 19 May, Teacher Training Agency, London

Riddell, S, Brown, S and Duffield, J (1996) The utility of qualitative research for influencing policy and practice, paper presented at the American Educational Association Annual Conference, New York

Robinson, P (1998) *The Tyranny of League Tables*, Institute of Public Policy Research, London

Sergiovanni, TJ (1992) *Moral Leadership,* Jossey-Bass, San Francisco

Sergiovanni, TJ (1994a) Organizations or communities? Changing the metaphor changes the theory, *Educational Administration Quarterly*, **30** (2), pp. 214–26

Sergiovanni, TJ (1994b) *Building Community in Schools*, Jossey-Bass, San Francisco

Sergiovanni, TJ (1995) *The Principalship: A Reflective Practice Perspective*, (3rd edn), Allyn & Bacon, Needham Heights, MA

Sergiovanni, TJ (1996) *Leadership for the Schoolhouse*, Jossey-Bass, San Francisco

Tierney, WG (1993) *Building Communities of Difference*, Bergin & Garvey, Westport, CT

Weatherill, L (1998) The 'Students as Researchers' Project at Sharnbrook Upper School and Community College, *Improving Schools*, **1** (2), pp. 52–53

5

School Management

Myth: Good Management Makes Good Schools

Stephen J Ball

In Chapter 3, Kogan argued for teachers to have greater professional freedom and in Chapter 4, Fielding linked this to equality, reasserting the need for open, democratic relations between teachers and students (pupils). In this chapter, Ball considers the relationship between teachers and school managers. He examines the 'new managerialism' that seems to have swept through the public sector, especially affecting hospitals and schools. He argues that the emphases on performativity, corporate culture, muscular leadership and competitiveness – each of them notions borrowed from industry – have undermined the important long-established values of public service and collective co-operation. Worse, by incorporating the ideology, teachers now police themselves; in an almost frighteningly Orwellian sense, 'we are all managers now'.

This chapter draws upon and extends a series of attempts to question the role and effects of managerialism in public sector organizations. It examines some of the social and moral costs of managerialism. It looks at the dark side of the new relations and new organizational forms which managerialism brings into play. I shall paint a grim picture, but some grimness is necessary in order to counter the powerful common sense of the discourse of managerialism. I am not asserting simple 'truths' here; rather, I intend to explore some complex paradoxes.

I use the term 'managerialism' in the sense that it is employed by John Clarke – 'the articulation of modes of organizational power and calculation that have displaced bureau-professionalism as the operating logics of public service organizations; and the creation of dispersed systems of organizational interrelationship and control' (Clarke, 1998, p. 175).

Managerialism represents the insertion of a new mode of power into the public sector, it is a 'transformational force' (ibid.). Managerialism has been the key mechanism in the political reform and cultural re-engineering of the public sector over the past 20 years. It has been the primary means 'through which the structure and culture of public services are recast. In doing so it seeks to introduce new orientations, remodels existing relations of power and affects how and where social policy choices are made' (Clarke, Cochrane *et al*, 1994, p. 4). Such changes affect all of us. They are as pervasive and potent in universities as they are in schools, local government, Whitehall, and voluntary sector organizations. We live and speak these changes; or should I say that these changes speak us. They are inscribed in our practices, and, as I shall go on to suggest, upon our bodies and emotions.

I want to concern myself primarily with the micro-politics of managerialism, the very immediate relationships and processes which pattern everyday life in the school. However, I also want to retain as a basis for my discussion the contention that the exercise of power within the organization is 'part of a larger ideological narrative and organizational strategy of the "enterprise culture" ' (Kirkpatrick and Martinez-Lucio, 1995, pp.10-11). In other words, we need also to recognise management as a technology of government – 'a generalisable model of functioning: a way of defining power relations in terms of the everyday life of men [sic]' (Foucault, 1979, p. 205).

I recognize that this is a somewhat paradoxical argument in so far as the insertion of managerialism into the public sector, along with the processes of financial devolution and institutional autonomy, take their impetus from an argument for rolling back the state – the call to replace bureaucracy with entrepreneurism, and planning with market forces. Nonetheless, I want to suggest that what we are seeing in the public sector is not a simple process of *deregulation* but the installation of *a new mode of state regulation and discipline*. This has its effects via the culture of managerialism, the values of enterprise and the logic of the marketplace. As I see it, devolution and autonomy, the market form, entrepreneurism, and managerialism together form a powerful and coherent ensemble of policies. They work together to blur the boundaries between the public and private sectors, and to insert new forms of social and political discipline into the relationships between, and practices of, educational and other public professionals.

In the education sector, the headteacher is the main 'carrier' and embodiment of managerialism and is crucial to the transformation of the organizational regimes of schools. That is, the dismantling of professional organizational regimes and their replacement with market-entrepreneurial regimes. Equally though, headteachers are strategically placed to stand against the inroads of managerialism. Some heads have been aggrandized and others damaged by the requirements of managerial leadership and its attendant responsibilities. However, I shall also make the point that one aspect of the effectivity of managerialism is its 'dislocation', that is, management is no longer identified simply with the activities of one group, or role or office.

Having sketched out the general terrain of my concerns, I want to home in on four inter-related features of the micro-politics of managerialism. I also want to stress their tight inter-relatedness; their separation here is solely for the purpose of presentation. They are as follows:

1. *Performativity*: This is the use of measurable performance outcomes as yardsticks of both individual and organizational 'achievement' and as ways of representing individuals and organizations. This includes the use of targets and performance indicators as a mechanism to steer and change organizations and increase productive capacity. Various data, especially comparative data in the form of national tests, league tables, inspections by quangos, audit, appraisal, and 'benchmarking' exercises are now used extensively throughout the public sector to determine organizational direction and embed substantive policies.

2. *Corporate culture*: This is used as a means of re-working the relationships between individual commitment and action in the organization, what Hugh Willmott calls 'the governance of the employee's soul' (Willmott, 1993).

3. *The gendered nature of managerialism*: We are witnessing an increasing de-feminization of the teaching profession, that is, the highlighting of qualities and practices which are stereotypically male. Nevertheless, certain forms of managerialism also involve the incorporation of aspects of femininity. That is, ' "Women's ways of leading" are held up in business and some educational systems as models of "best management practice". Women's "skills" as facilitators, communicators and in interpersonal relations are seen to be desirable attributes for educational managers in these complex times' (Blackmore, 1995, p. 49).

4. *The displacement of values-talk and of the 'service ethic'*: The struggle over values is subordinated to the imperatives of excellence, quality and survival. The practical meanings of excellence and quality as realized in the processes of comparison of and competition between schools remains largely unexamined. Comparison and competition are themselves taken to be value-free. In its crudest sense this can be reduced to the view that anything is OK, in relations within and between schools as long as it contributes to success or survival in the market place.

The effects of all this, I suggest, are that what it means to be a public sector worker, what it means to be a state professional and the nature of professionalism are all profoundly changed. We need to evaluate the desirability of those changes carefully. We need to ask the question – what are we doing to ourselves?

Performativity

In the case of education, performativity works in two main ways. First, it is a system of judgements, classifications and targets providing both the objectives and the criteria for evaluation of schools and their teachers. This is articulated and justified in the language of 'standards' and 'quality'. Standards are set and quality measured in terms of targets or performances required of schools, of departments or of teachers. Schools are left, at least to some extent, to decide how they will achieve their performance but in subtle ways performativity bites deeply and directly into classroom processes. The demands of performance – represented in examination attainments, corridor displays, open evenings, schools concerts and plays – often stand over and against professional judgement. Educational value and values are in danger of being subordinated to the requirements of image and impression (see Ball, 1998 and below). Second, these performance indicators increasingly 'represent' education in a form *for* consumption. Subtle and complex educational processes are translated into performance indicators and measurable outcomes. This feeds into a more general process – the commodification of education – through which understanding is represented as a package to be consumed and the process of learning is reduced to an act of private exchange. Both of these aspects of educational performativity are linked to the workings and effects of market form in education through choice and competition.

As the French philosopher Lyotard suggests, performativity or what he calls also 'context control' has other attractions as a technology for the management of complex social systems. He is writing ironically here.

> It cannot be denied that there is a persuasive force in the idea that context control and domination are inherently better than their absence. The performativity criterion has its 'advantages'. It excludes in principle adherence to a metaphysical discourse; it requires the renunciation of fables; it demands clear minds and cold wills; it replaces the definition of essences with the calculation of interactions; it makes the 'players' assume responsibility not only for the statements they propose, but also for the rules to which they submit those statements in order to render them acceptable. It brings the pragmatic functions of knowledge clearly to light to the extent that they seem to relate to the criterion of efficiency: the pragmatics of argumentation, of the production of proof, of the transmission of learning, and of the apprenticeship of the imagination.

(Lyotard, 1984, p. 62)

Lyotard's argument has a particular relevance to recent UK education policy (and public sector policy in general). Set within the framework of the market form in education, performativity requires a number of significant shifts and transformations in identity and purpose for schools and individual teachers.

Thus, for example, within the disciplines of choice and standards, the possibilities for *metaphysical discourses*, relating practice to philosophical principles like social justice and equity, are closed-down dramatically, and the *fables* of promise and opportunity which attend comprehensive education are also marginalized.[1] Instead, schools will become whatever it seems necessary to become in order to flourish in the market. The heart of the educational project is gouged out and left empty.

Pragmatism and cold calculation, as against fable and metaphysics, form the basis of managerialism. Professional judgement and debate over values – what schooling is for – are displaced by the requirements of maximizing income, balancing budgets, recruiting customers and marketing. Efficiency is asserted over ethics. Humanistic commitments like the service ethic are replaced by managerialism's promiscuity of values.

These shifts are not unrelated to the introduction in teacher training of new forms of de-intellectualized, competence-based training. The emphasis is on pedagogic skills and classroom management techniques and issues of values, equity and purpose are excluded from the teacher training curriculum. The teacher is re-constructed as a technician rather than as a professional capable of critical judgement and reflection.

There are now various mechanisms in place that allow description, measurement and comparison of educational and other organizations and of their individual members. Most obviously, as I have said, schools have GCSE/local league tables, national tests, attendance and destinations figures, inspection reports and Ofsted's Panda reports – the latter now of paramount importance to 'new' managers. Universities have the research assessment exercise, teaching audits and the likelihood of Certification of Teaching. There is a fundamental assumption embedded in all this that remains studiously unexamined. This is that the information or medium of exchange established in these social markets or systems of accountability does 'stand for' or 'represent' valid, worthwhile or meaningful outputs, that what you measure – what you get – is what you want. I will come back to this issue later.

These management activities drive performativity into the day-to-day practices of teachers and into the social relations between teachers. They make management ubiquitous, invisible, inescapable – part of, embedded in, everything we do. We choose and judge our actions according to their contribution to organizational performance. Examples include changes in pedagogy related to driving up GCSE examination performance, the targeting of students on the C/D grade boundary and the narrowing of the primary curriculum to concentrate on preparation for national tests.

Corporate culture: re-imagining work or 'small theatres' of discipline

The 'delivery' of efficiency, quality and the increase of productive capacity rests on the ability of the manager to relate outcomes to 'effort', that is to make the productive process transparent and thus make the worker 'accountable'. Increasingly, school managers search out data – whether 'residuals' derived from examination results, appraisal reports, or standardized classroom observations – which enable them to compare the performance of individual teachers. This parallels the more general methods of accountability aimed at schools as institutions – the publication of formal inspection reports, 'league tables' of examination results and the long lists of information required for inclusion in school prospectuses and annual governors' reports. The intention is to ensure the school is constantly visible. But management in its most potent form is not simply about describing and comparing teachers, however important that might be. It is also about creating an attitude and a culture within which workers – teachers – feel themselves accountable but at the same time committed or personally invested in the organization and its collective targets. The new teacher/workers are thus expected to internalize responsibility for their performance in relation to the well-being of the organization as a whole and take responsibility for their own short-comings and their own disciplining through mechanisms like appraisal.

Describing some of the leaders in management thinking like Peters, Waterman and Handy, Willmott writes:

> For the gurus of Excellence, the key to productivity and performance is to create a culture that fosters commitment by enabling individuals to think and feel that they are autonomous without simultaneously making them feel insecure ... The value of this accomplishment, from a managerial perspective, is that, by sparing individuals from a more existentially demanding sense of freedom, where values and practices are continuously problematized, the use of culture as a management strategy can 'be potentially very effective in promoting loyalty, enthusiasm, diligence and even devotion to the enterprise' [Ray, 1986 p. 289].

(Willmott, 1992, p. 62)

'Management' then is the collection of activities constituting the achievement of performance; it is not necessarily embodied in an organizational group of that name. It is not simply something done to us by managers. In so far as we internalize the imperatives of performativity we manage ourselves and one another.

Inspection and outcomes measures at the institutional level are direct parallels of appraisal and target-setting at the level of the individual and the team. The effect is that the members of teams increasingly become engaged in a process of self-reflection and self-discipline, in doing the work of management. In this close linking of group effort to organizational goals the individual is also expected to exhibit strong cultural affiliation to colleagues and to the organization.

Thus, one of the key techniques of new managerialism is the generation of 'new' forms of employee involvement, in particular through the cultivation of a 'corporate culture' which is often fostered via the use of symbols – badges, logos, slogans, uniforms, school colours, flags, flowers. It rests on the construction of new forms of institutional affiliation and 'community'. Corporate culture is a new focus of institutional allegiance. The institution, rather than the profession or 'service', is now the main point of reference for identity and commitment. In contrast, former colleagues in *other* institutions are now competitors. Success in the marketplace is the basis of common purpose – pragmatism and self-interest and personal commitment to the organization rather than professional judgement and ethics are the defining characteristics of the good teacher. 'Administrative procedures should make individuals "want" what the system needs in order to perform well' (Lyotard, 1984, p. 62).

This is the basis for what some management writers call the 'enchanted workplace' (Gee and Lankshear, 1995). ' "Enchantment" can mean "delightful" and, as such, stands for the claims that the new workplace will be more deeply meaningful and fulfilling than the old. But it can also mean "to be under a spell" ' (ibid., p. 8).

> In order to cash in on the meanings of the enchanted workplace... the workers must cleave to a set of ends... that is posited in advance. Workers rarely have the opportunity to influence the content of those ends.
>
> (Boyett and Conn, 1992, pp. 114–15)

Something of this is captured in a headline in *The Independent* newspaper (19 March 1998, p. 2): 'THERE IS PROFIT FROM PASSION: Studies show that people work better if they believe in what they are doing and are emotionally engaged with the company they work for... organizations need to manage the emotions, feelings and beliefs that motivate people'. The lifeblood of a successful company is its 'emotional capital'. This leads us to the issue of gender.

Making it a man's world: the incorporation of femininity

I want to comment briefly on the gendered nature of management and again explore some paradoxical aspects of contemporary educational manage- ment. In general terms I would support the assertion that male power has shaped the construct of:

> leadership, its culture, discourse, imaging and practice for centuries. Alterna- tive conceptions of leadership have to attempt to legitimate themselves against the pervasive influence of these established models.

> (Grace, 1995, p. 187)

Managerialism in education in many respects exemplifies and celebrates the masculine vision of leadership, for example, the technical focus on financial management, outcome control and accountability as key aspects of leadership. There is also the need for *strong* leadership, to make *tough* decisions in a *hard, cut-throat* world of institutional competition, and again the detached rationality of individualist, economic decision-making (Boyle and Woods, 1996; Grace, 1995; Pollard, Broadfoot *et al,* 1994; Riley, 1994). All these things reflect and endorse male attributes, capacities and modes of activity (Ferguson, 1984).This is the strategic/competitive rational- ity of the post-Fordist workplace (Kerfoot and Knights, 1993) – 'leadership is reduced to technique and not purpose, passion and desire' (Blackmore, 1996, p. 344). However, 'headteacher survival' (Pollard, Broadfoot *et al*, 1994) is not best achieved by reliance on a single style or mode of social relations, but rather in bringing off what Boyle and Woods (1996, p. 566) call 'composite headship'. Such headship is 'made up of many different aspects which work at different levels, and which can be attuned to different situations' and is full of 'apparent conflicts and contradictions'.

Thus, set against, or rather alongside, the sort of executive machismo outlined above is the current emphasis in school effectiveness and improve- ment programmes and TTA (Teacher Training Authority) literature on 'vi- sion' as a defining characteristic of 'good' headship. At face value, this is purpose rather than technique. However, viewed more cynically 'vision' can be seen as a key component of the technology of 'culture-building' and 'meaning-making' – the enchantment of the worker – discussed earlier. But in addition, 'leadership, particularly in a period of rapid change, is about emotions – desire, fear, despair, caring, disillusionment, pain, anger, stress, anxiety and loneliness...' (Blackmore, 1996, p. 346); is about 'emo- tional management'. For many teachers and headteachers, the line between the professional and the personal is 'increasingly blurred due to the emotional demands of the job and invasion of personal time and space' (Blackmore, 1995, p. 51). In effect, 'it is becoming harder to say when one is working' (Sabel, 1991, p. 43).

It is in the management of emotions and social relations, the 'valuing' of workers and the facilitation of more informal communication, that feminine qualities of management are apparently valued. This leads some writers like Valerie Hall to write in terms of 'the possible transformations of formal power when it is held by women' (Hall, 1996, p. 203). But there is a danger of romanticizing and decontextualizing management by women or feminist leadership here and of ignoring the primary task-oriented characteristics of school leadership roles. In other words, we have to question the role of feminine qualities in the current repertoire of management. Again, the issue is whether the adoption of such qualities indicates changes in technique or changes in purpose.

What we may be seeing in the celebration of 'women's ways of managing' may not be a basis of change but a process of incorporation. Indeed, these ways of managing, and the emphasis on emotional and inter-personal management, slip very easily into the sort of analysis outlined above. Part of the work of leadership involves instilling an attitude and a culture within which the workers feel themselves as accountable to and at the same time committed or personally invested in the organization. These new modes of management 'open up' more of the managed to control.

Values and competition, images and fabrication

I alluded earlier to the critique of bureaucratic provision and professionalism that underlies the advocacy of the market, entrepreneurism and managerialism (Bottery, 1992; Boyd, 1982). Much of this critique is rooted in a psychology of self-interest and interest maximization and a form of 'moral naturalism'. In other words, professional bureaucracies inevitably work primarily in the interests of professionals themselves as their natural inclinations are to fashion the workings of their organization to their own needs. The 'service ethic' (Marshall, 1939) which still underpins the work commitments of many teachers (Mrech and Elder, 1996) is discursively displaced in such critiques. As Hanlon (1998, p. 51) puts it, 'a social service professional ethos is perceived as a luxury which the state can no longer afford'.

The critique of professionalism draws upon free market economics and rests upon two basic assumptions. 'The first is that the market, and hence competition between people, is natural to the human condition... The second assumption is that humanity is composed of individuals, who are basically selfish... The market, then, merely gives expression to a basic urge' (Bottery, 1992, p. 86). Advocates of the market argue that in bureaucratic/professional systems 'self-interest' encourages complacency and unresponsiveness and 'tends to foster the maximisation of budgets rather than profits' (Boyd, 1982, p. 115) or attention to client satisfaction.

In this way, self-interest is the problem but it is also the solution. As an antidote to complacency and unresponsiveness the new public sector markets, in education, health, community services etc. are framed by a mix of incentives and rewards aimed at stimulating *different kinds* of self-interested responses from both producers and consumers. There is no recognition in these critiques of altruism or 'service' as aspects of the work or motivation of public professionals. The logic of the critique is also the logic of the alternative; that decision-making will be re-oriented and change brought about in response to the rewards and sanctions of the market framework. Thus, within the market, financial calculation and survivalism rather than principled educational thinking will drive decisions. Such calculation, it is argued, will link the practice of the provider to the satisfaction of the consumer and will thus lead to a rise in standards.

However, I would share the view that 'market-place institutions, instead of providing a structure for natural inclinations, in fact produce the conditions under which the mentality [of self interest] occurs' (Bottery, 1992, p. 87). The introduction of the market form and managerialist/entrepreneurial organizations are not just technical changes in the structuring of incentives and the form and means of delivery of services; they are cultural and values changes, and they produce a new mentality.

What is achieved in the establishment of the market form in education, as in other sectors of public provision, is a new moral environment for both consumers and producers. Thus, schools are being inducted into what Plant (1992, p. 87) calls a *'culture of self-interest'*. Within the market form, both consumers and producers are encouraged, by the rewards and punishments of 'market forces', and legitimated, by the values of the personal standpoint, in their quest for positional advantage over others, this is the 'cult of selfishness' (Kenway, 1990, p. 155). More generally, this is part of what Bottery (op. cit., p. 93) terms the 'pauperisation of moral concepts in the public sphere'. Fairness, probity and equality are all under threat as the differences between very distinct spheres of ethical life are collapsed (Plant, 1992). The idea of the deliberate and planned pursuit of the 'common good' is rendered meaningless within the disciplines of competition and survival. We can already see these market values, and the 'debased ethics' to which they give rise, at work in the UK school system (see Ball *et al*, 1994; Ball, Macrae *et al*, 1997; Ball, 1998).

Here I want to concentrate on one aspect of the values of the market, specifically as related to *the flow of information in the education market*. Market information in education generally takes four forms. First, there is performance information which is based on outcome indicators, which I began to explore earlier, and which is *required of* educational organizations and published. Second, there is judgmental information which is *generated about* educational organizations through processes of inspection and audit, founded on the notion of the measurement of quality and the integrity of procedures. Third, there is promotional information which is *produced by* educational organizations in order to give an impression of themselves for the purposes of marketing and recruitment – brochures, prospectuses, newspaper stories, web-sites, open evenings and other public events. However, both common sense and recent research tell us a fourth, qualitatively different reputational information, *circulates around* educational organizations by word of mouth through social networks. This last is often the most valued and most crucial sort of information for consumers in their choice-making (Ball and Vincent, 1998). I want to consider briefly the first three sorts of market information from a 'values perspective'.

Right across the public sector, 'performance information' is an important resource and one of the main disciplinary tactics of accountability. In the name of public interest more and more information about public sector organizations is required, recorded and published. In part, this provides 'information' for market decision-making but it is also a basis for 'official' judgements. Crucially, practice is re-focused upon those tasks that serve and are represented within the 'information' of performance. Tasks and activities less conducive to measuring and recording, or which do not contribute directly to performativity, are in danger of becoming 'valueless'.

One way in which we can see the relationship between market incentives, market values and information at work is around the 'production' (or what I would call the 'fabrication') of GCSE results and league table positions. The logic of market incentives would suggest that any school that can select its clients would do so – either formally or informally. Those schools that do select their students, either formally or informally, are more able to control their league table position and their reputation generally. Furthermore, those students who offer the best chance of GCSE success tend to be the cheapest to teach, and easiest to manage. Students who threaten the reputation or performance of the school will be de-selected – excluded – and we have seen a massive growth in the number of students excluded from school since 1991. Similarly, in some schools, poor-attending students, especially in years 10 and 11, are ignored in the hope that they will complete 40 days off-roll and can then be excluded. They then disappear from the school's GCSE returns and published figures for unauthorized absences, although the advantage of a small percentage increase in GCSE performance has to be weighed against loss of income. Generally, as explained by headteachers in our research on many occasions, the most effective long-term strategy for improving GCSE performance is to change the student intake. It is not so much what the school can do for its students but what the students can do for their school. Thus, GCSE attainment percentages and local league table positions do not in any simple sense represent the outcomes of teaching and learning. They are fabrications produced out of a complex set of policy strategies and practical tactics aimed at the enhancement of performance.

As another example, many schools appear to believe that the most effective short-term strategy to boost performance is to target energy, pedagogy and resources on students on the C/D boundary. They also focus pedagogy and classroom activities on the highly specific situated learning related to examination performance rather than transferable learning or real-world problem-solving skills and capabilities. This is one of the ways in which performativity penetrates into day-to-day classroom practices.

Within all this, there is a set of difficult and disturbing values-based issues struggling for recognition. Apart from concerns about equity and the differential valuing of students, we can also question *the values of representation* here, that is the *meaning of performance* as represented in local league table information. I am not simply rehearsing the critique of 'raw score comparisons' here. I am asking: First, how are these performances 'produced', what organizational processes are involved and what is represented? Second, are these performances worthwhile? What are the effects of performativity on the students' learning? Hugh Lauder makes a very important point. He says:

> the critical issue must surely be in part a question not only of test results but how they are arrived at... In England the problem of how to raise basic educational standards while preserving or developing creativity is not even part of the public debate. ... if we are not careful, policy settings which emphasise results at the expense of methods will lead to a trained incapacity to think openly and critically about problems that will confront us in ten or twenty years time throughout the system.
>
> (Lauder *et al*, 1998, p. 15)

Thus, we should not think of performance or judgemental 'information' as valid in any simple sense. The process of representation filters and interprets almost all forms of measurement. There is almost always latitude for presentational variation. The public importance attached to such measures in the artificial educational market only serves to increase the pressure for such filtration.

As noted, schools are also required to publish a variety of types of 'information' about themselves in prospectuses and annual reports including, examination passes, rates of attendance and students destinations. In addition, Ofsted inspections require documentation about a whole range of 'policies' and systems in use in a school. Again, these forms of representation invite schools to *fabricate* themselves. That is to say, performance indicators and other representations are used to 'stand for' or 'in place of' the organization as a set of day-to-day work practices. They 'fabricate' an organization that is *for* external consumption, they provide a focus for the gaze of quality and accountability, they are there *to be viewed, evaluated and compared*. Again the day-to-day practices of school and classrooms are not insulated from the performative requirements of fabrication, quite the reverse, but none the less there is a slippage or mismatch between fabric and core.

As part of this *fabrication*, within the context of the education market, schools are increasingly aware of the significance of the way they represent themselves to the relatively naïve gazes of 'lay' audiences. Schools have become much more aware of how they 'present' themselves to their current and potential parents, for example through promotional publications, school events, school 'productions', open evenings and local press coverage. There is a general tension or confusion in the education market between information-giving and impression management and promotion. The role of 'liaison' between secondary schools and 'feeder' primary schools is a case in point.

Two of the sixteen schools with which we have worked in recent research have employed Public Relations Consultants to help them with presentation and promotion. Most schools have marketing committees, and devote considerable time, energy and expense to the design of brochures, prospectuses and school events. We explored this is some detail in previous work and noted in the case of school prospectuses (Gewirtz *et al*, 1995, p. 127):

- the use of more sophisticated production techniques and the resulting 'glossification' of school imagery
- the commercialization of texts and an associated focus on 'visual images' and explicit indicators of 'quality', and
- a growing emphasis on middle-class symbolism.

The last point refers to the use of drama and music as social class surrogates, both as forms of appeal and as forms of indirect selection aimed at maximizing middle-class recruitment. It is interesting to note that 35 of the 41 Grant Maintained Schools (GM) which responded to the change of regulations in 1996 concerning selection of students indicated that they would select on the basis of aptitude or talent in Music or Drama (Parliamentary answer, 11 June 1996). As I have noted, the content and form of marketing texts produced by schools have also shifted away from print to softer and more immediate visual images in accordance with the aesthetics of advertising. The amount of information presented in such texts has reduced considerably.

There are now high levels of reflexivity and planning 'for effect' in the ways schools present themselves. That is to say, events and publications have both substantive and promotional purposes. More generally, the emphasis on 'selling' schools affects and inflects a whole range of interactions between schools and their social environment. Thus for example, Carol Fitzgibbon has drawn attention to the increasing use of consultants by schools preparing themselves for Ofsted inspections (*The Guardian,* 21 June 1996).

As a further variation on the fabrication of organizations many schools have used their new budgetary freedoms to re-design and re-decorate their entrance and reception areas – typically in open-plan 'building society' style. Again, the purpose seems to be to take control of and change the organizational messages conveyed. There is a detachment and confusion of signs; a shift from bureaucratic to business-like imagery; from something that is clearly 'represented' as a public service to something that *might be* a consumption good.

The further inter-related technology of performativity at work in our schools is that generated around the arrival, at some point, of the Ofsted inspectors. What is important here is again *appearances*; having policies *for ...*, being seen *to ...*, and making sure the figures look right. This not dissimilar from the ways in which public utility companies present their accounts and fabricate their performance targets.

Let me offer a couple of illustrations here. In fieldwork in schools, I observed several instances when the management of figures for public consumption was discussed. In one school at a year head's meeting with the senior deputy she talked about attendance figures and the need for 'the judicious use of authorized absences' (Deputy Head). At a SMT meeting on staffing analyses the Head asked the senior teacher responsible, 'How do we show the contact ratio in the best light [for Ofsted]?' And in interview, the head of one department talked about the very direct pressure coming from the Head to get the exam results presented in a particular way:

> I'm rushing around like a loony today trying to put together this exam results display she wants... I didn't have any data to do it with and I've had to collect that and then I've had to find a way of presenting the results in a way that looks good... GCSEs and A level results against the national average... that's presented us with some problems, because obviously with four subjects the results are uneven... I've found a way of doing the A level that looks alright, I'm struggling a bit with the GCSE.

(HoD2)

On the one hand, the issue again is that of appearances – an organization for 'the gaze', and for avoidance of 'the gaze'. But, on the other, the attempts to push up examination and test score performances and the organization of promotional activities have first-order effects on teachers' practice and second-order effects on students' school experience.[2] We simply take it for granted that they are beneficial.

Two further brief illustrations: The first is fairly subtle and is in the form of a quotation from a Head of Art in a secondary school, comparing the work of his students and the scope of his practice now with those of the pre-performance era.

> We have a different perspective, we're trying to sort of create excellence, a type of tacit competition within... between schools in a way... And if you pitch your sights that way I feel that you are not really encompassing the whole population... the students were producing very gutsy exciting work, which was not so much exam oriented.

What is suggested here is both that the requirements of performance reduce the possibility of producing artistically worthwhile work and that these requirements orient the teachers' work towards certain students and away from others. The second is another interview extract. This from a Head of Drama describing the way in which school productions have become less educational in nature, open to all students, and more promotional events.

> The Head takes a genuine interest in the Arts and we have a very good position in the curriculum, compared with a lot of other schools, but the quid pro quo if you like is a thriving kind of public face and most of the teachers are actually committed to that, funnily enough.... I mean they enjoy doing it, they get a lot out of it... but it's a lot of work, particularly to maintain the programme that they want... a problem with performance, the public performance in education, although it's educationally beneficial, very, for those students involved, it is inevitably selective, and what you're doing is concentrating on the able students... at the expense – well, you haven't got the time to spend so much on others, although of course we try and get... other people involved as much as we can....
>
> We've got so much keenness to be involved, and if you're doing what we're doing at the moment... like we're going into a thing... with the National Theatre, organizing a youth theatre project, we might be able to get... actually to the National.... The pressure's on and we're not gonna pick kids that can't do it, and anyway one of the things that the Head would say is, we don't want anyone who can't act involved really... she doesn't like people in the orchestra who can't play instruments, who've only just started, although you can get away with that to an extent, but she's against that, so there is that.... I think

it's unfortunate but performance is really aimed at – the kids who benefit are the ones who are able.

Here again performance requirements affect the nature and meaning of the 'educational' events and limit access to them for certain types of students.

Conclusion: what are we doing to ourselves?

I suggested at the beginning that management inscribes itself on our bodies as well as our practices. What I mean by that is the link between the increases in productive capacity, increased visibility, comparison and competition – within and between institutions – and the dramatic increases in teacher stress, ill-health and burnout.[3] Peter Woods and colleagues have summarised recent research on the horrendous impact of educational reform on teachers' health and morale. While they note that this may be a common condition of work in late modern societies, 'there is evidence that teachers in some respects have been worse off than other professions at risk' (Woods, Jeffrey *et al,* 1997, p. 143).

Indeed, they quote a national survey of work and ill health in which teaching is one of the 'big four' in terms of work-related health dangers – alongside mining, construction and nursing. Part of this stress is clearly material – the intensification of teachers' work – but part is also subjective. That is the increasing difficulty that many teachers face in putting their ideals into practice: the conflict between professional judgement and commercial expedience. Woods and colleagues argue that 'the integrity of living one's life according to the calling of one's occupation is now denied (ibid., pp. 194–6).

Once again, the untoward effects of one section of commerce provides new opportunities for other sections – in this case the explosion of business in fields like exercise and leisure, stress management, new-age therapies and particularly, the burgeoning field of educational consultancy!

The cold calculation of the management of reform is brought home by another comment made by Woods and colleagues: 'From a managerialist viewpoint, the disturbances in the profession of the last ten years or so might be considered functional on the basis of "no gain without pain". Many teachers are adapting, others are unable to and eventually leave, to be replaced by new recruits trained in the new order' (ibid., p. 164).

The act of teaching and the subjectivity of the teacher are both profoundly changed within the new managerialist systems of surveillance and comparison, and the new forms of entrepreneurial control through marketing and competition. Two apparently conflicting effects emerge. First, the teacher is increasingly individualized, including the destruction of solidarities based upon professional identity and trade union affiliation that cuts across schools. Second, new forms of institutional affiliation and 'community' are constructed – a corporate culture that also stresses the 'individuality' of schools and sets them against one another in the market (see also Chapman 1991).

Managerialism is pivotal in this duality. It is both an enactment of 'practical autonomy' and a technology of control. It represents a new mode of public administration, the freeing of institutions from direct bureaucratic controls, replacing these with local 'initiative', while, at the same time, it brings into play new and more immediate and pervasive controls over individual practice. It is central to the establishment of what Du Gay (1996, p. 186) calls 'entrepreneurial governance' – the use of market mechanisms to catalyse the public sector. And as I have tried to demonstrate, one of its most critical characteristics is that *we do it to ourselves and to one another*, we *are* all managers now. We are to be 'freed' and 'empowered' in the pursuit of entrepreneurial innovation. We become accountable for the improvements and achievements of our institution. Management redefines the nature of our endeavours and our very identities (ibid.). It becomes part of us and of our relationships. 'We are obliged to fulfil our political role as active citizens, ardent consumers, enthusiastic employees, and loving parents as if we were seeking to realise our own desires' (Rose, 1989 p. 258).[4] I have argued that as entrepreneurial management sweeps through the public sector it sweeps away the values of professionalism and of the 'service ethic'.

> If bureaucracy is to be reduced or abandoned and an entrepreneurial style of management adopted, then it must be recognised that while 'economic efficiency' might be improved in the short term, the longer-term costs associated with this apparent improvement may well include fairness, probity, complex equality and other crucial features of liberal democratic government.

> (Du Gay, 1996, pp. 189–90)

Notes

1. It could, however, be argued that these are replaced by the fable of 'the perfectly managed school' – the 'enchanted workplace' (see under 'Corporate Culture').
2. These are explored elsewhere in our research writing.
3. Between 1991 and 1997, days off work as a result of work-related ill health rose from 12 million to 20 million per annum.
4. This is a theme taken up later by Colin Fletcher (Chapter 10) in relation to the role of parents.

References

Ball, SJ (1998) Ethics, self interest and the market form in education, in A Cribb (ed.), *Markets, Managers and Public Service?* Occasional Paper No. 1, Centre for Public Policy Research, King's College, London

Ball, SJ, Bowe, R and Gewirtz, S (1994) Competitive schooling: values, ethics and cultural engineering, *Journal of Curriculum and Supervision*, **9** (4), pp. 350–67

Ball, SJ, Macrae, S *et al* (1997) The post-16 education market: ethics, interests and survival, ESRC project paper, King's College School of Education, London

Ball, SJ and Vincent, C (1998) 'I heard it on the grapevine': 'Hot' Knowledge and school choice, *British Journal of Sociology of Education*, **19** (3), pp. 377–400

Blackmore, J (1995) Breaking out from a masculinist politics of education, B Limerick and B Linguard (eds) *Gender and Changing Educational Management*, Hodder, Sydney

Blackmore, J (1996) Doing 'emotional labour' in the education market place: stories from the field of women in management, *Discourse*, **17** (3), pp. 337–49

Bottery, M (1992) *The Ethics of Educational Management*, Cassell, London

Boyd, W (1982) The political economy of future schools, *Educational Administration Quarterly*, **18** (3), pp. 111–30

Boyett, JH and Conn, HP (1992) *Workplace 2000: The Revolution Shaping American Business*, Plume, New York

Boyle, M and Woods, P. (1996) The composite head: coping with changes in the primary headteacher's role, *British Educational Research Journal*, **22** (5), pp. 549–68

Chapman, RA (1991) The End of the Civil Service?, *Teaching Public Administration*, **12** (2), pp. 11-15

Clarke, J (1998) Thriving on chaos? Managerialism and social welfare, in J Carter (ed.) *Postmodernity and the Fragmentation of Welfare*, Routledge, London

Clarke, J, Cochrane, A *et al* (1994) *Managing Social Policy*, Sage, London

Du Gay, P (1996) *Consumption and Identity at Work,* Sage, London

Ferguson, KE (1984) *The Feminist Case Against Bureaucracy*, Temple University Press, Philadelphia

Foucault, M (1979) *Discipline and Punish*, Peregrine, Harmondsworth

Gee, J and Lankshear, C (1995) The new work order: critical language awareness and 'fast capitalism' texts, *Discourse*, **16** (16), pp. 5–20

Gewirtz, S, Ball, SJ and Bowe, R (1995) *Markets, Choice and Equity in Education,* Open University Press, Buckingham

Grace, G (1995) *School Leadership: Beyond Education Management - An Essay in Policy Scholarship,* Falmer, London

Hall, V (1996) *Dancing on the Ceiling,* Paul Chapman, London

Hanlon, G (1998) Professionalism as enterprise, *Sociology*, **32** (10), pp. 43–63

Kenway, J (1990) Privileged girls, private schools and the culture of success, in J Kenway and S Wilks (eds) *Hearts And Minds: Self Esteem and the Schooling of Girls*, Falmer, London

Kerfoot, D and Knights, D (1993) Management, masculinity and manipulation: from paternalism to corporate strategy in financial services in Britain, *Journal of Management Studies,* **30** (4), pp. 659–77

Kirkpatrick, I and Martinez-Lucio, M (1995) *The Politics of Quality in the Public Sector*, Routledge, London

Lauder, H, Jamieson, I *et al.* (1998) Models of effective schools: limits and capabilities, in R Slee and G Weiner with S Tomlinson (eds) *School Effectiveness for Whom? Challenges to the School Effectiveness and School Improvement Movements*, Falmer, London

Lyotard, J-F (1984) *The Postmodern Condition: A Report on Knowledge*, Manchester University Press, Manchester

Marshall, TH (1939) A recent history of professionalism, *Canadian Journal of Economics and Political Science*, **5**, pp. 325–40

Mrech, RA and Elder, G (1996) The service ethic and teaching, *Sociology of Education*, **69**, pp. 237–53

Plant, R (1992) Enterprise in its place: the moral limits of markets, in P Heelas and P Morris (eds) *The Values of the Enterprise Culture*, Routledge, London

Pollard, A, Broadfoot, P *et al* (1994) *Changing English Primary Schools? The Impact of the Education Reform Act at Key Stage One*, Cassell, London

Ray, CA (1986) Corporate culture: the last frontier of control?, *Journal of Management Studies*, **23** (3) pp. 287–97

Riley, K (1994) *Quality and Equality: Promoting Opportunities in Schools*, Cassell, London

Rose, N (1989) *Governing the Soul: The Shaping of the Private Self*, Routledge, London

Sabel, C (1991) Moebius strip organizations and open labour markets: some consequences of the reintegration of conception and execution in a volatile labour market, in P Bourdieu and JS Coleman (eds) *Social Theory for a Changing Society,* Westview Press, Boulder, Colorado

Willmott, H (1992) Postmodernism and excellence: the de-differentiation of economy and culture, *Journal of Organizational Change and Management*, **5** (1) pp. 58–68

Willmott, H (1993) Strength is ignorance; slavery is freedom: managing culture in modern organizations, *Journal of Management Studies*, **30** (4), pp. 215–52

Woods, P, Jeffrey, B *et al* (1997) *Restructuring Schools, Reconstructing Teachers,* Open University Press, Buckingham

PART IV

Curriculum and Assessment

6

The Quality of Learning
Myth: Standards are a Measure of Quality

Michael Armstrong

We now begin to focus particularly on the learner. It was always possible that the introduction of a national curriculum would homogenize the experience of schooling and drive out innovation. In this chapter, Armstrong shows that even in the first years of primary schooling, originality and meaning in children's expression are discounted by an unimaginative national orthodoxy. Teachers are as much the victims as their pupils or students. They must struggle to overcome the dead weight of conformity and to encourage individual expression.

Standards

What do we mean when we talk about standards? Everyone is in favour of higher standards. No one seems to doubt that the concept of a standard is appropriate as a sign of educational worth or achievement. It seems self-evidently so. I want to challenge this easy consensus. I will argue that the standards laid down in the National Curriculum – targets and levels of attainment measured at the end of specified key stages by tests and teacher assessments – fail to represent the most significant features of intellectual performance. I will suggest that there are better ways of evaluating children's learning.

The concept of a standard is troublesome in several ways. For a start, a standard is a measure. Certain aspects of education may be more or less susceptible of measurement, particular routines, for example, or factual recall, or certain kinds of problem-solving, but the most dynamic characteristic of learning, which for want of a better term I will call its creative aspect, cannot be measured, as I will show. Moreover, a standard is a measure of conformity whereas education is as much, if not much more, concerned with non-conformity: with exception rather than rule; with the novel, the unexpected, the re-described and reconstructed; with the revival of learning no less than its transmission, and with innovation as well as tradition. In short, education is a critical practice.

These deficiencies point to a deeper problem. The concept of a standard seems to imply that education is essentially preliminary to culture, the necessary training for a subsequent engagement. Once the basic skills are in place, as measured by a succession of tests at a variety of ages – 5, 7, 11, 14 – then and only then are children equipped to launch out culturally on their own. But education at any and every age is always more than cultural training. To watch a class of children struggling with narrative, or working out the means of visual representation, or puzzling over some problem of behaviour, is to be made aware that education is as much a matter of making or re-making culture as of absorbing a culture that has already been defined. Contrary to the expectations of the Secretary of State for Education and his advisers, notably the Chief Inspector of Schools, one way or another each new class of children necessarily re-invents the wheel.

The guardians of the National Curriculum have always been uncomfortable with the innovative nature of learning. Occasionally they pay lip service to the values of creativity and imagination, only to ignore them in the detailed prescription. It was the original English Working Party itself that first recognized the problem when at the end of a discussion of writing in their first report (NCC, 1988) the authors candidly acknowledge their failure to include significant cultural expression within their allotted framework: 'The best writing is vigorous, committed, honest and interesting. We have not included these qualities in our attainment targets because they cannot be mapped onto levels. Even so, all good classroom practice will be geared to encouraging and fostering these vital qualities' (ibid., p. 48). That final sentence is deeply ironic in the light of all that has happened since. In the years that have followed this early report, several attempts have been made to supply the missing ingredient. Predictably, all have failed. Anyone who doubts this need only consult the report by QCA on *Standards in English at Key Stage Two* (QCA, 1997). Discussing the results of the previous summer's writing test, the authors draw attention to children's punctuation, paragraphing and syntax, the length of their writing, the choice of 'conventional and unexciting openings to stories', the overwhelming use of a chronological structure, the absence of figurative language and the generally poor understanding of 'the role of dialogue in narrative'. That is all. Not a word about the children's literary intentions or ambitions, the way they formulate their ideas or work out their plots, the themes they explore, the patterns they create. The quality of the children's thought and expression is quite simply irrelevant. Nor is this in any way surprising. After all, the standard measure is no more than a single piece of writing to a set theme to be composed within a given time on a particular day under examination conditions. The chances that such a procedure might identify whatever is distinctive or characterful or of interest or value in any child's writing are negligible. This might not matter so much if the targets and tests that define the National Curriculum were regarded as minimal requirements of a system whose fundamental values lay elsewhere. But that was always wishful thinking. The tests have already become the chief, if not the only, criterion by which individual schools, and, more damagingly, individual children are judged.

How, then, might we better evaluate children's learning? I will try to answer this question by examining one short picture story, composed by a child at my own school who had just turned 6 years old. In analysing this one particular narrative my intention is threefold: to explain what I mean by the creative aspect of learning; to show how a child, in one of her earliest engagements with the culture of narrative, exploits tradition even as she absorbs it and *in order to* absorb it; and to suggest how such an achievement might properly be recognized, appreciated and judged. I have deliberately chosen one slight but significant text to stand for many. My aim is, as Walter Benjamin put it in outlining his plans for a study of the Paris arcades, 'to discover the crystal of the total event in the analysis of the small particular moments' (Morss, 1991, p. 74). I have chosen a story, rather than a non-narrative text, because of the central role of narrative in children's early education. Bruner describes narrative as 'the mode of thinking and feeling that helps children (indeed people generally) create a version of the world in which, psychologically, they can envisage a place for themselves – a personal world' (Bruner, 1996, p. 39).

Narrative

The Little Girl Who Got Lost was composed by Melissa Warwick in the winter of 1996, shortly after her sixth birthday. The circumstances of its composition are easily told. Melissa's teacher had given her class small hand-made booklets in which she had asked them to write a story. There was no set theme, no defined genre, no prototype and no advice about how, if at all, the story might be illustrated. But there *was* one particular oddity about Melissa's booklet that may have had a significant effect on her tale, as we shall see. Whereas all the other children's booklets contained eight pages in all, Melissa's, by accident, contained twelve. Melissa wrote and drew alongside her friend Jessica. No doubt they looked over each other's work and chatted as they wrote. There are certain similarities: the placing of illustrations, always underneath the text; the hair style given to the characters, male and female; the choice of a girl such as themselves as heroine; the opening of each story with a walk; the focus on family life. These common features seem insignificant though, when set alongside the striking differences in the two girls' respective visions.[1]

Here is Melissa's story.

The Litte drel who got Lost BY Melissa

One day a Little drel came out side and she Deolded to do out for a Woir

But soon the Little drel got Lost and she Woonted her mummy then her Mummy cane

The Little drel Was very Happy

then one day the whole family went out for a wolk Little girl the and to her mum and dad sticked

then they went home

and wen we got home we had tea

then it was nily tim for my bed tim

then it was
my bed tim

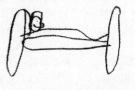

then it was nily
tim for my mums
and dads bed tim

then it was 10
minytes antil my
mums and dads
bed tim

then it was tim
for my mums and
dads bed tim

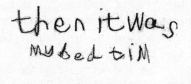

the end

Let's start with the title page. In one sense, the title is misleading. This is not a simple story about a little girl who got lost but an extended celebration of family life, set in motion by the opening incident. However, in another sense the title is central to the tale. Getting lost is the consequence of an act that ignores the reality of the child's dependence on her family. That dependence is not seen as a threat but as a support, and the point of the story is to reaffirm family solidarity. Getting lost is the rupture that Melissa's tale sets out to heal. The illustration below the title dramatizes this rupture. The figure of the girl looking out at us and saying, 'I want my mum' is the figure whose first person voice will eventually move from speech bubble to become the voice of the narrator herself. But it is only at the point of resolution, two-thirds of the way through the tale, that this shift is manageable, as we shall see.

The story of getting lost occupies just three pages. On the first of these, the heroine asserts her independence. 'One day a little girl came outside and she decided to go out for a walk.' The vocabulary is deceptively simple. The words 'came outside' draw attention to the girl's leaving home. Here in the outside world she is apparently free to decide for herself. 'I love walking' she insists as she steps boldly out, justifying the decision she has taken by the smile on her face, the spoken thought and the determined stride. Crisis and resolution follow swiftly on the second page. 'But soon the little girl got lost and she wanted her mummy then her mummy came.' The narrator chooses not to linger over the details of the abortive adventure, not, I suggest, because she has nothing to say, or insufficient skill to say it, but because the adventure is incidental to the narrative as a whole. Perhaps, as well, Melissa could not bear to leave her heroine in suspense for a moment longer than she needed to. At any rate, as soon as help is sought, there it is, at hand. The wish is father to both thought and deed, as if it were possessed of magical power, a hint of the fairy tale in Melissa's family saga.

I love the absence of any full stop before the word 'then'. It is true that there are no full stops in Melissa's story and yet she is careful with her punctuation, making use of the movement from page to page to separate her sentences one from another. Every other time that the word 'then' is used it opens a page, no fewer than seven times in all. On this occasion, however, the effect Melissa requires is of the immediacy of aid when called for. The absence of a break between 'mummy' and 'then' precisely suits her purpose. I want to be clear here. I am not arguing that Melissa self-consciously chose to ignore the full stop at this point. I am suggesting that the variation in her use of the word 'then' in the story indicates a subtlety in the use of the written language which it is easy to ignore. Imagine a teacher who persuaded Melissa to put a full stop between the words 'mummy' and 'then'. The meaning of the page would change significantly. The drawing below the text redoubles this effect. Child and mother stride confidently towards each other, all smiles. The girl shouts in recognition, as if she has just realized she needs her mum when, lo and behold, there she is before her. Melissa drew the speech bubble twice. She told me she had redrawn it because she could not fit the word 'mum' into her first bubble. This second bubble, with its long tongue-like ribbon, becomes the visual sign of recognition, a symbol of identity closing the space between mother and child.

With this, the first part of Melissa's story comes to an end. Her lettering gets larger. 'The little girl was very happy.' For the first time, excepting the title page, the drawn figure faces the reader, beaming. She is no longer on an adventure. It's over, she's happy, she's free to be herself once more, but only under the protection of her family, as we are now to learn.

The following three pages recapitulate the girl's adventure but this time she is not on her own. 'Then one day the whole family went out for a walk and the little girl sticked to her mum and dad.' The formula is the same, 'one day... out for a walk', but the circumstances have been transformed. It is 'the whole family' that now sets out as one. 'Sticked' is perhaps the single most important word in the entire narrative, partly by virtue of its irregularity – I hesitate to describe the word as incorrect. It simultaneously confirms the deliberateness of Melissa's usage and draws an adult reader's attention to the force of this particular word in this particular context. The girl is free to be herself only when she is inseparable from her family. The drawing is a minor masterpiece, three figures marching as one, identical smiles on their faces, identical postures, one foot forward, arms by their sides. Only the hairstyles are different, distinguishing male from female. I asked Melissa which was the girl. 'The one in the middle,' she replied, 'because she's sticking to her mum and dad.'

Turn the page and the family return – 'then they went home' – in the same order and with identical expressions and gestures. The drawing is a mirror image of the previous page, surely a brilliant narrative stroke. Melissa herself gave a somewhat roundabout explanation. She said it was just that when you turn the page and look through the paper you could see that the dad was now on the other side of the page. So is it by chance that there happened to be a page turn between departure and return? Maybe, but the accident is organized. As William Blake put it in a marginal note on a page of his poem, *The Four Zoas*: 'Unorganiz'd Innocence: An Impossibility. Innocence dwells with Wisdom, but never with Ignorance.'

'And when we got home we had tea.' What are we to make of the sudden change from third to first person, a change that is sustained throughout the closing pages of Melissa's narrative? When she recorded her story on tape later in the year, Melissa at first read 'they' and then corrected herself. She would not admit that she had deliberately chosen to write 'we' rather than 'they'. Yet the change, whether or not it is symptomatic of a young writer's insecurity in the use of person, becomes a central element in the narrative.

It would be impossible to regularize person here and in the succeeding pages without damage to Melissa's thought. Imagine replacing the word 'my' on each of the remaining pages of the story with the word 'her', or worse still, with the words 'the little girl'. The aura so carefully established would vanish. It seems to me that at this precise moment, when the terror of the first adventure has been resolved by recasting it as a family outing, the narrator is able to enter her own tale in imagination, becoming herself – the little girl. Perhaps she thought of herself as the girl all along. But now she can afford to dispense with concealment. This movement into the first person opens the way for the long, slow epilogue, the winding down of the day and the story, even of time itself.

Teachers tend to encourage children, even in their earliest writing, to be regular in their use of person, especially in a post-National Curriculum environment. But this is to suppose that the irregularity is aesthetically pointless and at best no more than a confusion. Melissa's story shows the mistake to be ours rather than hers. As she grows older as a writer there will be time for didacticism but not here and now. It is hard not to wonder how many aspiring literary imaginations may have been blunted by adult pressure to conform to what are, as yet, irrelevant norms.

I asked Melissa if the food on the table, in the picture of the family having tea, was biscuits. No, she said, it was beans; she always drew fish and chips and beans when she was drawing tea. Tea: the appropriate conclusion to an afternoon walk. But there are still five pages of the book to fill. Does the available space explain Melissa's drawn-out ending? Partly, perhaps, for as I indicated earlier, Melissa's teacher had included an extra folded page in Melissa's booklet inadvertently. I doubt that is the whole explanation. It might be more accurate to say that this accident of circumstance provided Melissa with an added opportunity. She chooses to compose a five page epilogue, closing the story down frame by frame, creating the effect of a quiet and solemn ritual in elegant contrast to the excitement of getting lost, finding mum and setting out a second time as a family.

When Melissa first read these pages in public, at a school assembly, her audience laughed. Afterwards she told her teacher, somewhat irritably, that she didn't know why they laughed. She was right, of course, except that it was not a mocking laughter so much as an expression of delight at Melissa's naïve but controlled sense of an ending. Succession is the key to these pages: the succession of beds, now empty, now filled; the successive appearances of 'then it was', 'time', 'nearly time' and 'bedtime'. When at last we reach the words 'the end' on their own separate page, unaccompanied by any kind of illustration, we know that the tale is told. Whatever comes next can only be another time, another story. Melissa seems well aware of the ritual character of these closing pages. Identical beds appear four times, the sentences repeat themselves, over and over, while time is intoned on every page with the regularity of a clock chiming the midnight hour. The single exception to the repetitive format occurs on the penultimate page, which at first seems to prolong the ending somewhat pedantically. 'Then it was ten minutes until my mum's and dad's bedtime.' In school assembly, Melissa's audience broke into gentle laughter at this moment. But this page is important in so far as it gives Melissa one last opportunity to picture the intimacy of family life which her narrative has set out to explore. Father and mother sit side by side on armchairs in front of the television while, alongside a lamp on a shelf behind them, a clock ticks off the last ten minutes. It is the end of the day, though not of the little girl's day, for she is already asleep, safe in the knowledge that mum and dad are downstairs watching TV. So many times are invoked here: the time of the clock, the time for bed, the time to close the tale. It is almost as if, at the end of her story, Melissa is brooding on the nature of time itself, her final trick in a narrative that delights throughout in its own semantic play.

Quality

Melissa's story is neither unusual nor extraordinary. I present it as a characteristic example of a young writer's critical practice. As a 6-year-old, Melissa may seem at first sight to have almost everything to learn about the art of storytelling. But the more closely we examine her text, the more we are impressed by her control of narrative within the limitations of her present experience. The narrative means available to her may be slight but she uses them to considerable effect. Close reading is the only sure way to recognize Melissa's achievement. Yet it is this that sets the quality of her writing against the National Curriculum in its present guise. A close reading is incompatible with standard measures. Partly this is a matter simply of time. Tests of achievement, affecting entire cohorts of pupils nationwide, have to be prepared, administered and marked in short order. There is no opportunity to consider individual performance in any depth. Can teacher assessment provide what is missing? Hardly. Teacher assessments are equally constrained and compromised by the requirements of the standard tests. Moreover, standard measures call for uniformity of judgement and of the performances that are to be judged. Close reading, by contrast, is responsive to children's individual circumstances: to their developing interests, their distinctive frames of mind, their intellectual and emotional stance, their personal style. But above all else, close reading calls for the suspension of judgement while measured standards are defined by a numerical score which is in effect a summary judgement.

The purpose of close reading is to seek out the significance of a particular work by entering its world and following its incitements. What it calls for is interpretation rather than judgement, which is not to say that individual judgements are invariably out of order, but rather that they can never be final, let alone universal or uniform. The appropriate model for an evaluation of children's critical practice is the portfolio rather than the test. By the term portfolio, I have in mind quite simply a body of work which celebrates a child's achievement year by year. It exhibits the child's distinctive interests and character, and demonstrates the elaboration and extension of the child's thought over time. For the most part, portfolios must stand by themselves as evidence of a child's considered *œuvre*, to be interpreted by the interested reader. But there is a place for annotation too as teachers or pupils look back over a body of work to reflect on its continuing and developing significance. Still more important is the conversation that takes place between pupils and their teachers and parents as they read and respond to the work. Nothing would be worse than to mark the portfolio, with a number or a letter, or to ascribe a level to it, tempted though we may be. For that would reduce the portfolio to yet another test.[2]

I will end as I began, more confidently now in the light of Melissa's tale. As I see it, the pursuit of standards can never be reconciled with the evaluation of creativity. That is not to say that testing is irrelevant to education. It is simply that tests, however subtle, never reach the heart of what learning and teaching are all about. The tragedy is that our contemporary obsession with the myth of standards has obscured this truth.

Notes

1. Jessica's story is published and described elsewhere (Armstrong, 1997).
2. For an interesting discussion of a child's, or, more exactly, a school's, or a classroom's, 'works' or '*œuvres*', see Bruner (1996, pp. 22ff).

References

Armstrong, M (1997) The leap of imagination, *Forum*, **39** (2) Summer
Bruner, J (1996) *The Culture of Education*, Harvard University Press, Cambridge, MA
Morss, SB (1991) *The Dialectics of Seeing*, MIT, MA
NCC (1988) *English for Ages 5 to 11*, Report of the English Working Party of the National Curriculum Council, HMSO, London
QCA (1997) *Standards in English at Key Stage Two*, Report of the Qualifications and Curriculum Authority, QCA, London

7

Curriculum and Assessment

Myth: Testing Helps Learning

Bob Moon

With school tests now consuming hundreds of millions of pounds each year, national assessment is in danger of becoming the tail that wags the dog. Beginning with an historical perspective, Moon shows that this is a very recent British obsession. Developing Armstrong's criticism of the limited and limiting reach of such tests, Moon exposes ten separate fallacies associated with testing. He argues for more holistic and human assessment techniques that can be used to help learning rather than simply to judge schools and their pupils.

Formal testing is a 20th-century phenomenon in education. We should be cautious of its translation into the 21st. There is, of course, a longer lineage for formal assessment. Examinations can be traced back at least to Chinese dynasties attempting to defeat blatant nepotism. But the main Graeco-Roman tradition from which most western education systems grew eschewed any form of formal assessment up to the present century.

There were exceptions. The notorious and short-lived experiment in England and Wales to 'pay elementary school teachers by results', introduced through Robert Lowe's Revised Code of 1862, would be one. Generally speaking though, particularly within the higher status public schools formal tests and examinations hardly existed. Indeed, one attempt by the Clarendon Commission of the mid-1860s to test fifth form boys in nine leading public schools was strongly resisted. Headmasters were terse and to the point in their response. Rev. Charles Scott of Westminster replied, 'Your letter appears to be so seriously objectionable that I must beg to decline to entertain the proposal. The Dean of Westminster concurs with me,' and Dr

Elwyn of Charterhouse described it as 'objectionable both in principle and detail'. Other objectors were more precise, such as Moberley of Winchester: 'We should be deeply and unnecessarily wounded by having it put on record that we had passed a bad one'; and Balham of Eton: 'This interference with the authority of the headmaster is calculated to cause evil' (Moon, 1990).

How some headteachers would relish such autonomy today. Up until the early years of this century the formal paraphernalia of tests, certificates, let alone standardization and moderation, were relatively unknown. The French sociologist Emile Durkheim wrote that even the most cursory historical glance is enough to make us realize that degrees and examinations are of relatively recent origin and that there was nothing equivalent in classical times.

> We are so accustomed to believing that emulation is the essential motivating force in academic life, that we cannot easily imagine how a school could exist which did not have a carefully worked out system of graduated awards in order to keep the enthusiasm of pupils perpetually alive. Good marks, solemn statements of satisfactory performance, distinctions, competitive essays, prizegivings, all these seem to us in differing degrees, the necessary accompaniments to any sound education system. The system that operated in France and indeed Europe, until the sixteenth century, was characterised by the surprising fact that there were no rewards at all from success in examinations. What is more, any candidates who had assiduously and conscientiously followed the course of studies was certain of success.

(quoted in Broadfoot, 1996, p. 80)

The preoccupation with testing is a twentieth-century phenomenon. I want to suggest that there are ten fallacious assumptions about testing which permeate current educational debate:

1. Tests measure ability.
2. Tests are predictive of future educational performance.
3. Tests are neutral in terms of gender and ethnicity.
4. Tests give parents accurate information about their children's progress.
5. Tests can be genuinely criteria based.
6. Tests allow the monitoring of standards over time.
7. Tests allow us to judge how good a school is.
8. Tests allow us to judge national level of achievement against other countries.
9. Tests can be easily applied across the full range of educational experience.
10. Tests are essential to underpin a modern education system.

In one sense, I am playing devil's advocate. Let me be allowed one qualification, however. I am highly pro-assessment. One of the most important developments of the 1980s was the integration of ongoing modes of assessment into daily classroom teaching. Implicit after all in any meaningful pedagogy is the language of assessment. One of the most significant developments in recent years has been to make explicit the formative process of assessment. This process is crucial to successful teaching and learning. Neither am I entirely opposed to formal testing *per se*. The work of the Assessment of Performance Unit in the 1980s (scandalously closed down by the Thatcher administration) was setting an international lead in showing how 'dip stick' testing and assessment could feed back into meaningful teacher development programmes. My argument is with the wholesale spread of individual testing across all phases of the education system and the negative impact this has on so many children's self-esteem. Feeling confident in our selves and secure in our learning, I see as prerequisites to high levels of achievement. Rather than offering opportunities and rewards, the present arrangements, for many, confirm failure. Let me turn to the fallacies.

Tests measure ability

I put this first because it seems one of the most crucial issues. Let me give you three quotations, the first to illustrate nineteenth-century attitudes to grading:

> we shall call these the Third, the Second, and the First Graded education respectively... It is obvious that these distinctions correspond roughly, but by no means exactly, to the gradations of society.
> First Grade: This class appears to have no wish to displace the classics from their present position in the forefront of English education.
> Second Grade: ... though most of these parents would probably consent to give a higher place to Latin, they would only do so on condition that it did not exclude a very thorough knowledge of important modern subjects, and they would hardly give Greek any place at all.
> Third Grade: ... belongs to a class distinctly lower in the scale... The need of this class is described briefly by Canon Moseley to be 'very good reading, very good writing, very good arithmetic'.

> (Taunton, 1868, pp. 15–21)

A second quote indicates how very similar ideas are manifest in the build-up to the Education Act of 1944:

Intellectual development during childhood appears to progress as if it were governed by a single central factor, usually known as 'general intelligence, which may be broadly described as innate all round ability'. It appears to enter into everything which the child attempts to think, or say, or do, and seems on the whole to be the most important factor in determining his work in the classroom. Our psychological witnesses assured us that it can be measured approximately by means of intelligence tests... The average child is said to attain the effective limit of development in general intelligence between the ages of 16 and 18... Since the ratio of each child's mental age to his chronological age remains approximately the same, while his chronological age increases, the mental differences between one child and another will grow larger and larger and will reach a maximum during adolescence. It is accordingly evident that different children from the age of 11, if justice is to be done to their varying capacities, require types of education varying in certain important respects.

(Spens, 1938, pp. 357–81)

Still, in the last decade of the century, the linking of class and ability prevails:

While ABC 1s can conceptualise, C2s and Ds often cannot. They can relate only to things they can see and feel. They absorb their information and often views from television and tabloids. We have to talk to them in a way they understand.

(Leaked Tory party election proposals by former minister John Maples)

The apparently common-sense nostrum that children should be educated according to their abilities is deeply ingrained in the English educational system. Aptitudes, testing, selection and individual categorization co-exist in truly deferential, even reverential, style.

Out of such beliefs have come those self-defining determining labels of the high ability, low ability ('dull', 'thick') and the average child, labels that pervade the language of too many schools and politicians. This, of course, is the language of the bell curve, the shape or curve of normal distribution that purported to allocate grammar school places, positions in class or set and, that passport to success, the university place. Every adult in England today has been labelled in this way. Around half by definition 'didn't do very well at school' and more than half, caught in the slipstream of the high status examinations, still harbour a sense of failure about their school achievement.

The separate schools proposed for the mid-19th century became a reality in the mid-20th century. The selection of children through testing dominated the post-war period. In most parts of the country, the idea that the test

test measured aptitude was misconceived. The number of places available in grammar schools varied markedly from one town or county to another and tests were a bureaucratic means of allocating scarce resources. Despite this, the system ground on relentlessly. The examination system neatly came to mirror the divided school system GCE, CSE or 'non exam'. GCSE, created in the mid-1980s, perpetuated the distinctions with the grade distinction between C and D effectively creating a dual system.

The conviction that different *types* of individuals need different *types* of school and a different *type* of curriculum pervades educational discourse. The school curriculum, and especially the secondary school curriculum, is relentlessly framed by the scholastic subject-based traditions of the 19th century, regulated now through a national curriculum. More significantly the examination and testing system is now firmly based upon that curriculum, made statistically sound by assumptions about a distribution of performance every bit as bell-like as the allocation of IQ scores. Caroline Benn and Clyde Chitty have explored this myth more fully in Chapter 1.

The whole school population still marches to the tune of high, low and average. The symbols change, IQ to National Curriculum levels, but the *distribution* remains the same. Seven-year-olds are sorted into National Curriculum levels 3, 2 and 1 – high, average and low. Five-year-olds are given baseline grades A, B, C. High, average and low repeated like a mantra. High, low, average, seeping into every nook and cranny of our educational experience. High, low, average, defining opportunities and more importantly self-esteem for a lifetime. England and Wales are the only countries in the world that officially suggest that 1 child in 5, 20 per cent of the population, has learning difficulties or special needs. The cult of the satisfactory, the average, places a dead hand on creativity, depressing expectations across the board.

How can this be challenged? First, an offensive should be mounted against the plainly wrong idea that any child's ability is innate, finite or measurable in any general way. The evidence exists before our eyes. The brain is an amazingly complex organism, more subtle and powerful than any computer yet conceived. We know as well that the brain has its geography. Howard Gardner (1984) has brilliantly pointed out the educational implications of this in his conceptualization of multiple intelligences. As Gardner's colleague David Perkins (1995) has shown, our intelligences evolve and stretch through interplay with specific contexts in an ever more complex way. Other powerful commentaries (Damasio, 1994; Goleman, 1995) further demonstrate the intricate architecture through which our mind works. Such creativity cannot be categorized into two or three general levels and certainly not into a numbered score around 100.

For me, therefore, this first fallacy is the crucial and underpinning one. I will move more quickly through the remaining fallacies.

Tests are predictive of future performance

Our minds, our intelligences, evolve and develop over time. Yet out of the innate concept of ability grew the notion of fixed potential. In how many schools do you see the aim that the school seeks to educate all children to their full potential? Potential must be understood, like intelligence, as open to development rather than a vessel of a predetermined size.

The Open University provides perhaps the best evidence to challenge the notion of prediction. Hundreds of thousands of adults over the past 30 years have gained degrees, an achievement their school results would never have predicted. The OU demonstrates clearly how potential can change and intelligences evolve. When I left school in the 1960s less than 10 per cent of my age group were assumed able enough to go on to higher education. Now, in my children's generation, it is more than 30 per cent. As I have indicated in relation to secondary school places, normal test and examination pass rates became tied to the availability of university places too. There will be demand for an Open University well into the next millennium.

Tests are neutral in terms of gender and ethnicity

Quite simply they are not. My colleague, Patricia Murphy, in a series of publications (for example, Gipps and Murphy, 1994), has pointed to the problems of finding gender-neutral tasks in test design. There is voluminous research to show that this applies equally to different ethnic groups, particularly where the children have recently arrived in a new environment. This inevitably interlinks with expectations. Jerome Bruner (1996), for example, has recently pointed to the way in which Korean children arriving in west coast USA, where expectation of Pacific Rim children's performance is high, are quickly achieving high test scores. However, the children of Korean immigrants to Japan, where the expectations are culturally different, achieve much lower scores. The culture of schooling inevitably infuses what are often purported as fair or neutral, valid and reliable tests.

Tests give parents accurate information about their children's progress

At the level of formal national tests, many different items have to be aggregated together to create simple scores. Scores calculated across reading, writing and oral work when manipulated statistically to give an overall level, tell parents little about specific areas of achievement. For the information to be meaningful, you would need to gain insight into the sub-scores of each of the component parts, and this requires explanation and qualifications. In attempting to do this, the first National Curriculum tests became too complex to administer or understand. For political reasons, we have reverted to simple scores, as in GCSE and A levels. While these may provide a rudimentary normative indication of how a child performs compared to their peers, it provides little accurate information about strengths and weaknesses within the subject.

Tests can be genuinely criterion-referenced

It may be possible for tests to give grades against specific criteria for some very specific tasks, 'Attach the wires to the correct pins on the plug', for example. Beyond that, everything becomes more complex, particularly when tests are to have nationwide significance.

National tests and examinations must be created with the expectation that the questions and tasks are fair and that their outcomes comparable from one part of the context to another. The prevailing view of humanity is that it fits a bell curve. Hence, in order to be fair, tests are standardized with this in mind. They are norm-referenced. Items that do not conform to the bell curve have to be rejected. This enhances the bias in tests because they exclude items that might recognize wider achievement, including the achievements of students who might be in a minority of the 'test' population. In this way, tests purporting to measure a wide range of achievement are actually constrained to a narrow range of measures.

For example, some maths questions actually measure children's language skills first, while some foreign language tasks presume everyday experiences that only some children have access to, such as family holidays. We take the performance on items to define the criteria. This is not criterion-referenced achievement, but test-referenced achievement dictated by the test writer's view of human ability.

There are many consequences of this approach. Perhaps most detrimental is that items or scores in a test are altered until each produces a similar profile of performance. Hence, neither teachers nor children can be seen to be achieving 'improved' levels of performance. Yet we would expect improvement to be possible if we set no limits on children and assume that as we research learning and teaching we become more effective as practitioners.

Tests allow the monitoring of standards over time

One of the problems with the current educational mood is the resolutely backward-looking approach of so many politicians and policy-makers. There really is a belief that standards used to be higher. Comparisons over time, however, are fraught with difficulties. Social conventions and linguistic usage change imperceptibly from one year to another. The test language of 1950 seems archaic in the late 1990s, and the test tasks can often read straight out of a 'Janet and John' book. There really is no conclusive evidence about any significant drop in overall standards. There is some evidence to say that the broader curriculum that emerged in primary and secondary schools in the 1960s and 1970s has had a positive impact on standards widely interpreted. Recent, as yet unpublished, work by Professor Maurice Galton and colleagues at the University of Leicester suggests that during the decade since the introduction of the National Curriculum, overall achievement may have dropped.

Tests allow us to judge how good a school is

This is, of course, the subject of intense debate. For professionals, I think that this myth has been demolished comprehensively. It still lives on, however, in many parents' minds and presents a serious challenge to those working in socially and economically challenged environments. The unfair way in which some schools are evaluated cannot just be addressed by changes in the testing regime. In fact, this prevents something of a quandary for me. I am firmly of the belief that the sort of standardized tests now in use wrongly categorize hundreds of thousands of children. For this reason, I am opposed to the sort of deterministic reliance on individual scores that has now invaded English classrooms. At the aggregated level of school scores, the margins for error undoubtedly become less. That, however, makes no allowance for the socio-economic factors that are so influential. My solution, tentatively put, if tests there must be, would be to surround individual scores with ample health warnings and to make sure that testing points should come midway, rather than at the end of each stage of schooling. Around that, other policies of community commitment and responsibility to local schools would have to be developed. Living with the fallacy that tests judge how good a school is makes the working lives of a proportion of teachers and headteachers more difficult than most of us could imagine.

Tests allow us to judge national levels of achievement against other countries

Tests can only illuminate international comparisons if you reduce the items tested to those that appear on *every* country's curriculum. In Mathematics, for example, this tends to mean that arithmetical operations predominate over problem solving or investigative assessments. Importantly, tests are age-specific. The hothouse atmosphere of a Japanese High School may display high performing 14-year-olds. But what happens to them seven years on? Students in the USA, outperformed at the earlier age, and experiencing the slower build-up and an extended education, appear to catch up over time. Age standardized tests cannot report this.

We have already discussed the problems of finding tasks that cross cultures, even within a single country. International comparisons are bedevilled with such difficulties. The wringing of hands consequent upon the publication of some international tables amounts to sheer media indulgence. Some more sophisticated research in this area has been taking place. The QUEST programme at the University of Bristol (Planel *et al.*, 1998), for example, has looked at the Mathematics and Language achievements of English and French primary children. There are differences in attainment on different items of the curriculum. English children do better at problem solving, whilst French children are more skilled in procedural skills. Overall, however, the achievement is comparable. What is interesting about the QUEST study is the way this is linked to an exploration of how the best features of the pedagogy of English and French classrooms might be brought together in looking for new approaches and methodologies.

Common tests can be applied comprehensively across the school system

State education systems, almost inevitably, develop uniform and standardized testing systems. Recent moves to measure standards and ensure accountability have reinforced the bureaucratization of teaching and learning. But as I have indicated, the simplified scores used (1–3, A–E, or 1–10) so distort the achievement being recorded as to render their accuracy for individuals highly dubious. As we move into the 21st century I anticipate a backlash. Increasingly knowledgeable parents will want to delve beneath the grades and categories we use today. They will demand systems of assessment that are more formative, providing a broader reach through a greater variety of techniques. The idea that tests can be applied comprehensively and meaningfully across the school system may in time look as dated as the recommendations of the 19th-century Clarendon Commission do today.

Tests are essential to underpin a modern education system

As currently conceived, I believe that tests represent the end of a long era: tests fitted in with the needs of the first part of the twentieth century and meeting bureaucratic needs of an emergent state education system. We are reaching saturation point. We spend more money now testing and examining children than we do on the books and materials they need to prepare for the examination. That really is scandalous! More critically, the important aim of raising levels of attainment has somehow become divorced from the question of what ends that process is serving. The rallying cry of 'Standards, standards' has substituted for a reasoned debate about which standards matter as we enter the twenty-first century. Certain 'standards', devised as benchmarks, appear to be becoming ends in themselves – proxies for collectively determined values – simply because they are easily measured. This process raises tests, which are inherently fallible, to the status of an educational touchstone. And the importance of certain symbols (GCSE A–C, National Curriculum Level 4) is inflated absurdly.

In that context, the quest for unproven standards can easily drift into an enforced standardization. Testing fallacies underpin this conservatism. But perhaps the retrenchment of the 1980s and 1990s is waning. Richard Elmore has talked about the 'noble lie' of conventional policy administration and analysis (Elmore, 1989). That is the unquestioned assumption that policy-makers control the organizational, political and technological processes that affect the implementation of any particular reform. Two decades of *dirigiste* and costly central intervention in the running of the education system has reaped scant reward.

Over the next few years, I think it inevitable that the pendulum will swing towards more school-based, localized forms of innovation and change. The other chapters in this book represent a healthy questioning of the *status quo*. Testing, like inspection, has become the main instrument of governmental control. As the new loci of power begin to emerge, so then styles and forms of testing will change. Assessment designed to help, encourage and reward, rather than testing to sort, rank and divide may gain the ascendancy.

References

Broadfoot, P (1996) The history of assessment in advanced industrial societies, Chapter 4 in *Education, Assessment and Society: A Sociological Analysis*, Open University Press, Buckingham

Bruner, J (1996) *The Culture of Education*, Harvard University Press, Cambridge, MA

Damasio, AR (1994) *Descartes' Error: Emotion, Reason and the Human Brain*, Crosset/Putnam, New York

Elmore, VR (1989) Backward mapping: implementation research and policy decisions, in B Moon *et al*, *Policies for the Curriculum*, Hodder and Stoughton, London

Gardner, H (1984) *Frames of Mind: The Theory of Multiple Intelligences*, HarperCollins, New York

Gipps, C and Murphy, P (1994) *A Fair Test? Assessment, Achievement, and Equity*, Open University Press, Buckingham

Goleman, D (1995) *Emotional Intelligence: Why It Can Matter More than IQ*, Bloomsbury, London

Maples J (1994) Leaked Tory Party election proposals by former minister John Maples, quoted in the *Financial Times*

Maples, J (1994) quoted in *The Financial Times*

Moon, B (1990) The National Curriculum: origins and context, in T Brighouse and B Moon *Managing the National Curriculum: Some Critical Perspectives*, Longmans, Harlow

Perkins, D (1995) *Outsmarting IQ: The Emerging Science of Learnable Intelligence*, Free Press, New York

Planel, C, Osborn, M, Broadfoot, P and Ward, B (1998) A comparative analysis of English and French pupils' attitudes and performance in Mathematics and Language, unpublished report available from the University of Bristol Graduate School of Education

Spens (1938) *Report of the Consultative Committee on Secondary Education With Reference To Grammar Schools & Technical High Schools,* (The Spens Report), Board of Education, London

Taunton (1868) *The Taunton Report,* Schools Enquiry Commission, London

8

Curriculum 14–19

Myth: A Levels Cannot be Radically Reformed

Ken Spours

Armstrong and Moon have criticized a reified conception of assessment in which tests have become an end rather than a means of educational progress. In this chapter, Spours shows how in the post-compulsory sector even, the qualifications available and their associated methods of assessment effectively determine syllabuses. There is thus a very direct relationship between qualifications reform and curriculum reform. The peculiarly English attachment to academic exclusivity has hampered qualification reform throughout the last 50 years. Each attempt to introduce a framework that will meet the demands of the rapidly expanding student population and the future economic needs of the country has foundered on the rock of the impervious A level. Radical reform will require sensitive staging, but a clear vision of the journey's end will also have to be articulated.

New Labour and A levels

In her letter of 3 April 1998 to Bill Stubbs, Chairman of the Qualifications and Curriculum Authority, Baroness Blackstone, Minister of State for Education, outlined New Labour's attitude to advanced level qualifications (DfEE, 1998). She restated the government's manifesto commitment to broaden A levels and upgrade vocational qualifications, underpinned by rigorous standards and Key Skills. Moreover, she saw the government building on the recommendations of Lord Dearing's *Review of Qualifications for 16–19 Year Olds* (Dearing, 1996), while taking into account the implications of changes to advanced level qualifications.

132

The letter contained a brief analysis of the current problems of advanced level study, which was described as narrow, overspecialized and inflexible. The Minister went on to observe that young people in England are taught for less time and follow a narrower programme of study than they do in most other European countries. New Labour wants to encourage more young people to follow broader programmes; for instance, studying up to five subjects and the first year and three in the second. The main instrument of this approach to broadening advanced level study will be a new 3-unit Advanced Subsidiary (AS) qualification representing 50 per cent of a full A level. However, New Labour have been at pains to convince the public that the broadening of A level programmes will not involve any compromise on A level standards. So accompanying the new AS are a series of tough curriculum measures – limits to the number of module resits, little relaxation of the maximum coursework assessment allowed and a suggestion that advanced level study, whether academic or vocational, should normally be restricted to two years.

In the letter to Bill Stubbs, the Minister was also lukewarm about reform in the future being more radical. She stated that unitization (breaking down qualifications into smaller units of attainment) may be appropriate for adults but younger learners (16–21 year olds) would have to achieve whole qualifications. Furthermore, despite widespread support for overarching certification, such as an Advanced Diploma consisting of A levels, AS levels and GNVQ qualifications expressed in responses to *Qualifying for Success* (QCA, 1998), she said that Ministers recognized that there were conceptual and practical difficulties to be resolved, and QCA should undertake more research and consultation in this area.

The Minister's response to the *Qualifying for Success* consultation constituted a much more diluted approach to A level reform than signalled by Labour's policy document *Aiming Higher* (Labour Party, 1996). Published at the same time as the Dearing Review, this had argued for the staged development of a unified and flexible qualifications system over a period of a decade. It is still possible that New Labour will keep to the spirit of *Aiming Higher*, but the time-scales now look much longer than were envisaged prior to the general election.

As far as the reforms scheduled for implementation in the Year 2000 are concerned, a great deal rests on how the new AS/GNVQ qualifications will be implemented by schools and colleges. For their part, post-16 institutions will also be keeping a close eye on whether the idea of five subjects in the first year of advanced level study will be accepted by all the universities. So there are hearts and minds to be won.

This is the core of New Labour's dilemma concerning A levels. Ministers believe the qualifications system needs reforming. They recognize that the debate amongst the education profession over the last decade has culminated in widespread support for a more flexible and unified post-14 qualifications system. However, they also believe it to be far ahead of popular opinion which, in the words of Professor Alan Smithers, 'knows where it is with A levels' (Smithers, 1998). While New Labour wants to see reform, it is not currently prepared to lead opinion. It is content, at least for the present, to be situated somewhere between those who want to push on at a faster rate to a more unified system and those who remain sceptical.

Many in the education profession are, nevertheless, asking why New Labour with a 179 parliamentary majority, appears to be 'chickening out' on A level reform.[1] The reasons for the extreme caution are not just about keeping in touch with popular opinion, crucially important though this is to New Labour. The fact is that the radical reform of A levels is not a top political priority during this Parliament – it is regarded as an area with many potential pitfalls and little immediate payback. Attention is focused instead on the more politically important areas of school standards and the New Deal to tackle unemployment for 18–24 year olds.

However, I am going to suggest that New Labour's dilemma about A levels is not simply the result of a preoccupation with remaining voter-friendly or because of its political strategy of not fighting on too many fronts at once. I will argue that their cautious attitude is also a reflection of a more fundamental issue of the historical role of A levels within the English system or what has been described as 'A level tenacity' (Tomlinson, 1997). The resilience of A levels will be explored by focusing briefly on the history of A levels and their evolving relationship to the English education and training system since their introduction in 1951.

A levels and the English system: a changing relationship

It has been difficult to have a rational debate about the strengths and weaknesses of A levels. During the late 1980s, the Conservative Government elevated A levels to represent the 'Gold Standard', thus making them into an ideological totem. The result has been that the debate about the reform of A levels in England has been far more politicized that the debates about the reform of 'Highers' in Scotland (Howieson *et al,* 1997). The political spectre of A levels would be a problem for any reforming government but it positively haunts New Labour.

I will argue that the main problem with A levels is their relationship to the education and training system or what can be called their 'system effect'. IPPR, in their document *A British Baccalaureate*, suggested that the system effects of A levels were the division between academic and vocational qualifications, curriculum narrowness and early specialization (Finegold *et al,* 1990). While this analysis is widely accepted, there is a debate about how A levels currently serve the education and training system. Tomlinson (1997), argues that the divisive triple-track system (A levels, GNVQs and NVQs) is deepening because it corresponds to what Will Hutton (1995) has described as the 40/30/30 society in which only the top 40 per cent are in secure employment. This 'correspondence' approach sees A levels continuing to function smoothly as a selector in the context of emerging new divisions between secure, insecure and marginalized workforces.

Many educational analysts take a less deterministic view and see A levels as increasingly out of step with changes which have taken place over the last 30 years both in society and in the education and training system. A levels were introduced in 1951 for the grammar schools and independent schools to prepare students for single subject honours degrees. Since then, the education and training context has changed out of recognition. These changes include rises in full-time participation[2] and the changing nature of the post-16 cohort (Gray *et al,* 1993); international comparative analysis, which shows that students in more successful systems experience broader learning programmes and achieve more highly at advanced level (Ryan, 1992; Green & Steedman, 1993); the growing focus on the demand for more applied skills (CBI, 1989; Finegold *et al,* 1990; NCE, 1993) and arguments for increasing levels of achievement, meeting national targets and promoting parity of esteem of academic and vocational qualifications (CBI, 1991; NACETT, 1994). A levels are increasingly in tension with the growing aims of the rest of the education and training system even though they are still highly regarded by university admissions tutors and employers as a screening device.

The relationship between the selection role of A levels and rising levels of participation can be better understood by the process of 'divisive expansion' or 'homogeneous differentiation' (Richardson, 1991). This describes a situation in which growing numbers of students in full-time post-16 education and training are segmented into different qualifications tracks such as A levels, GNVQs and NVQs. However, the lines of division between these tracks have being continually redrawn (Edwards, 1997). In the 1980s, the term 'tertiary tripartism' was used to describe the relationship between the academic track, the technical vocational track and the newly emerging pre-vocational track (Ranson, 1984). In the 1990s, however, and under pressure from rising participation, national targets and new qualifications such as GNVQs, A levels are being slowly drawn into a reciprocal relationship with vocational qualifications. Moreover, the close relationship between A levels and undergraduate admission is gradually weakening as more students with vocational qualifications enter university and as adult access grows. So amidst a divided and track-based qualification system, there is a constant search for mechanisms to promote system coherence and student progression. This dynamic creates further pressure for A level reform.

The other argument for the retention of A levels is support for A level-type study. It has been widely recognized that A levels play a valuable role in promoting specialist study which can be intellectually challenging, provides choice and can be motivating for some students (DES, 1988). In the next section, I will argue that in the past, A levels have kept up-to-date at syllabus level by incorporating new content and modular structures and methods of assessment. However, A levels do not in themselves constitute an advanced level curriculum. They are single subjects, there is no common core of learning, they lack applied skills and students normally only take between two and three subjects. So the strong features of A levels – in-depth study and intellectual challenge – are accompanied by features of narrowness. Over the last decade, these limitations have become more apparent as international comparisons have shown education and training systems to be more successful where qualifications offer both breadth and depth of study (Finegold *et al,* 1990; Green and Steedman, 1993; Lasonen and Young, 1998).

The resilience of A levels is due, therefore, to the inter-relationship of two features – an approach to study which is choice-based and specialized and the A level system effect which supports selection and division. Both of these features are now under pressure. A levels, have proved, nevertheless, to be an adaptable beast. Through the 1980s they went through a process of 'internal adjustment' to absorb rising levels of participation in the academic track. A levels have been continually reformed but never radically restructured. In the early 1990s, A levels began to coexist with GNVQs and became part of a national qualifications framework. Accordingly, New Labour now talks of advanced level qualifications and not just A levels. The questions are, how much further A levels can go on adapting and at the end of this process will they remain A levels in essence? How this process of change has taken place and what it means for future reform can be best analysed historically.

A levels over the last 30 years: incremental reform and failed structural change

Over the last 30 years, A levels have experienced a series of internal reforms whereas their structures have remained largely unchanged (Kerr, 1992). The internal changes include the introduction of new subjects, the development of subject cores, new forms of assessment such as assessed coursework and the growth of modular syllabuses. These reforms can be seen as a way of A levels coping with the 'expansion' of the education and training system by absorbing higher numbers of A level candidates. Furthermore, these incremental changes have helped to keep A levels in touch with wider changes in the curriculum introduced through other changes in the 14–19 curriculum such as through GCSE and TVEI. This type of reform can be regarded as a process of 'creeping modernisation' (Higham *et al.*, 1996). On the other hand, since the early 1960s, there have been repeated proposals for reforming the structure of A levels; that is, to broaden A level study. Unlike the internal and incremental reforms, the proposals for structural change have been a relative failure.

Phase 1 (1951–79): Proposals without reform

In 1951 when A levels were introduced, they were seen as a post-16 curriculum for a very small section of the cohort. By the 1960s, the growth of comprehensive schools and changing sixth forms, pressure began to mount for change. Kerr (1992) reports that in 1961 there was an *Agreement to Broaden the Curriculum (ABC)*, signed by 360 schools pledging to maintain a full range of subjects and to keep at least a third of the sixth form timetable for non-specialist work. In 1968, the *Dainton Report* (DES, 1968), which focused on the shortage of scientists, recommended the broadening of the sixth form curriculum as the best way of increasing the number of students studying science. However, Young and Leney (1997) remark that it attracted little attention. In 1966, the Schools Council recommended a combination of full and half subjects – 'Majors and Minors' – and in 1973, 'Normal (N) and Further (F) Levels'. Universities and schools reacted negatively to both proposals on the grounds that they would be an inadequate preparation for short and specialized degree courses and that broadening would dilute the standard of academic achievement.

Phase 2 (1979–91): Incremental change and failed structural proposals

During the 1980s, and in response to rising levels of participation, a series of incremental changes to A levels took place. Six types can be identified:

1. the introduction of new subjects
2. the introduction of new half subjects (the Supplementary AS level)
3. the development of modular syllabuses
4. changes to assessment approaches and the growth of coursework assessment
5. local integrative experiments linking A levels and BTEC awards, and
6. the core skills initiative of the late 1980s.

During the 1980s, certain reforms were allowed, such as more modular syllabuses and increased levels of assessed coursework, providing they did not threaten to overall A level system. The more radical structural proposals were opposed including the Higginson Report and the core skills initiative to bridge A levels and NVQs.

The Higginson Report (DES, 1988) was the most robust structural challenge to A levels since the failed broadening proposals of the 1960s and 1970s. Nevertheless, it represented both continuity with and a break from the A level tradition. Continuity could be seen in the arguments for the preservation of some element of choice and of A levels standards. However, the arguments for breadth and more subjects challenged one of the central principles of the A levels – their narrow specialization (Young and Leney, 1997). The Government's rejection of the Higginson Report reflected a growing perception amongst politicians on the Conservative Right that participation in A levels, which by now had reached about one-third of the age group, had gone far enough. Narrow specialization was associated with a view of a more elite A level cohort and therefore with the preservation of standards. The scene was set for the next phase of development.

Phase 3 (1991–96): A levels within a triple-track national qualifications framework

The 1991 White Paper *Education and Training for the 21st Century* (DES/DoE/Welsh Office, 1991), created the national qualifications framework based on different types of qualifications. The White Paper set about reforming post-16 qualifications in three ways:

1. by 'retrenching the academic track', for example, through restrictions on assessed coursework in A levels (Spours, 1993);
2. by introducing GNVQs as an alternative full-time qualification to A levels, and
3. by proposing overarching diplomas to promote parity of esteem between academic and vocational qualifications.

The White Paper aimed to preserve A levels within a triple-track qualifications system where rises in participation rates could be absorbed by the new GNVQs and not by A levels (Hodgson and Spours, 1997).

In the period following the 1991 White Paper, further changes to A levels focused on consistency across different syllabuses. There were proposals to establish new subject cores, to introduce a new code of practice for A and AS levels and to ensure modular courses matched the standard of conventional linear syllabuses (SCAA, 1994). This policy emphasis did not halt the growing popularity of modular syllabuses. Schools and colleges found that they provided shorter-term learning goals and opportunities to bank credit, which encouraged students (Higham *et al*, 1996). In terms of curriculum development however, the era of 1980s A level-style innovation came to an end. GNVQs took up the baton of innovation.

Phase 4 (1996–97): The Dearing Review of 16–19 qualifications

The development of National Targets, in particular the foundation target of 60 per cent of 21 year olds achieving Level 3 (advanced equivalent) by the Year 2000, renewed the pressure for reform (DTI, 1994 and 1995). Non-completion rates in A levels, highlighted by the Audit Commission Report *Unfinished Business* (Audit Commission/Ofsted, 1993), remained stubbornly high. Moreover, successful completion rates of GNVQs were far worse than the traditional vocational qualifications they were meant to replace (Spours, 1995). So in 1995, the Conservative government invited Sir Ron Dearing to 'consider and advise... on ways to strengthen, consolidate and improve the framework of 16–19 qualifications' (Dearing, 1996, p. 1). He was also asked whether there was scope for measures to achieve greater coherence and breadth of study without compromising standards.

Sir Ron's answer came in the form of 198 recommendations for action of which arguably the most significant was a proposal for a 'reformulated AS'. The reformulated AS, to be known as the Advanced Subsidiary, was to become deliberately horizontal. In contrast to its predecessor, it would represent achievement after one year of A level study. Its primary purpose was to encourage breadth of study but it could also be used as a means of gaining credit if a student did not want to follow a subject through the second year of an A level course. The Dearing approach to A levels, however, continued to display all the ambivalence of previous reform attempts: trying to retain the rigour of A level standards while promoting breadth and greater flexibility. The task of implementing the Dearing reforms, with their ambivalence and technical complexity, was left to a Joint SCAA/NCVQ Committee. The general election of 1997 interrupted their work and it fell to New Labour to decide what to do about Sir Ron's proposals.

Observations on the history of A level reform

A levels have been propelled through various phases of internal reform by successive rises in post-16 participation. These were occasioned first by an initial expansion of comprehensive school sixth forms in the 1960s and early 1970s, and then by a more concerted rise in full-time participation in the 1980s. Throughout this period, proposed reforms to the structure of A levels were resisted by the universities and schools and then, more politically, by the Conservative government in the late 1980s and early 1990s. The more far-reaching internal reforms of the last decade – diverse assessment, modularity and local integrative experiments – began to test the boundaries of A levels. The 1991 White Paper attempted to halt these developments and to use broad vocational qualifications as the means of expanding participation.

Several observations can be drawn from this historical analysis.

- Policy has tended to be reactive to changes in the participation context which has allowed A levels to changed slowly. However, during the late 1980s, the pace of change quickened which began to threaten the position of A levels within the education and training system.

- The Thatcher administration reacted politically and ideologically to the changing context by 'politicizing' the issue of A level standards. This has made the A level debate in England more difficult to discuss in a rational and educational way.

- The adaptability of A levels has come from their incremental internal changes but the basic pattern of study – two or three A levels – remains largely unchanged.

- The attempt to preserve A levels by including them within a national qualifications framework may be creating the conditions of the eventual dissolution of A levels by developing the notion of 'advanced level qualifications'.

- Over the last decade, reform proposals such as the vertical AS, the introduction of GNVQs and recent proposals for a 'horizontal' AS, can be seen as 'demand-led'; that is, their development was premised on student choice.

The key issue in late 1997 was whether New Labour would build on the Dearing proposals in such a way that would radically reform A levels.

Appraising New Labour's approach: muted pragmatism or phased reform?

The fifth phase of A level reform came with the *Qualifying for Success* consultation about the reform of advanced level qualifications in late 1997 (DfEE, 1997). In early 1998, QCA offered its advice to Ministers and, following this, New Labour announced its reforms, which would take effect from the Year 2000 (DfEE, 1998). The main proposals for advanced level were the introduction of the following:

- a three unit 'Subsidiary AS' which will be at full A level standard and will count as 50 per cent of an A level
- three and six unit GNVQs to parallel the structure of A/AS levels
- a common grading system for A/AS levels and Advanced GNVQs
- a Key Skills qualification at advanced level focusing on communications, numeracy and IT
- a marginal relaxation of the maximum amount of assessed coursework in A levels from 20/25 per cent to 30 per cent in most cases, and
- some changes to modular syllabuses including accreditation of individual modules and the introduction of synoptic assessment.

The proposals can be seen as a threefold approach to broadening advanced level programmes. Students will be encouraged to study five subjects in the first year of sixth form and they will have more opportunities to combine vocational and academic qualifications. At the same time, students will be encouraged to take the new Key Skills qualification. However, the delivery of broader advanced level programmes will be firmly in the hands of schools and colleges. They will not be required to offer five subjects at Year 12. Moreover, they will only be encouraged to offer the new Key Skills qualification – through the funding mechanism, the attachment of UCAS 'points' for access to higher education and the likely judgments of the Ofsted and FEFC inspectors.

It is difficult to tell, at this point, whether New Labour's proposals will work effectively. Schools and colleges will need funding incentives to time-table broader programmes. The preferred approach of five subjects in the first year and three in the second will mean a four A level workload for more students. This will require more teaching contact time, particularly in FE where in recent years it has fallen sharply because of the effects of the FEFC funding mechanism (Spours and Lucas, 1996). The reception given by end-users such as higher education establishments will also be crucially important. Nevertheless, the new AS looks potentially flexible but at the same time of credible standard. As such, it has a chance of being given a good reception.

However, there is a downside to New Labour's policy – a tough stance on A level standards and reliance on a demand-led approach. Proposals that limit modular resits, increase the amount of external assessment overall in advanced level programmes[3] and limit the duration of advanced level study to two years, will make the advanced level standard less accessible to some students. These restrictions are an attempt to make modular qualifications adopt the same rules as linear A level syllabuses. Unaltered, these measures could also hold back any improvement in successful completion rates.[4] New Labour appears to be sacrificing greater access to advanced level study to maintaining public perception of the A level standard.

Like the Higginson proposals of a decade earlier, New Labour's approach to A level reform is both a continuation and a break with the past. The Conservatives became ideologically obsessed by A levels as the 'Gold Standard' and equated this with narrow specialization. New Labour is very concerned to maintain the advanced level standard but seeks to broaden advanced level study. New Labour does not particularly like A levels but it is very wary about their reform because they are deeply rooted in the popular psyche. That is why the government has decided to put the consumer in the driving seat. It sees A level reform, promoted through student choice as a long-haul approach and one in which public understanding of the system will slowly catch up with the ideas of the reformers.

If successful, New Labour's approach to broadening advanced level study will represent an advance greater than that of the Higginson proposals. However, a mixed and voluntaristic strategy based on introducing the new, while retaining the old, is risky. Moreover, we will only know if it has worked when the pattern of institutional provision and student choices have become established, by which time we could be confronted with a policy failure. We could face a situation, which is all too familiar, where government policy is being propelled by reactions to past policy weaknesses.

A phased and planned approach to radical change

New Labour's reform package could, with widespread professional support, become the first stage in a much more radical plan for post-16 change (NAHT, 1995; AfC *et al,* 1994; Richardson *et al,* 1995). Such a flexibility/unification strategy could consist of the phased introduction of three radical measures yet to be considered by New Labour:

1. The modularization/unitization of both the academic and vocational curriculum which can create a basis for credit accumulation.
2. The introduction of overarching certification (OAC) which eventually could replace both A levels and broad vocational qualifications, and could encompass both school-based and work-based learning.
3. The introduction of a curriculum and qualifications system starting at 14 rather than 16 that promotes achievement and progression through a variety of levels, additional to the three we have at present.

Together, these could provide the framework for both breadth and depth of study combined with a more flexible and accessible structure. The cumulative effect of these more radical strategies would place England on a path of convergence with the Scottish system which, in 1999, will implement *Higher Still* (Scottish Office, 1994) – a single modular framework covering both academic and vocational courses.

Creating the conditions for the successful reform of advanced level qualifications

Even if New Labour can be persuaded to relinquish a pragmatic demand-led approach in favour of the phased and planned more radical approach it recommended in *Aiming Higher*, success will depend on the right kind of context being created. I refer briefly to three important contextual factors.

1. *A policy process with vision*: First, it is important to have a well-managed and phased approach to reform where students, parents, teachers, end-users and policy-makers know where they are heading and how they can prepare for change. This is not what we have at the moment. New Labour is moving carefully, but there is little sense of vision or of ultimate destination.

2. *Funding reform:* A broader and more flexible curriculum will require more teachers, and they will have more contact time. New Labour has pointed to the fact that advanced level students in Continental systems typically enjoy about 25 per cent more taught time (Labour Party, 1996; DfEE, 1998). Moreover, many students there take a third year to achieve the advanced level standard. More support and extended study result in over 60 per cent of young people achieving Level 3 equivalent – a figure that is still rising. This compares with about 45 per cent in England (Spours, 1995). Reaching these levels of achievement will not be possible without more funding and it being better targeted.

3. *Recognition by end-users*: The third contextual factor concerns the role of the labour market and HE end-users. If more young people are to undertake and successfully complete broader advanced level qualifications, in both schools, colleges and the workplace, then they have to be encouraged to do so by both universities and employers. Universities will be more inclined to support the broader approach to advanced level study if success is the result of harder work, and not just less specialized study. Employers in the work-based route should become involved in encouraging high levels of qualification. For example, they should insist that modern apprentices complete their studies and they should not employ young people still at school or college for such long hours in casual or part-time employment. Government can show it is determined

to see the proposals contained in *Qualifying for Success* succeed. It should make clear that it expects the reformed qualifications to be accepted as a means of entry to higher education and to be recognized in the labour market.

Conclusion

Once more, A levels are at a watershed. Through incremental reform they have evolved over 40 years but without significant structural change. Hence the perception that A levels cannot be radically reformed. Very cautiously, New Labour is taking A levels into new territory, in the guise of smaller advanced level qualifications. But its voluntaristic and demand-led approach, while promising more evolutionary change, could still fail to produce the structural broadening of student programmes which have eluded previous reform attempts.

New Labour must realize this danger now. It is not sufficient to wait for signs of policy failure three or four years hence. The answer is a phased approach to a unified diploma at 18+ which integrates the strengths of A level specialist learning with greater breadth and flexibility of study. The QCA can use the remit offered to it by government to develop a robust model of overarching certification and unitization by the Year 2002. This would allow the first wave of reforms, due to be implemented in the Year 2000, to be reinforced by more radical measures once New Labour has completed its first term of office.

If we do not take this more radical but phased path of change, we risk becoming more out of step with the rest of the world. Our isolation will become starker as both Scotland and Wales take advantage of political devolution to move towards more flexible and unified post-compulsory qualifications systems. In doing so, our most immediate neighbours will expose the myth that you cannot reform advanced level qualifications radically.

Notes

1. The reaction of the education professional associations to New Labour's position on A level reform has been quite hostile. The NAHT has accused the government of 'chickening out' from requiring breadth of advanced level study (*Times Educational Supplement*, 10 April 1998), and the Joint Association Curriculum Group (JACG) has

complained that its proposals will be impossible to timetable (*TES*, 17 April 1998)

2. Participation in A levels has risen from 37,000 candidates in 1951 to 400,000 candidates in the mid-1990s, and from about 3 per cent to 35 per cent of the 16-year-old cohort.

3. The assertion that the QfS proposals constitute an overall increase of external assessment in advanced level programmes is supported by the combined effect of a marginal increase in internal assessment in A levels and a large increase in external assessment in GNVQs.

4. The number of students successfully completing full awards of Advanced GNVQs after only two years of study remains low at about 50 per cent. GNVQ successful completion rates for the full award rise significantly when students are allowed an extra year to complete their assessments.

References

AfC *et al* (1994) *Post-Compulsory Education and Training, A Joint Statement by the Association for Colleges, The Girls' School Association, The Head Masters' Conference, The Secondary Heads' Association, The Sixth Form Colleges' Association and The Society of Headmasters and Headmistresses in Independent Schools*, AfC, London

Audit Commission/Ofsted (1993) *Unfinished Business*, HMSO, London

CBI (1989) *Towards a Skills Revolution: Report of the CBI's Vocational Education and Training Task Force*, CBI, London

CBI (1991) *World Class Targets,* CBI, London

Dearing, R (1996) *Review of Qualifications 16–19 Year Olds*, Schools Curriculum and Assessment Authority, London

DES (1968) *The Dainton Report*, HMSO, London

DES (1988) *Advancing A Levels*, (The Higginson Report), HMSO, London

DES/DoE/Welsh Office (1991) *Education and Training for the 21st Century,* HMSO, London

DfEE (1997) *Qualifying for Success,* Department for Education & Employment White Paper, DfEE, London

DfEE (1998) *Qualifying for Success: The Response to the Qualifications and Curriculum Authority's Advice*, DfEE, London

DTI (1994) *Competitiveness: Helping Business to Win,* Cmnd. 2563, HMSO, London

DTI (1995) *Competitiveness: Forging Ahead,* Cmnd. 2867, HMSO, London

Edwards, T (1997) Foreword, in S Tomlinson. (ed.) *Education 14–19: Critical Perspectives,* Athlone Press, London

Finegold, D, Keep, E, Miliband, D, Raffe, D, Spours, K and Young, M (1990) *A British Baccalaureate: Overcoming divisions between education and training*, Institute for Public Policy Research, London

Gray, J, Jesson, D and Tranmer, M (1993) *Boosting Post 16 Participation in Full-Time Education: A Study of Some Key Factors England and Wales,* Youth Cohort Study No 20, Employment Department, Sheffield

Green, A and Steedman, H (1993) *Education Provision, Education Attainment and the Needs of Industry: A Review of the Research for Germany, France, Japan, the USA and Britain,* National Institute of Economic and Social Research Report No 5, NIESR, London

Higham, J, Sharp, P and Yeomans, D (1996) *The Emerging 16-19 Curriculum: Policy and Provision,* David Fulton, London

Hodgson, A and Spours, K (1997) From the 1991 White Paper to the Dearing Report: a conceptual and historical framework for the 1990s, in A Hodgson and K Spours (eds) *Dearing and Beyond: 14-19 Qualifications, Frameworks and Systems,* Kogan Page, London

Howieson, C, Raffe, D, Spours, K and Young, M (1997) Unifying academic and vocational learning: the state of the debate in England and Scotland, *Journal of Education and Work,* **10**, 1, pp. 5–35

Hutton, W (1995) *The State We're In,* Vintage, London

Kerr, D (1992) The academic curriculum – reform resisted, in T Whiteside, A Sutton and T Everton (eds), *16-19: Changes in Education and Training,* David Fulton, London

Labour Party (1996) *Aiming Higher: Labour's Plans for Reform of the 14-19 Curriculum,* Labour Party, London

Lasonen, J and Young, M (1998) *Strategies for Achieving Parity of Esteem in European Upper Secondary Education,* Institute for Educational Research, University of Jyvaskyla, Finland

NACETT (1994) *Report on Progress,* National Advisory Council on Education and Training Targets, NACETT, London

NAHT (1995) *Proposals on 14-19 Education, National Association of Head Teachers,* NAHT, Haywards Heath

NCE (1993) *Learning to Succeed: A Radical Look at Education Today and a Strategy for the Future,* Report of the Paul Hamlyn Foundation's National Commission on Education, Heinemann, London

QCA (1998) *Summary of responses to 'Qualifying for Success',* Report of the Qualifications and Curriculum Authority, QCA, London

Ranson, S (1984) Towards a tertiary tripartism: new codes of social control and the 17+, in P Broadfoot (ed.) *Selection, Certification and Control: Social Issues in Educational Assessment,* Falmer, Brighton

Richardson, W (1991) *Education and Training Post-16: Options for Reform and the Public Policy Process in England and Wales,* VET Forum Report No 1, Centre for Education and Industry, University of Warwick

Richardson, W, Spours, K, Woolhouse, J and Young, M (1995) *Learning for the Future: Interim Report,* Institute of Education and University of Warwick

Ryan, P (1992) (ed.) *International Comparisons of Vocational Education and Training for Intermediate Skills,* Falmer, London

SCAA (1994) *Post-16 Briefing Note,* Schools Curriculum Authority, Edition 2.2, 24.9.94, SCAA, London

Scottish Office Education Department (1994) *Higher Still: Opportunity for All,* HMSO, London

Smithers, A (1998) View from here, *The Independent,* 9 April 1998

Spours, K (1993) The reform of qualifications within a divided system, in W Richardson, J Woolhouse and D Finegold (eds), *The Reform of Post 16 Education and Training in England and Wales,* Longman, Harlow

Spours, K (1995) *Post-Compulsory Education and Training: Statistical Trends,* Learning for the Future Working Paper No. 7, Post 16 Education Centre, Institute of Education, University of London

Spours, K and Lucas, N (1996) *The Formation of a National Sector of Incorporated Colleges: Beyond the FEFC Model,* Post 16 Education Centre Working Paper No 19, Institute of Education, University of London

Tomlinson, S (1997) 14-19 education: divided and divisive, in S Tomlinson (ed.) *Education 14-19: Critical Perspectives*, Athlone, London

Young, M and Leney, T (1997) From A levels to an advanced level curriculum of the future, in A Hodgson and K Spours (eds), *Dearing and Beyond: 14-19 Qualifications, Frameworks and Systems,* Kogan Page, London

PART V
School and Community

9

Home and School

*Myth: A Home–School Curriculum is Incompatible
with a National Curriculum*

Tim Brighouse

Noting that children spend 85 per cent of their waking hours outside school, in
the home and the community, Brighouse laments the narrowness of the
National Curriculum. To maximize learning, the school should add its own
curriculum and a third, home-and-community curriculum, he argues. Examples of the activities that might be included exist already, and could be combined to make an entitlement for all, with citizenship at its core. He outlines
the respective parts that the local education authority and the school could
play in such a democratic entitlement.

'Education never did me any good. Just keep your nose clean for the next nine
months. I have had a word at the works and there is a job for you when you
leave school.'

'School? A waste of time. Look what it did for your dad and me. We are both
out of work. You had better learn to 'do the double' like us.'

'What more can you expect from kids with a background like this?'

'The families of the children in this class are from Mirpur so they have no language.'

'Our sort of children do not go on to higher education.'

We can catch the divide and incompatibility between the home and the
school in conversations, and in the words of parents and teachers. So too
with our habits: historically, it has been convenient to assume that school is

the only place where education happens. The richest in society seemed to act in that belief by sending their children away to privileged residential schools, while earlier employing governesses to educate their offspring. The very rich still do. Meanwhile, within the state sector, 'care' – a matter for the family and Social Services – was counterpoised with 'education'. So, right at the beginning of life, the poorest were encouraged to see 'day nurseries' as care institutions to park their children and 'nursery schools and classes' where education took place.

Perhaps it is the way we define the curriculum in terms of *subjects*. We have always done so, and more especially since 1988 when the Education Act gave subjects even greater credence as the correct framework for seeing the curriculum. So national and school curricula have been formulated with increasing precision and have been detailed predominantly by reference to subjects, few of which relate to the mapping of the rest of a child's or any adult's life. For example, outside a school who would say 'I have just been to French, now I am going to German', or confess that what they have got next is 'Double Science'?

At one time, of course, it was fair to make such assumptions. Knowledge, even in my childhood, was sufficiently limited that CP Snow could describe those people who mastered and straddled the Sciences and the Arts so impressively as 'Two Cultures' Renaissance people. They appeared on programmes such as *The Brains Trust* to impress us all with their polymath propensities. As the architect of the revised code and a handmaiden of the 1870 Education Act, Robert Lowe was instrumental in creating the first national curriculum. He once confessed that 'the education of the lower classes should be only sufficient to give them that sense of awe for higher education as the leaders of the nation demand'. *The Brains Trust* did that all right.

But that world of deference has changed. My own mother was part of a generation where one half of 1 per cent enjoyed higher education. Of my generation, 3 per cent enjoyed that opportunity. Having risen to 12 per cent by the time my eldest son attended university in 1981, the figure has now reached 30 per cent. Over the same period, the proportion of all permanent paid jobs available for unskilled and semi-skilled work has dropped from 98 per cent of the total workforce to just over 15 per cent. Small wonder that we have seen all modern developed societies emphasize the overwhelming importance of education as an opportunity that all, not a few, should grasp for success.

More surprising, however, is how we have reacted in terms of our conservative attitudes to school while acknowledging that change. For while there has been such an explosion of knowledge that the subject map of higher education has had to be totally redrawn, the national school curriculum of 1988 was framed in terms of the very same subjects (Technology apart) that described the 1903 grammar school curriculum, which was itself drawn from the model of higher education of the time. This fatal design flaw is especially surprising when one reflects that HMIs' publications during the fifteen years before 1988 had been getting away from such an inadequate curriculum map and had explored different ways of describing it. Moreover, we have continued, even in the face of this major explosion of knowledge and ambition, to invest all the education of a child's upbringing on the school alone. The copious 1988 legislation, for example, makes no mention of the parents' complementary educational role as opposed to their role in governance and as consumers. Scarcely a month goes by without some reference to the role of schools as the press metaphorically wring their hands about some current national, moral or performance crisis. So whether it is cricket, drugs, athletics, crime or economic well-being, some reference to the school as part of the solution always crops up. It is as though school and home are not complementary – two distinct and independent worlds.

We could look at things differently. We could consider the curriculum not as a list of discrete subjects, but as that set of experiences through which an individual acquires and understands information, concepts and other knowledge, develops and practises skills, encounters ideas and adopts values.

What is the implication of looking at the curriculum in this way? First, it is clear that children spend *all* their waking life in activity that is part of such a curriculum. As it happens, the proportion of a child's waking life spent in lessons in school between birth and age 16 is roughly 15 per cent of the whole. The balance of 85 per cent is spent in the home and community.

If we want to make the most of the 100 per cent, we would be wise to consider how the national and school curriculum fits with the home and community curriculum. Clearly, the classroom 15 per cent is focused time: collectively, society provides modest sums of money for experts whom we call teachers and support staff, to work together for 38 weeks of the year for six hours a day, Monday to Friday. They attempt, as the Victorian Headteacher of Uppingham put it, to 'unlock the minds and open the shut chambers of the heart' of the youngsters whom we entrust to them. In an attempt to help the individual pupil learner make the most sense of that curriculum, however, the successful teacher is forever probing into the home and community curriculum. They do this in childhood by many means: they receive gifts at the beginning of the school day during the growing child's infancy and childhood and they enthuse with interesting questions as the child talks of home and community experiences. They garland their explanations to pupils with chance arrows of fortune towards pupils' everyday experiences whether in terms of popular songs, sports, 'soaps' or other vernacular culture to hook the interesting connection that will help the learner's motivation or understanding. In a multi-lingual context for example, as part of her learning plan for the year, the teacher decides to extend their vocabulary of the various first languages of her pupils, to surprise and delight them by her very knowledge. I witnessed this in one of Birmingham's schools as excited children attempted to help the developing Urdu inflection of one of our star teachers who was extending her multi-lingual skills. She knew that in doing so, she was increasing the receptiveness of her own pupils' learning in the process.

The successful school goes much further though. Just as pupils suspend disbelief through their unique trusting relationship with the teacher, in order that he or she can acquire a skill or understanding hitherto beyond reach, so the wider local community knows when its school is going beyond what it strictly has to do. Local conversations illustrate local communities' approval and ambition. 'It is all right at such an such a school' they say to each other, 'they are always doing things for the kids'. 'Doing things for the kids' is shorthand for what many successful schools would recognize as a coherent set of interventions that when taken together add up to their contribution to the home and community curriculum. In short, they go beyond the timetabled 15 per cent the pupils spend awake and in lessons and invade the 85 per cent, which strictly speaking they do not need to occupy. Let us illustrate some of these interventions.

Homework

The regular setting and marking of relevant extension and reinforcement tasks of appropiate length. Clearly, this will vary with the age of the child and the stage of learning, ranging from home/school reading pacts in infancy for example, to the completion of GCSE coursework in Years 10 and 11. Communities judge schools by the consistency of their homework practice – for example, whether they sustain it throughout the year rather than simply part of it. So the leadership of the school, whether as a whole or departmentally, reinforces homework consciousness by showing interest in it, even having prizes for it at Awards Evenings.

Responsibility points are used for the staff who lead on homework. They know that by Key Stages 3 and 4, school-influenced homework can add between a quarter and a third to lesson time when account is taken of 'holiday tasks' too. In Key Stages 1 and 2 there is greater potential for using homework more overtly to promote the 'joint educator' role which is so necessary if the parent is to be 'good enough'. The most advanced example of this I have seen comes from the Greenwood School in Nottingham, with its graduated tasks for four days a week throughout Key Stage 2. Most of the tasks involve parent and child in necessarily joint activities.

Extra-curricular clubs and societies

The expectation is that committed members of staff – teachers and support staff alike – contribute in some way to extension, supplementary and enriching activities outside the formal school timetable. It is part of their professionalism. So 'chess clubs', 'dance and drama', 'debating', 'computers' vie with each other on a menu that in a well-run school owes less to serendipity and more to a coherent recruitment and development policy for staff and pupils alike. Learning is not restricted to lessons.

Residentials

A residential experience during their primary and secondary education should be part of what the school offers automatically to each and every child, not just ski-trips for the wealthy few. So the school monitors that each child has a week's residential in each of Key Stages 2, 3 and 4, for the experience of 'under canvass', 'environmental' and 'outdoor' challenges.

Homework clubs

Secondary schools frequently offer an 'out of school day' facility for children to find a place to do their homework where support and reference materials and resources are readily available in a quiet and purposeful atmosphere. To its great credit of course, the Prince's Trust has supported the creation and the rapid expansion of such 'study support centres' – an initiative now consolidated by the government's decision to earmark Lottery money to the same purpose. In a school I visited recently, Saturdays were available for Key Stage 3 pupils, while Monday to Thursday was for Key Stage 4.

School performances and sporting activities

Schools are places where there are opportunities within the sports and arts for youngsters to find their talent and give expression to it. School concerts, plays, musicals and sports teams flourish in the evenings and at weekends, often by deliberate linkages to local amateur adult clubs who see the links as lifeblood for their future health.

Holiday learning

Successful schools find ways to minimize the 'learning loss' so often incurred during long, and sometimes short, holidays from school. So Easter revision courses or summer holiday tasks set by teachers who are to take the children from September are features of some schools' activities.

For schools to take stock of the whole of these activities, they need to set them out as part of their vision, which necessarily needs to be shared with their partners in education – the parents or carers. Many schools do this through a home/school compact or understanding that sets out each side's responsibilities rather than through the school prospectus whose marketing/consumer slant may inhibit the full appreciation of the parental education partnership.

A small example of practice glimpsed in one primary school recently illustrates the point. The Head saw that parental consultations about pupil progress suffered from being scheduled in the middle of the school year. By then, so much of the time had already passed in which the partners – parent and teacher – could join in a concerted effort to improve the child's learning. Instead, the school now starts the year with a discussion involving parent and teacher, and if necessary the previous year's teacher. Their review takes in the results of the pupils' summer holiday learning assignments, targets for learning experiences and outcomes for the forthcoming year, the home learning and experiences expected, for example spelling games, numeracy treasure hunts, family environmental projects, extended reading and video criticisms. It concludes with a clear exposition of what will happen in school, including a review of the extra-curricular activities and some anticipated pupil gains in skills and understandings. At this school, the process results in what is, in effect, a written individual learning plan for the year. The school in question was doing this from Year 3 onwards and was planning to involve the pupils in the review in Years 5 and 6. As a result, the subsequent mid-year parental consultation took place in a more focused light. There is sharply focused debate of the contribution of each – pupil, teacher and parent – to the progress made. I know of no school, however, that has conducted this process for a sufficient length of time to be certain of its outcome in terms of measurable gains whether in attendance, academic attainment or behaviour. It is hard to believe, however, that the outcome of it all will be anything but positive.

It is an example drawn from primary school practice of course, but it is easy to see that secondary schools can do something similar. At the secondary level though, if the partnership is to make best use of the home and community curriculum as well as the school and national one, it will require continuity of tutorial responsibility from year to year, as well as a systematic intention by faculties to take measures of individuals' progress forward from year to year.

In this respect, it may be sensible for schools to focus on progress up to Key Stage 3 results as well as Key Stage 4 GCSE outcomes, at least in the core subjects. If this were done from the moment of pupil entry, it might be possible to catch the sense of accelerated progress from the end of childhood at Key Stage 2 through adolescence in Key Stages 3 and 4 to GCSEs. After all, since some individuals turn a modest Level 3 at KS 2 into a Level 5 at KS 3 and then a Grade C at GCSE, such progress must surely be tantalizingly within the grasp of 80 per cent of pupils. At the very least, such close tracking would minimise the likelihood of a pupil's progress stalling suddenly.

So far I have shown how schools can extend the 15 per cent of waking time that is spent in lessons perhaps to 25 per cent, by including a wide range of extra-curricular activities in their offer and their practice. In doing so, they set out their stall in such a way that is appealing to most parents. Ironically of course, participation in clubs, societies and homework correlates strongly with social and economic advantage. In short, the discerning and articulate parent is only too willing to encourage the school to be more ambitious about its task. Indeed, in the great public schools, Eton and Harrow, for example, the notion of 15 per cent is misplaced for the residential school assumes responsibility for as much as 65 per cent of the child's waking time, at least during the impressionable adolescent years. In these schools, the home and community curriculum experiences of the youngster are quite different and restricted. Not for them a holiday spent knocking round with mates in familiar local surroundings, for their mates come from the four corners of the United Kingdom and beyond.

Nevertheless, 95 per cent of our youngsters are at day boarding schools. Of that 95 per cent, two-thirds are educated in challenging urban environments. There, the home and community curriculum is both important and potentially more hazardous than that enjoyed by the better off and those living in more stable neighbourhoods.

I want to advance the argument that it is here in the urban landscape that somebody else should take a strategic view of the home and community curriculum for children between birth and the age of 16. Preferably, this should be the local education authority as the democratically accountable body. Schools in such settings need encouragement and extra resources to take on the range of extra-curricular activities outlined earlier in this paper. The resource is necessary because their teachers have to expend far more energy, enthusiasm, skill, drive and commitment than their colleagues in more affluent surroundings do to achieve the same results. Extra resources are essential.

Nor is it a commentary on the generosity of teachers to argue that what might be done voluntarily in more salubrious surroundings needs extra money here. Moreover, in such surroundings they need encouragement to acknowledge those points in the community pulling in roughly the same direction. I shall refer here to one example to make the point. In Birmingham there are over 200 supplementary schools providing extra tuition. In some, this covers the basics of the English language or Maths. Others teach religion or cultural studies relating to the family's community of origin, or the language of the home. Between age 7 and 12, many youngsters can spend about half as much time again in supplementary schools as they do in the mainstream itself. Yet shamefully, as the city's education officer, I have not yet made arrangements enabling mainstream schools to acknowledge the achievements of pupils made in supplementary schools. I need to repair that omission, urgently.

In heavily urban areas therefore there needs to be a view of how and when to intervene beyond the extra the individual school may do in what is the home and community curriculum. Clearly it is possible, for example, by play or learning schemes during the holidays and in after-school care clubs, to take both a complementary and a supplementary view of what goes on, rather than a disjointed one. However, very few local authorities plan either their holiday play schemes or their provision of after-school care in order to fit in either 'catch up' or 'enrichment' activities for what goes on in schools.

Given that such a strategy is desirable, how might a local education authority look at it? They would need to start by examining the home and community curriculum with more precision. For example, for the first three years in life, except for the working family, the home and community curriculum is exclusively in the hands of one or other parent. In contrast, from 3 onwards it is likely that nursery schools or classes and then the primary school offers a substantial curriculum until the age of 11, the usual age of secondary transfer. Even so, the time spent in lessons in primaries is less than it will be in the secondary years, and the tradition of the school extending its curriculum is less strong. Moreover, from birth to 3 the home and community curriculum is 100 per cent of the time. There is therefore a case for a first-time parenting service with a focus on birth to 3. This would involve the practice nurse, the health visitor, child minder and pre-school workers.

What might that look like? A school in Walsall, for example, takes the trouble to give a congratulatory card, via the health visitor, to the mother at birth. It follows this up with books and tapes at nine months and access to a toy and pre-school learning library in staged steps leading to school. In Birmingham, the health clinics become centres of children's book collections provided by the libraries. The health visitor delivers the first infant book and membership of a library and of the centre for the child as well as entitlement to the parent for the use of swimming pools and other museums and recreational facilities. In Manchester, the WILSTAAR project provides an enormous bonus between nine and eighteen months for babies who appear to be experiencing undue difficulty with language development receptively, expressively or behaviourally.

The period from birth to 3 is where the education battle is won or lost. As well as education, the agencies involved in the home and community curriculum for that age group include health, housing, leisure, community and social services, benefits advice. GP commissioning groups hold out the tantalizing prospect at last of enlisting the public service commitment of doctors collectively as opposed to individually.

Awesomely, what these developments illustrate is the complicating factor of trying to make sense of inter-disciplinary and multi-agency work. To meet this challenge in Birmingham, we are creating an over-arching strategy framework – the family support team – to sustain the difficult task of maintaining such working practices.

In later childhood, a different encouragement is appropriate from the LEA for the home and community curriculum. Children at that stage are inveterate collectors, as well as insatiable tasters of new experiences. The Children's University within Birmingham is a loose association of schools, their teachers and other adult educators. They design modules of four, five and six sessions which can be taken by the 7 to 11 year-olds either at weekends or in holiday periods. Within the design of the modules and programmes, differentiation to suit different levels of interest and competence ensures that there is progression for those wishing to take studies further. The whole community celebrates successful participants in the programme at a graduation ceremony in the city hall. Over three years, 10,000 children have taken part.

The University of the First Age is a different model targeting early adolescence. It aims to combat the disaffection and lack of motivation that seems to emerge in the first years of secondary education, between Years 7 and 9. The UFA has two features so far. There are interest-led intensive summer schools committed to multi-sensory and accelerated learning. They model themselves on learning and teaching based on Howard Gardner's theories of multiple intelligence (Gardner, 1984). The second feature, funded by the Paul Hamlyn Foundation, enables UFA school-based fellows – teachers – to work on the implications of such an approach for existing school practice. UFA is also trialling tutorials by e-mail and distance learning. It will begin to breathe reality into the national grid for learning in the City as we seek to build the infrastructure. It has also been the vehicle for the City's literacy summer schools, backed by the multi-million pound 'core skills' programme, which is being funded through Single Regeneration Budget (SRB) for seven years. The whole is co-ordinated in partnership with the Training Enterprise Council (TEC) to provide a skeleton lifelong learning network.

The source of the idea for the current Education Action Zones is the same as that which stimulated education priority areas (EPA) a generation ago. It is a realization that in some areas of great challenge the tide of despair runs so strong and so deep that however good school becomes, something more is necessary. As Ofsted said, 'schools in such areas have insufficient resources within themselves to achieve and sustain consistent improvement' (Ofsted, 1993).

What must be different this time round is the realization that merely to tackle education issues, even within a complementary national/school/ home/community curriculum, is insufficient. What is needed is a co-ordinated set of social and economic programmes with education at the heart of the action, to change the local climate and local habits. So joined-up thinking is needed to give a school improvement package the chance to work. By school improvement I mean adopting programmes of proven interventions which improve results in the schools, but incorporate ingredients and practices which affect their learning outside school. For example, housing refurbishment schemes can have built-in lifelong learning training facilities and a family team of existing staff embracing inter-disciplinary working, and can come equipped with a 'foyer' – a first-time parenting service linked to a healthy living centre in the GP clinic – and a local forum with real influence over the way some local money is spent.

There are two further challenges to be examined – first, the position of teachers as a profession, and second, the need for an over-arching set of curriculum experiences unifying school, home and community.

As we have seen, the school used to be an island: it was insulated from real life in the view of other adults whose children were entrusted to the skill of teachers who were in turn respected and sometimes feared. *Dominie* is how the Scots describe the teachers. It should not be forgotten that Scotland also had the tawse. It suited both sides to see it that way. Apart from using the tawse, the *dominie* was a feared and respected gate-keeper to knowledge, and through that, to power and privilege. He or she operated in a world that limited access to the fruits of success: pre-ordained percentages found entry into higher education only if sifted first through pre-selection at 11+. That world has gone and will not return. Collectively, the teaching profession has been defensive about this change regarding the passing of the age of deference which may, as we have seen, been one of rather more fear than respect. After all, among the majority that was failed, whose memories were of 'respect' rather than 'fear'?

Now is the time to reduce, not to expand the number of teachers. Every teacher deserves not one or two, but three support staff. These para-professionals would be drawn from the local community and trained rigorously to act as support or assistant educators. They would posses many of the qualities, skills and characteristics of teachers, but they would not be the active researcher and skilled questioner, the curriculum designer and orchestrator of all learning experiences, which the good teacher always is. Teachers would remain the leaders of debate and direction, but the support educators might well be the people whom an individual child sees as special, and in whom the individual child trusts as a valued 'learning guide'. They would also provide examples of learning and they would lead learning activities under the direction of a teacher. As 'learning guides' they would know the children well, live locally and provide continuity. There would be one of these 'learning guides' or 'support assistant teachers' to every 15 pupils. Thus, in a school of 575 secondary pupils there would be 35 or so, as well as the current number of technicians, librarians and other support staff of course. They would be on contracts of 44 weeks of the year, as would the teachers, who would be fewer in number, with a ratio of 1 to 40 pupils. Teachers would be very highly paid and highly qualified. They would orchestrate and organize extensive use of video link teaching and would deploy the latest technology. They would have regular opportunities for updating, and sabbatical entitlement.

Finally, there is the issue of what the curriculum should include, whether national, at school level, or in the home and community. Earlier, I argued that it should not be designed by way of subjects, but by knowledge, skill, understanding of concepts, values and attitudes. But whatever the definition, there will be great argument about what should be in it.

I confess that I have never been one who gets excited by the fruitless and tiresome debates about which information or concepts should be prescribed. There are so many, only an arbitrarily small fraction of them can be chosen. It certainly makes the older generation comfortable to specify some warm and familiar cultural knowledge that they want the next generation to learn. There is a warm sense of continuity in such prescription. Given so much change, it seems sensible. However, we just try to squeeze more and more quarts into the same pint pot.

Nevertheless, certain skills and competencies are necessary in any youngster. And while Maths, English and Science represent competencies any parent can help develop, there comes a time when we parents can no longer travel the same journey as our children, particularly in Maths and Science. It goes 'beyond our ken'. There is, however, one aspect of curriculum where a parent can trade ideas on equal terms: it is the question of developing 'attitude' and 'values'. As we have noted, it is that part of the curriculum where the subject imperialists suddenly become shy.

There is now much talk of 'citizenship' being taught in schools. If ever there were territory suitable for shared partnership between home and school, parent and teacher, it is citizenship because it is about nothing if not attitudes, values and behaviours.

Learned people are about to cram citizenship into the PSE slot on the timetable and/or the tutorial time, however it may be organized. Certain information and concepts will be prescribed. And who will lead this debate? It will be academics, 'experts' in this new specialist territory by dint of their supposed expertise, trading concepts, information and research. Yet this is to fall into the same trap that leaves values and attitudes so neglected. Citizens contribute. You can tell them by their deeds as well as their words.

Surely the time has come to talk of the 'experiences' that we want our youngsters to take part in, many though not all of them guided or supervised by teachers, parents or others. They are experiences that can happen outside the school or outside the home. The cumulative purpose of the experiences is to increase the likelihood of a youngster developing an emerging realisation of their own limitless potential and the contribution it can make to their own well-being and that of others.

What should those daily, weekly or annual experiences include? The following is a purely illustrative list, to start the debate as it were:

Very young children should experience:

- looking after animals (regularly)
- taking part in nursery rhymes
- playing in groups at shops, fire stations, hospitals
- dressing up in groups
- caring for a younger child
- carrying out tasks that contribute to the life of the family on a daily and weekly basis.

Primary children should experience:

- visits at least annually to museums, environmental centres and public service outlets, eg fire, ambulance, police
- making a book (then a multi-media presentation) as part of a team as an infant and as a junior
- visits to a council house, churches, temples and mosques in the course of the primary years
- an overnight residential under canvas when a junior
- a visit to a theatre/sporting event at least twice in their time in primary school
- team games
- a challenge involving 'field work' and canvassing the views of adults regarding a local and a global environmental issue
- taking part in a public performance every year
- the responsibility of a 'job' for which they must apply in order to sustain the classroom organisation and which requires their daily contribution
- looking after animals regularly for a sustained period
- mediation to solve a dispute at least once a term
- circle time to understand others' feelings and viewpoints
- being part of a 'team task' each year as a junior
- an ICT simulated challenge, perhaps of an environmental or scientific nature
- having an e-mail partner in at least one other continent
- carrying out tasks which contribute to the life of the family on a daily and weekly basis.

Secondary pupils should experience:

- responsibility of a classroom 'job' for which they must apply in order to sustain the work of the tutorial group in Year 7 and Year 8
- a visit to a theatre at least once in Years 7–9

- tutorial responsibilities from Year 9 for a younger pupil in a partner primary school (or the lower school)
- contributing on a long-term basis to the needs of a group or an individual in the wider community
- between Years 7 and 11, take part in at least two outdoor education challenges
- ongoing communication by e-mail with 'pen' pals in each continent
- visits to a distant community to compare different societies
- belonging to a class 'moot'
- the chance to be elected to a 'school council'.

With their peer group, pupils should experience:

- the chance to be a representative in a Young People's Parliament organized by the local council
- in Years 7–9, taking part once a week in term-time in a regular self-organized tutorial discussion of a contemporary news item
- arguing a case 'in public' that they believe in, and then taking the opposite viewpoint
- work placement and work shadowing
- taking part as a team in an urban and rural 'research' project and presenting the outcome to others
- visiting exhibitions of art and performances of music as spectator and participant.

We need to view education as more than the school, and the curriculum as something to be shared between the school, the home and the local community. The debate about rights and responsibilities, about reviving a sense of democratic solidarity is urgent in all societies, especially one like our own which appears to have lost its sense of certainty. Citizenship, embracing as it does matters affecting values, attitudes and behaviour, is the ideal vehicle for that debate to happen.

References

Gardner, H (1984) *Frames of Mind: The Theory of Multiple Intelligence*, HarperCollins, New York
Ofsted (1993) *Access and Achievement in Urban Areas*, HMSO, London

10

Parents, Teachers and Governors

Myth: Parents Don't Care

Colin Fletcher

For Fletcher, it is not just that, under pressure from the National Curriculum, schools and teachers fail to make use of the home in their curricula; they positively freeze the home and the parents out. Thus, the school becomes insular, marooned from what should be its mainland. Schools have failed to adapt to the changing patterns of family life and even behave like estranged partners, heaping blame on parents and vying for the children's affections. Parents still involve themselves in their children's learning, but many follow a 'career' that leads them to become 'warriors' because schools deny them roles that are more collaborative. Even the government, supposedly championing parents' rights, has actually reduced the complexity of open democratic relations to a formal 'contract' that gives parents additional duties and diminishes their freedom.

We are obliged to fulfil our political role as active citizens, ardent consumers, enthusiastic employees and loving parents as if we were seeking to realise our own desires.

(Rose, 1989, p. 258)

The myth *parents don't care* usually goes like this: parents' home–school contact often begins with enthusiasm but their engagement usually slackens as their children get older; eventually there are just a few loyalists left. The myth is 'proved' by the difficulties of getting parents into meetings. 'Those few loyalists,' say teachers, 'are not the ones we really need to see.'

An alternative interpretation might be, 'Parents do not seem to take much notice of Ofsted, as was perhaps expected or intended... parents are generally satisfied to leave the process to the professionals' (Brimblecombe *et al*, 1996, p. 1).

On the one hand, there is a public and largely unquestioned version of the myth, and on the other a privately circulated, less acceptable and more strident version. In the public version, it is said that many parents do not support the school, its teachers or its aspirations: they condone bad behaviour, low motivation and poor achievement. In the private version, it is said that some parents are bad at being parents; they are not fit to have children.

The public version describes exasperation and frustration. It can be reinforced, however, by the private version that is full of annoyance and even anger. The more strongly these versions are felt in a school, the less it is likely that the school has a comprehensive vision and strategy. The view that our 'parents don't care' identifies a dysfunctional comprehensive school, one that has the atmosphere of being under siege and which strives for the success of a select few.

Both public and private versions draw strong support from changes in parenting and family life. The myth points to the diseases of family life and the decline of the extended family and its support. Indeed, government rhetoric and legislation purporting to counter and correct these perceived defects have fuelled the myth. 'Getting them and their parents to accept their responsibilities' is a common theme for Prime Ministers, Education Secretaries and Home Office Ministers. Yet those very responsibilities are the 'sites of contest'. Are parents' responsibilities the same as, or different from those of comprehensive schools?

The making of the marooned school

Parents sense already that they are *the* problem for the twenty-first century. Malthus was right. He said we would have to control childbirths. Modern nation–states want to be vigorous, to have healthy, well-educated workers and to have a culture that expresses national pride. At the same time, however, there are too many mouths to feed. The children parents bring into the world then become both wanted and unwanted. Whole civilisations procreate and become damned. The twenty-first century is already populated with billions of potential parents. Many of the children yet to be born to those who have themselves been born at the end of the twentieth century, will themselves outlive the twenty-first century.

At the same time, there can be real tensions between parents and their child's school. Teachers have a duty *in loco parentis*: they *are* effectively the parents of children during school times. Parents and schools share children, almost like divorcées. Parents fight to get the best for their children, including custody and access. Even when they secure a good school, they often fight with the staff over what is best for their child. It is no wonder that many schools, probably even the majority, speak as if parents were the estranged partner. They pretend to the children, and may even try to convince them, that their parents do not exist for most of the time, and rarely do what is best for them. Schools that exclude parents in this way are rivals for the child's affection. For such schools, parents are either a pain because of their interference or a problem because of their indifference.

If it excludes local parents, a school can become like a frontier trading post. It erects a virtual stockade; it becomes marooned, surrounded by its setting. The school door closes and parents have to shout at an intercom. The scene at the car park outside says it all. Nosing up to the school entrance are the senior teachers' new saloons – fashion statements issuing declarations of determined recreational intent; behind, an outer ring of the rugged roadsters favoured by the long distance teacher-commuter. The school car park says, 'when we are here, this is our school but at other times we are as far away as possible'. Little wonder if parents, both fearing and admiring the teachers, go on to both undermine and emulate the school.

Home–school links are a minority interest, even an esoteric one, in most secondary schools. The responsibility for 'the links' is often delegated to a single member of staff, usually someone quite senior with other more substantial and urgent duties. They are good at handling people and quickly become responsible for dealing with the difficult cases. The more specialized the responsibility, the more substantial its problems. But only when *all* teachers are responsible for their own links is there room for significant learning *from* parents. And only when teachers are learning from parents is it possible to see how parents *do* care, despite their often seemingly paradoxical words and actions.

Myths and fallacies are resistant to the force of research findings, so on top of the evidence I will present I may have to advance the antithesis: that parents do care about their children's education but they don't care about schools because of what schools have done to them. Only when pupils have enjoyed their schooling are they likely to become pro-school parents. Schools' or teachers' hostility towards their pupils today returns hauntingly as parental scorn a generation later.

I want to deal with the myth directly, by examining:

- What is happening to parenting?
- What do parents do for learning?
- What are the 'golden rules' of parenting?
- What is the policy framework for parenting?

What is happening to parenting?

In its *Social Focus on Families*, the Office for National Statistics recently pulled together some facts about parents and their children to show how extensive recent changes have been.

> In one generation the numbers marrying have halved and the numbers divorcing have trebled while the population of children born outside marriage has quadrupled.
>
> Most children live with both parents whether they are married or cohabiting, but there has been a substantial growth in lone parents over the last 25 years. Lone parents now head almost a quarter of all families with dependent children, three times the proportion in 1971. There are many more lone mothers than lone fathers, and this generally reflects the tendency of children to remain with their mother when a partnership breaks up.
>
> The traditional model of 'breadwinner husband and homemaker wife' has been eroded – the dual income family.... Women are now much more likely to return to work after childbirth than in the past.'

(Office for National Statistics, 1997, pp. 6-7)

All available data point in the same direction, a move from traditional forms of nuclear and extended families to transitional forms of being a family. The fixed form of the nuclear family prevalent during a period of European wars has given way to more fluctuating forms. More children now experience more diverse types of family life than previously. One of their carers may remain throughout, but other carers will change. Multi-family households are a thing of the past. Married couples with dependent children are more common in non-manual classes and in rural areas, while cohabitation and lone parenthood are more weighted towards manual classes and urban areas (ibid., p. 13).

The following can be said about women's lives:

- Many women are choosing to cohabit either before or instead of marriage (ibid., p. 14).... One in five women aged between 20 and 24.
- Most women have children at some stage of their lives (ibid., p. 21).
- Lone mothers are generally younger, and have younger children than lone fathers. In 1995, there were twelve lone mothers to every lone father, the latter representing less than 2 per cent of all families with dependent children.

Modern family life displays some continuities:

- Most births occur to mothers who have a partner (ie are registered by both parents living at the same address) (ibid., p. 23).
- 80 per cent of children grow up in a family with two parents, and 80 per cent are in families where there are other children.
- South Asian families have the largest proportion of couple families, and the largest proportion where two or more families make up a single household.

But there have also been changes:

- The average number of children has declined, and the average age of their mothers has increased (ibid., p. 22).
- Divorced people tend to cohabit for the longest time (ibid., p. 16).
- In 1995, local authorities in England and Wales were looking after just over 50,000 children, two-thirds of them in foster placements.
- Just over half of families with dependent children from the black community are lone parent families (ibid., p. 12).

Pulling these facts together to sense the new formations reveals the transitional nature of every form of family and parenting. Whilst the vast majority of children are still brought up by two parents, the parents themselves may be divorcing, cohabiting or separating. A small minority of children are brought up by lone parents, who also tend to cohabit and then separate. The smallest minority, lone fathers, may be the 'loners', older and less likely to cohabit and remarry.

All parents are under pressure, even the two-income, non-manual rural parents who seem to be at the top of the Lifestyle League. Being just a couple on their own is the source of this pressure – having to cope on their own, with whatever hand life deals them. In effect, the less the support from kith and kin, the more intense the pressure. This pressure itself is to live an economically active, happy and healthy life. The irony of the twentieth century is that this simple achievement depends directly upon the support of others. It cannot be achieved in isolation, or by accumulating wealth. The family, whatever its form, is both symbolically detached and socially dependent.

Good comprehensive schools, then, make connections with the transitional forms of parenting, with the difficulties of solitary families and with the kaleidoscope of their pupils' parents. For many children there is more continuity to their schooling than there is to their parenting. In their turn, schools become confused as to which of the child's 'parents' they should expect to be the carer. A child may have a natural father, an adopted father and a current carer who does not act like a father, whilst the adopted father has access rights but the natural father does not. Schools also become concerned about how the current care for the child relates to their learning and achievement. Like their pupils, schools have had to adjust to a changing landscape of parenting – either that or they have become alienated and cynical about those changes.

Transitional forms of the family and of parenthood are clear expressions of contemporary sexual freedoms. These expressions and their complexities may offend those who believe in the traditional form of a nuclear family embedded in a wider extended family offering practical and emotional support. In particular, those in two-income, non-manual nuclear families can be angry that children in transitional forms seem to have been abandoned, at least in part.

Nevertheless, who the parents are is often a matter of current domestic arrangements as much as historical or biological fact. The family is most definitely changing. Transitional forms are challenging traditional forms and good schools have changed their attitudes towards parents in order to accept transitional forms and to work with them for the child's benefit.

What do parents do for learning?

This question is neither facetious nor easy to answer. It is a commonplace to describe learning at home as informal as distinct from the formal learning at school. But the folksy view, of old wives' tales being told at home and young learners' tasks being set at school, is now being challenged by the fact that audio-visual and computer-assisted learning have essentially the same characteristics wherever they take place. In 1997, 60 per cent of households with children had a computer and 99 per cent had a TV. Acres of anxious prose have been written on the effects of TV watching, especially exposure to pornography and violence. Calculations have been made comparing time at school and time in front of the TV or video games. Such calculations suggest that weekend watching is extensive and that the total 'electronic hours' per year could well equal the total formal 'educational hours' which the child experiences. But computers and video can also be used to highlight the significance of parents' contributions to informal teaching and learning, as the following example shows.

Margy Whalley and Cath Arnold developed a pilot project at Pen Green Centre, Corby. Staff and parents at this early-years centre 'produced a CD ROM of video clips. These video clips were of parents with their children at home and at nursery and of nursery staff involving parents and children in the nursery. These video clips were then analysed by staff and parents in informal discussion groups' (Whalley & Arnold, 1997, p. 3).

From their observations, they identified key features in the parents' behaviour (ibid.):

- *Anticipation* – parents seemed intuitively to know what to do next when a child needed something physically or emotionally
- *Recall* – parents could share past experiences and relate them to what the children were doing or saying now while they played
- *Mirroring experience through language* – parents reflected back to the children verbally what they were doing
- *Extending experiences and accompanying the child* – parents were quick to think about and show children new ways to approach things; they were also willing to follow their children's interest and give them the time and space to explore things
- *Asking the child's view* – parents seemed interested in what their children were thinking and feeling about things
- *Encouraging autonomy* – parents encouraged their children to make choices and decisions
- *Boundary setting/ encouraging risk-taking* – parents seemed to know when to step in and how to encourage their children to have a go
- *Judicious use of experience of failure/making mistakes* – parents supported their children's right to experiment, to make mistakes and occasionally to experience failure.

Are these valuable contributions from parents restricted to the early years, diminishing as their children get older? Or *do* parents at every age of their children's lives aspire to the same *involvement,* albeit with decreasing certainty and *intensity* as their children mature? It is instructive to consider parents of children with special educational needs or learning difficulties.

In their most positive moments, maturity in the form of independence, intimacy, imagination, integrity and insight is what parents strive to develop in their children. Parents of children with severe learning difficulties are explicitly concerned with these attributes. They watch their children for all the signs of learning ability. When few, if any, of the signs are discernible, they go into action.

Linnea Glynne-Rule (1995) visited the parents of children with severe learning difficulties over three years. From their words and actions, it was clear that these parents had gone through three stages as advocates on behalf of their children's learning. They had found themselves driven to study, and were now struggling to secure an entitlement for their child.

In the first stage, they became *experts.* Parents developed skills in both observation and clear description. Parents learned through observation what they thought the child was unable to do but *might* be able to do next, possibly with some assistance. The next stage was to discover the words possibly with some assistance. The next stage was to discover the words medical and social professionals used and their real meaning. Applying this vocabulary to their broad and deep experience of the child's behaviour, they became *advocates* about what their child could do, arguing for learning rights. Emboldened by advocacy and sustained by expertise, parents finally became *warriors*. They joined specialist interest groups and they campaigned for improved services.

None of these parents had had any formal education after their school-leaving age. They were self-taught, without wealth and toiling in isolation until they met up with other warriors. The vocabulary broadened with each stage as they felt compelled to take another step 'for the sake of their child'.

Many parents of mainstream children probably go through similar stages, becoming an expert, an advocate and a warrior, albeit that their child's difficulties are less well defined. As Michele Wates says, 'those who are hardest hit by challenges are often those who have gone furthest towards finding solutions' (Wates, 1997, p. 7). Her study is of parents with disabilities bringing up able-bodied children. 'In a society in which so much store is set by being normal, there is a strong pull upon disabled and non-disabled alike to pass as such. Being a parent enshrines, perhaps more than any other social role, the right to participate in mainstream life. It is an initiating role, an active and adult role' (ibid., p. 15). The study's perspective is to 'see disability as a social experience first and foremost rather than a personal characteristic' (ibid., p. 101).

From the interviews, she found the four main characteristics of good professional–parent relationships were (ibid., p. 104):

- Providing encouragement
- supporting a parent's way of doing things
- helping to find solutions to practical challenges, and
- opening doors to resources.

It is immediately apparent that few teachers would give themselves these responsibilities directly. The learned wisdom is to get parents to help the school, not the reverse. Perhaps the phrase 'unlearned wisdom' would be more appropriate here:

> Most of us who have trained to work with children have received relatively little training for working with adults – parents or professional colleagues. Many of us just don't know how to engage parents in an equal and active partnership.

(Whalley, 1997b, p. 1)

Some teachers in community comprehensive schools *do* see themselves as having a responsibility to help parents to help their children. That is one of Pen Green's purposes, and the theme has been taken up regularly in primary school projects such as the Belfield Reading Project (Hannon and Jackson, 1987) and in secondary school practices such as Sutton Centre's Eleventh Session where parents and children learn together (Wilson, 1980).

Case studies such as these do not prove things, still less do they break down myths, but they do point to possibilities. In themselves, case studies rooted in early years and in disabilities do not make possibilities any more realistic for mainstream schools. What they do achieve is to reverse the lens of perspective: What are schools doing for parents so that their caring counts towards their child's maturity? Why have parents' skills been marginalized by the National Curriculum when at the same time child development has become an academic subject? How perverse to talk to pupils about becoming parents, but not to talk to their parents about their experiences. Is this, again, a projection of failure upon the many and the idealization of a few?

What are the 'golden rules' of parenting?

Parenthood has many uncertainties. Most parents worry about their child's progress, the development of their personality, and their own adequacy as parents. Partly to wrestle with these uncertainties, parents engage with their child's school. In particular it is possible to speak of having a 'career' as a parent. The idea of parents having a career as a carer acknowledges how their relationship with their child's schools changes over time. The intensity of their involvement comes and goes. The involvement itself alters from holding formal positions and undertaking voluntary functions to giving informal help with hardly a word having been said.

Mary Stacey positively identified some of the ways in which parents' uncertainty is invested in schools. There is a process of investment for both their rational and emotional capabilities – for both learning about children in general and loving their child in particular. There are good objective grounds for parents' uncertainty. To take an example, if a child is listless and unable to concentrate, it could be because something has gone wrong at home. In the same way, all children, particularly young children, can be whipped into a frenzy by a high wind. Parents know their child in detail day by day, but teachers know children by their ages and their actions. 'Teachers have a "public" and generalised "theory" about child development whilst parents have a "personal theory" about the development of a particular child' (Easen *et al*, 1992). They need each other's knowledge and so parents embark on a career of involvement at their child's school. They become, in turn and by alternations:

- *Supporters,* eg at fund raising, social events, religious and cultural festivals
- *Learners,* eg at curriculum workshops and computer days
- *Helpers,* eg designated tasks in the classroom, listening to reading
- *Teachers*, eg home reading schemes, and
- *Policy-makers,* eg governors, governors' annual meeting.

(Stacey, 1991, Chapter 4)

In one sense this list of roles is like Arnstein's 'Ladder of Participation' (quoted in Robbins and Williams, 1980), in that there is a progression towards the professional and political aspects of schooling. Some – a very few – do indeed climb such a ladder, but most do not. To begin with, there are forms of glass ceilings in parental careers in schools. There are also feelings of 'connection fatigue', with anxieties about spending all one's time going back and forth to meetings and not spending enough time with one's own children.

Essentially, parental involvement waxes and wanes. Getting into things at the school opens up links with occupational careers, which then compete for available time. By far the most popular involvements are events with parents of other children in the same class. Workshops, issue specific meetings and class group meetings touch the nerve ends of uncertainties. Again, a personal dependence on others is obvious: only discussion and comparison with others resolves the doubts about the efficiency and effectiveness of the parents' own care.

Some parents do feel a deep sense of failure and long for the day that their child/children will leave home. Some parents are bullied by their children and yet still love them.

The Heisenberg Principle therefore has a partial application to the principles of parenting. This Principle says that it is not possible to know exactly what something is, and at the same time know how it is changing. The study of essential properties and emergent processes reveals different characteristics and different insights. When applied to parenting, the Heisenberg Principle proposes some interesting paradoxes for how parents can relate to their child as a school child and to their child's school. The following suggestions can be made:

- Accept and use your own uncertainty about your child's character and capabilities.
- Contribute fully your particular knowledge and carefully consider the school and its teachers' knowledge about children in general.

■ Range through the roles available, getting in deeper when needed, and getting out when in too deeply.

■ Anticipate a conflict between having a parent-school career and having an occupational career.

■ Never assume that the present state is an end or final stage, neither in relationships with children nor in relationships with schools.

These suggestions have some significance when considering the policy framework for parenting.

What is the policy framework for parenting?

As I noted earlier, every major government ministry produces legislation on what is required from parents. Successive Home Secretaries have taken up the theme that parents must take on more responsibilities for the control of their children. The 1989 Children Act represents a milestone in making parental responsibility a legal requirement. With respect to the Education Ministry, however, the simplest view is that in Britain under the conservatives, parents were consumers and that under New Labour, they are custodians. Interestingly, both emphasize the parent's role in the present: the Conservative version expressing rights and choices; New Labour expressing responsibilities and control. But 'being a consumer is not just about choice: it is also about the continuing *relationship* between parents and schools once the initial choice has been made' (Hughes *et al.*, 1994, p. 76).

Within a month of returning to power, New Labour produced the White Paper *Excellence in Schools* (DfEE, 1997) with Chapter 6 specifically addressed to parents. Fifteen extracts from this chapter are listed opposite in the sequence in which they appear. I have starred those that emphasize responsibilities rather than rights. The balance is weighted towards parents being required to contract with schools, to be involved with reading and arithmetic, discipline, attendance and homework. Spin-doctors use the phrase 'tough love' to describe such strictures and their supports. In effect, consumerism has been overlaid with custodialism, possibly even to be incorporated within it.

Excellence in Schools: Chapter 6

Parent support

The best early years' centres... already offer support and learning opportunities for parents alongside their children.

*We will look to every primary school to have a plan for involving parents in the way their child learns to read and goes on to learn broader skills of literacy and numeracy.

Family learning can go wider than parents – foster grandparents, child minders, health visitors and school nurses.

Home–school contact

*All schools should develop, in discussion with parents, a written home-school contract: not legally binding but powerful statements of intent.

Information for parents

Annual school report, annual child's report in the clearest possible form.

Giving parents an effective voice

*Encourage governing bodies to ensure that the school has a home-school association.

Increase the number of elected parent governors.

Discipline and attendance

*Detailed new guidance on school discipline policies, after-school detention and advice on good practice (eg assertive discipline).

*We will consult on further means of bringing home to parents – through home-school contracts and more effective use of legal sanctions – their responsibilities for ensuring regular and punctual attendance.

Exclusions

We will be consulting shortly on new detailed guidance for schools and LEAs about appropriate circumstances for exclusions... appeals... pupil's subsequent education, and financial incentives for schools to admit pupils excluded by others.

School leaving date

From Easter 1998 young people will not leave school before the end of their GCSEs.

Homework

*Parents should know what homework their children are expected to do and the support they themselves should give... we will issue national guidelines on homework.

Study support centres

Regular out of school hours learning activities in half of all secondary schools and a quarter of primary schools by 2001.

Parenting

We want all secondary schools to help teach young people the skills of good parenting, both formally and through contact with good adult role models.

School meals

We propose to specify minimum national standards for inclusion in school meal contracts.

The tone of the responsibilities discounts the tender complexity of a more highly developed home–school relationship. It leaves out the care and love evident in the earlier case studies. The tender complexity to which I refer brings together all the roles which parenting has within it. Parents have concerns both for their child's present experiences and for their future prospects. Parents have rights over their children as well as responsibilities for them. There is no dominant role. Rather, there are four roles as shown in Table 10.1.

Table 10.1 Parenting roles for school involvement

	Responsibilities	Rights
Present concerns	**Custodian**	**Consumer**
Future concerns	**Carer**	**Citizen-maker**

As *custodian,* the parent has a *responsibility* look after the child materially and morally. In relation to school, this means that the child has food to encourage physical and mental growth, shelter and space in which to study, sufficient sleep to be able to learn to the best of their ability, support for regular attendance and punctuality, and sanctions for misbehaviour. At times this conventional parent role can be idealized and misrepresented as the main role.

As *carer,* the parent has a *responsibility* for compassion towards the child's character development. With respect to school, this means not expecting the child to be good, or the best, at everything but rather expecting them to have social skills, communication skills and consideration for others. At times, this conventional parent role can also be idealized and misrepresented as if to produce a quiescence comparable with that also produced by the custodial role.

The role of *consumer* is rooted in present *rights* of choice, criticism and complaint. When it comes to school, this means balancing the choice of school with the choice of special subjects at each point of change – nursery, infant, junior, secondary and tertiary. The parent as consumer criticizes the school if it 'fails to deliver', complains if the child fails through no fault of their own. At times, this conflict-laden role condenses to a state of continuous hostility, so it is rare for it to be the main parental role in relation to school.

The *citizen-maker* demands the *right* to retain and develop political, religious and sexual beliefs, and above all freedom of expression. Parents have a right to 'bring up their children' within the framework of these freedoms in such a way that their chosen expressions are perpetuated by their children (or freely rejected by them when themselves adult). At times this conflict-laden role can be intensified too, leading to three-cornered conflicts between parents, their children's school and their children themselves. Again, it is rarely the main parental role, though it can never be overlooked or ignored.

These four parenting roles are in danger of being fudged by the government's rhetoric into the metaphor of parent as *coach*: a role involving training children for tasks, shouting encouragement to them from the sidelines and urging extra effort from them in order to achieve targets. It is most unlikely that the role of unpaid coach is all that parents care for, or care to do. It is this aspect of containing and controlling that parents don't care for, particularly when it has primacy and crowds out their concern for their child's future. Parents don't care to be exclusively custodians or consumers; they want a more balanced mix of roles with a view to a more balanced adulthood for their children. They feel the school excludes their emotions, along with their wishes for their children to learn to appreciate justice, fairness and good humour.

Wolfendale (1989) acknowledged that mutual support and conflict are both aspects of parental involvement, and that the potential for conflict can be uppermost when there is no explicit home–school contract

> The message... is that the existence of a written agreement between home and school will clarify rights and responsibilities, and will be a positive basis on which all joint activities can rest. In so doing, it will reduce the possibility of friction and conflict.

> (Wolfendale, 1989, p. xi)

Good comprehensive schools share the vision held by all parents, of their children becoming independent, sociable, productive and challenging adults. However, comprehensive education has yet to produce a generation of such adults who, as parents in their turn, will express through school partnerships the way in which their own parents cared for them. This failure is not due to the lack of will, vision or capability (Fletcher *et al*, 1985). It results from the dominance of national government's present concerns and requirements in the policies and practices of comprehensive schools. An opportunity has been missed to express the goals of literacy and numeracy not just as intrinsic requirements for a skilled workforce, but also for active modern citizenship. These goals have been expressed in a way that also requires schools to manage themselves like a business, and to command their participants like an army. Since 1978 or thereabouts, schools have had no choice but to subordinate pupils and to regard home–school relations as an optional luxury unless there are big problems with some pupils. Schools have had to risk 'turning off' a high proportion of their pupils in the interests of turning in test and examination results. The exaggerated emphases on the consumer and custodial roles are steps in the wrong direction. The full productive potential of home–school partnerships has yet to be realized.

Conclusion

Pascal and Bertram (1994) suggest five questions for schools. These questions acknowledge that parents do care, and lead to answers in which good practice can be found. Practitioners will recognize them:

1. What is the policy on parental partnership? A clear commitment to seek out and spend on parental partnerships is required. A contract on its own can become another useless piece of paper full of unenforceable expectations, dominated by what parents should do for schools, rather than what both could do for each other.

2. How are parents involved in learning? Involvement in learning is pivotal. The school must take account of the learning that takes place at home, and the parent must understand and underpin the child's learning in school.

3. How are liaison and co-ordination achieved between the different settings? This is a perennial problem, requiring active engagement at all levels in the school. It has to be a part of everyone's job, and not an extra. It is also fraught with all the dangers of exposure and misunderstanding of each party's expressions. If liaison and co-ordination are the sole responsibility of either main grade teachers or the senior management team, then the inherent tensions will become impossible to handle.

4. How do the learning activities reflect awareness of the home and community environment? In addition to the learning that takes place in the immediate home, referred to above, the local community and environment are proper subjects of study. More 'empirical teachers' can be found within them. Children learn about life from their locality all the time. This learning can become more systematic, more reflective and more embedded through appropriately linked activities in the school.

5. Does the school offer any means of support to families? Family support is needed because of the uncertainties and transitional modern forms of parenting. Teachers and parents need to work together to produce the first generation of adults who will recall their own school experiences as having been overwhelmingly positive. Whalley's (1997a) four supports are: home visiting, parent spaces, parents' groups and parents' roles.

What is emerging from good practice in parental involvement is a challenge to the idea that parents are the owners of children. In its place, the idea has formed that all adults should see themselves as 'quasi-parents'. By this I mean that parenting should be seen as a right and responsibility which all adults share because the isolated or nuclear family is too stressful for all concerned with it. A policy needs to involve parents actively. Whalley sets out the needs from the perspective of early childhood educators:

> You need to recognise the great untapped energy and ability of all parents using our settings. You need to have high expectations of their interest in and commitment to their children's learning. You need to develop mutual understanding and share experiences with parents.

> (ibid., p. 177)

Thus Ofsted's criterion for judging schools, item 5.5 in its *Handbook for Inspections*, is a pitifully narrow one-way street: 'Relations between home and school are supportive and co-operative. Parents get actively involved in their children's work and in the life of the school.' It emasculates so much in its superficiality. The contrast is with adults who act as parents giving their best and receiving the best support and encouragement for this essential social service. Such a conclusion parallels that reached by Tim Brighouse in Chapter 9. The necessity of shared parenthood comes from stewardship, or what Michael Fielding calls 'authorship'. Neither parent-carers nor the nation-state 'own' children, they are the first and last links in a chain of care. Such a principle is neither romantic nor sentimental, but it *is* an optimistic feature of good comprehensive education.

References

Brimblecombe, N, Ormston, M and Shaw, M (1996) What role does Ofsted Inspection have in Meeting the Government's Aims for Parents and Schools?, paper presented at BERA Conference, Lancaster

DfEE (1997) *Excellence in Schools,* HMSO, London

Easen, P, Kendall, P and Shaw, J (1992) Parents and educators, dialogue and development through partnership, *Children and Society,* **6** (4), pp. 282–96

Fletcher, C, Williams, W and Caron, M (1985) *Schools on Trial: The Trials of Democratic Comprehensives,* Open University Press, Milton Keynes

Glynne-Rule, L (1995) The family as a learning environment, PhD thesis, Cranfield University

Hannon, P and Jackson, A (1987) *Belfield Reading Project Final Report,* National Children's Bureau, London

Hughes, M, Wikely, F and Nash, T (1994) *Parents and their Children's Schools,* Blackwell, Oxford

Office for National Statistics (1997) *Social Focus on Families,* HMSO, London

Ofsted (1993) *Handbook for the Inspection of Schools,* HMSO, London

Pascal, C, and Bertram, A (1994) Defining and assessing quality in the education of children from 4-7 years, in F Laevers (ed.) *Defining and Assessing the quality in Early Childhood Education: Studia Paedagogica,* Leuven University Press, Leuven

Robbins, W and Williams, W (1980) Developing community participation, in C Fletcher and N Thompson *Issues in Community Education,* Falmer Press, Brighton

Rose, N (1989) *Governing the Soul: The Shaping of the Private Self,* Routledge, London

Stacey, M (1991) *Parents and Teachers Together,* Open University Press, Buckingham

Wates, M (1997) *Disabled Parents, Dispelling the Myths,* National Childbirth Trust, Cambridge

Whalley, M. (1997a) *Parents' Involvement in their Children's Learning,* Pen Green Centre Conference, Corby

Whalley, M (1997b) *Working with Parents,* Hodder and Stoughton, London

Whalley, M and Arnold, C (1997) *Parental Involvement in Education,* Pen Green Centre for Under-5's and their Families, Corby

Wilson, S (1980) The eleventh session at Sutton Centre as a community involvement, in C Fletcher and N Thompson *Issues in Community Education,* Falmer Press, Brighton

Wolfendale, S (ed.) (1989) *Parental Involvement,* Cassell, London

11

Schools and Beyond

Myth: Good Schools Are All We Need

Tom Wylie

Wylie agrees with Fletcher, that schools misjudge parents if they believe the latter only want examination successes, the league table's 'good school'. Actually, most parents consider the development of character and values to be more important. This is most particularly true in socially deprived areas, where the task is more challenging and schools need additional resources. Community education offers the chance to find 'joined-up' solutions to the interconnected and self-reinforcing problems of the neighbourhood, because education alone cannot remove poverty, and in any case poverty removes the hunger for education on which real learning depends.

Education is carrying a great burden as the centrepiece of policy. It is seen to hold the key to economic success and social stability, although few speak now of its role in individual fulfilment. In a globalized economy a country no longer needs coal, iron or steel – having human capital is what makes the difference and the way to increase the stock of a country's intellectual and skill assets is to improve education.

To this end, we are awash with initiatives – New Start, New Deal, Education Action Zones, The People's Lottery. A state which has rediscovered the possibility of intervening pulls the levers of power with great enthusiasm. If we cannot build a new Jerusalem in England's green and pleasant land, we'll settle for Taiwan in the Dales. Good schooling is now at the heart of the construction of this new Britain. This paper will explore the nature of the good urban school; will suggest that good schooling is a necessary but not sufficient condition for human development; will examine the claims of schooling within a context of community education, but will conclude that the latter also has to be reshaped if it is to meet the needs of young people.

First, how are we defining the good school? Our Victorian forefathers, the Matthew Arnolds of yesteryear, used language; our contemporaries use figures. Even in the notorious period of 'payment by results', HM Inspectors were still able to discover some of the innate curiosities of pupils. One such was inspector Rev. W H Brookfield, formerly a fashionable preacher in Mayfair: his witty and outspoken reports brought criticism from both the Department and school managers. In one of his reports, Brookfield wrote:

> It is my custom to ask the children of a first class to write impromptu upon their slates about different subjects which I mention to them, an elephant, a swan, a monkey, etc. To one little boy of eleven years of age I had, perhaps somewhat imprudently, proposed a racehorse. He gave up his slate, inscribed, with very good writing and spelling, as follows:
>
> 'The racehorse is a noble animal used very cruel by gentlemen. Races are very bad places. None but wicked people know anything about races. The last Derby was won by Mr I'Anson's Blinkbonny, a beautiful filly by Melbourne, rising four. The odds were twenty to one against her; thirty started, and she won only by a neck.'
>
> I handed this dissertation to one of the managers. He returned it to me with a perplexed look, saying, 'I am very sorry indeed for this. He was always a very good little boy till now.'

(Brookfield, 1905)

Such discursive writing is no longer fashionable in inspectors' reports!

Government now is fascinated by targets, by performance indicators. In consequence, we have narrowed the definition of the good school – especially in the secondary sector. The benchmarks – even the new-fangled 'improvement index' – have become academic assessments, notably tests in English, Mathematics and Science and 5 A*–C in GCSE. Schools, and the young people they serve, have become bedevilled by shallow comparisons.

Of course, literacy and numeracy matter, and all schools need to focus their efforts on enabling young people to be competent in both. It is not making an excuse to acknowledge that it is harder in some settings to achieve such goals. A study by Ofsted of the 100 secondary schools having the highest proportion of free school meals indicated that only three (all of them girls' schools) achieved the national GCSE average point score of 35, that 15 are subject to special measures and a further 15 are known to have serious weaknesses. Pupils at urban comprehensive schools serving the 10 per cent most advantaged areas are twice as likely to achieve 5+ A* –C at GCSE as those at comprehensives in the 10 per cent most disadvantaged areas. This gap is widening, not narrowing. Many of the reasons for this are well known.

High levels of unemployment create poverty, which in turn affects health and attendance and achievement. They also diminish the perceived relevance of schooling in these communities and help to sustain a subculture of derision for those adolescents concerned to achieve. Students expect to go into short-term, casual jobs – if they get work at all – and they are not persuaded that learning is either fun or brings its own reward. As HMI (1993) wrote a few years ago in their unique study of urban schooling:

> Poor levels of education and qualification among many parents complete a cycle of under-achievement which continues to affect the lives of their children. The community does not acquire sufficient numbers of people able to offer role models of educational success.

School improvement in urban areas can be fragile – difficult to achieve, and hard to sustain – especially if the schools concerned are facing substantial mobility of population and/or pressures to take disproportionate numbers of excluded children. It is not surprising that many who teach in such settings are driven to put their concern for welfare and self-esteem of the young people in their charge before their academic achievement. The HMI report went on:

> Concern and commitment are necessary but not sufficient conditions for improvement. It is not enough to offer educational safe havens, secure against other social pressures and temptations. Raising the achievement of children needs to be acknowledged as the central purpose of schools, to become the systematic focus for their endeavours, and to set the targets for action by all... [but] success has depended on individuals' strengths rather than on shared purposes and concerted teamwork. Often, policies and projects are not sustained long enough to make an impact.

> (Ibid.)

The measures promoting good schooling need to be those that will assist urban schools directly to develop their pupils' key skills and civic literacy – values and understandings necessary for participation in our democratic society. We need schools to adopt sharp targets and benchmarks for their own improvement and to work deliberately towards achieving them. In response to the powerful 'performance indicator' lobby, schools and other educational services should consciously construct and publicise indicators that reflect wider educational goals. We could use some of those entitlements Tim Brighouse has suggested (Chapter 9), such as the percentage of students who take part in a residential experience, or gain a Duke of Edinburgh Award. But beware of Goodhart's Law. Goodhart was a chief economist at the Bank of England who pointed out that perfectly good economic indicators could go grievously wrong if adopted as policy targets.

Hence, during the 1980s, control of money supply became a target and the economy was driven into the deep abyss of recession, with levels of structural employment from which it has still to recover. We need to avoid a similar fate befalling education by the excessive use, for example, of 5+ GCSE grades A*–C as the key criterion. We do well to remember the ironic lines of Brian Patten's poem *The Minister for Exams*:

> Q1 how large is a child's imagination?
> Q2 how shallow is the soul of the Minister for Exams?'

(Patten, 1996)

We need a wider view of the role and purposes of education, and performance measures which sustain and reflect these wider purposes, not least those of social inclusion. Good schools seek a range of developmental goals:

- increasing both knowledge and skills – now reaching levels far higher than previously imagined possible for many pupils
- developing cognitive ability through a range of subjects and areas of experience
- enhancing interpersonal skills including the ability to manage feelings and conflicts, so important in a diverse society
- liberating young people from the givens of authority and tradition, so that they can participate fully in changing society for the better
- promoting self-motivation which will enable pupils to learn and to sustain lifelong learning.

To put it more simply and more profoundly, in the words of Sir Edward Boyle, the best of post-war Conservative Ministers of Education (not a long list, it should be said!): 'the purpose of education is to enable people to bear for themselves the cross of being human'.

Schooling matters for all young people, not just for their cognitive gains but for its effects on individual self-esteem and for the promotion of a wider sense of citizenship. Michael Rutter put the case clearly:

> experiences in childhood do make a substantial impact on children's psychological development and the qualities of the schools attended by children make a big difference to their levels of scholastic achievement. It is no easy matter to create a happy, effective school and there are a variety of influences outside the control of schools. Nevertheless, schooling does matter greatly. Moreover, the benefits can be surprisingly long-lasting... because experiences at one point in a child's life tend to influence what happens afterwards in a complicated set of indirect chain reactions... these long-term benefits rely on both effects on cognitive performance (in terms of learning specific skills,

improved task orientation and better persistence) and effects on self-esteem and self-efficacy.

(Rutter, 1991)

Parents already know this about their own children and should be helped to resist simplistic league tables purporting to rank the quality of schools. As Rutter indicates, we need, both in primary and secondary schools, to address pupils' self-esteem and the arena highlighted by Goleman in 'Emotional Intelligence' (Goleman, 1996). The latter expresses the basis for a set of essential skills concerned with self-control, creative thinking, decision-making, political awareness and team working. The development of such values and skills is the core of youth work and of schools. An emotionally intelligent school would offer some of the following characteristics – children are listened to; they work co-operatively in groups, as the staff do; good citizenship is the norm; anti-social behaviour is discouraged and constrained, not simply removed by expulsions.

Over the last twenty years, schools have changed less than young people have and we need to recognize the great potential of young people themselves. We should judge schools by how far they have been able to tap into this potential, to give opportunities for its expression and to demonstrate rates of improvement across a range of educational endeavours, not just the formal subjects.

It has to be acknowledged, however, that not all young people enjoy their school days. Various reports remind us that:

> A significant number of the disaffected young people... laid the root cause of their problems at the door of weaknesses in the education system. They said they felt excluded, psychologically and then physically, from school at an early age.

(Aspire Consultants, 1996)

A number of factors within the school system have been found to contribute to a sense of exclusion, including:

- difficult relationships with teachers
- a perception that school is irrelevant
- changes in examination and assessment procedures including a reduction in coursework
- a sense of failure accruing from the academic orientation of the National Curriculum framework
- an inappropriate pedagogy.

If such weaknesses are to be remedied, we need teachers who can light a fire for children's learning. But we also need a much more relevant curriculum, one that connects with young people's experiences, their world, their aspirations and the stories they tell about themselves. Of course, we must raise their aspirations and move them on in their personal narratives, but first, schooling has to connect with them. Some young people use their insights into the teaching process to avoid learning: they turn work into play. They need to be helped to see its value. To this end, young people should be given a greater say in their own learning, in determining and developing the orientation skills they need; to be helped, especially after 14 years, to become independent learners. They should be treated as co-producers, co-creators of their own learning and not simply as its consumers. In short, what they do should become congruent with what they hope and think. This is not to be promiscuous in pedagogy; rather, it is to deploy the authority of the teacher in stimulating and sustaining responsible learning, a task so much more demanding than didacticism.

Good schools, including good community schools, take readily to such goals. Moreover, a good community school is a neighbourhood school. It should accept and work with all the children of the neighbourhood. It should not select – or seek to retain – only the most intelligent, the most biddable. We have already seen the emergence and consolidation of a new hierarchy of esteem about schools, especially in urban areas. The distinction between 'Foundation' and 'Community' schools is not helpful. On the contrary, this new categorization risks further stigmatizing and dividing schools.

But schools of all kinds – whatever their title – carry expectations that they will play a wider role in developing citizens and communities. This is particularly important in those areas that have suffered the flight of public and private capital in the last few decades. You know the ones I mean: most shops boarded up, the bank long since closed, no doctor's surgery, the small youth and community centre vandalized, crime expected by all, and the young and the poor robbing themselves. Within a year or two of construction, the soulless shopping precinct is almost derelict and the design faults of the cheaply built housing units are evident – roofs leaking, damp penetrating, security doors broken and lifts no longer functioning. Multiple entrances open onto long, dark internal corridors and the open spaces around the tower blocks become bleak deserts across which the discarded packaging of modern consumerism blows carelessly. A collective depression overwhelms all who live there.

They have become the communities of the left behind. As conditions worsen, residents migrate if they can. The homeless take their place – younger, poorer families with twice the rate of unemployment and three times the rate of lone parenthood. There is no obvious escape from these underclass estates. The spiral wears down the local schools, the health and social services, and the police. What were services for the poor become poor services.

And what happens to the young in such places? Studies published by the Joseph Rowntree Foundation illuminate the position:

> The areas contained a dangerous combination of large numbers of out of work young males with no status or stake in society, living in low-income work-poor households, in areas suffering from a high social stigma. The physical conditions, ethnic make-up and tenure of the areas were no different from some neighbourhoods which have not experienced such problems. The special characteristics of these areas concerned the economic and social status of inhabitants and, in particular, the young men. Levels of unemployment were three times as high as for the local authority areas as a whole and higher than other areas of social housing. Causing trouble was a commonly known way of asserting an alternative, defiant, anti-authority and destructive image to compensate for the inability to succeed or participate in a more organised way in mainstream society. There was constant reference to the problem of lack of jobs. Many young men did not see any harm in stealing cars, attacking the police, intimidating older residents or forming gangs to strengthen their control of outdoor spaces. They accepted and some claimed to admire violent, aggressive, illegal actions which set them apart from the mainstream from which they felt excluded.

> (Power and Tunstall, 1997)

Such reports tell of the particular needs of disaffected young males – 'men behaving badly'. However, it is also the case that the lowest achieving young women, including those who failed at age 11, are the most likely to become young single mothers.

Not surprisingly, schools are expected to play their part in at least helping young people to handle and survive such circumstances, if not to find individual ways to escape them. Meanwhile, some of us still try to cling to the old maxim *rise with your class, not out of it*. The National Curriculum has damaged attention to personal and social education and active tutorial work. What spaces remain for teachers and pupils together to explore questions of values, except when rules are broken? The school is a microcosm of society, and its role as a learning resource needs to be rediscovered.

What is that role? Clearly, at its heart must be promoting individual achievement in key skills and personal development, the prerequisites for full citizenship. As well as re-vamping their curriculum, schools can offer encouragement to sustain learning. Study support, promoted by the Prince's Trust, can play a useful role. It is important also to draw parents into the process and a number of schools engage in parenting classes and much more. In some projects developed by the Community Education Development Centre, parents gain accreditation from the Open College Network for helping their children with KSI Maths and English. In Chapters 9 and 10, Tim Brighouse and Colin Fletcher have explored the parental and community agenda in more detail.

All this activity plays a part in re-building communities, in linking generations, in challenging the received codes of disadvantage and of social classification, in breaking down the enclave of social exclusion that can disable parents and their offspring. It reflects the ethic of creating a just and truly democratic society.

Time will tell if the 1997 general election result will signal the re-emergence of the role of community. If so, it will not be too soon. For the 'habits of the heart' have been loosened. The impulse to intervene against anti-social or violent behaviour has been in retreat in the face of violence and a culture of privatized indifference – 'it is not my/your business'. The communitarian writer Amitai Etzioni, says that the 'values that command our support because they are morally compelling have been thinned out and must be stiffened once more' (Etzioni, 1995).

This is where the concept of 'community education' begins to deploy its beguiling rhetoric: the school as the site for community learning, social integration and renaissance. It paints a portrait of the disaffected adolescent wired to the Internet rather than on the school roof and the arch exponent of the local underground economy teaching adult classes in social entrepreneurship.

Of course, rhetoric can sometimes become reality. In some places, for instance, youth work is:

- extending the formal curriculum – in drama, arts, sports, outdoor activities
- promoting personal and social development – fostering social skills, health awareness
- providing study support
- encouraging active citizens through volunteering, and political education.

Together with our sister organization the National Institute of Adult and Continuing Education, the National Youth Agency, is currently working on a Young Adult Learners Project. This is designed to illuminate and replicate community-based learning with a curriculum that promotes achievement in disillusioned adolescents. Some authorities – Leeds, for instance – have used imaginatively the knowledge gained through their administration of benefits to target resources and offers of training to particular neighbourhoods and families.

Schools can offer a neighbourhood base for the holistic delivery of local services. They can be a focus for community empowerment and democratic action and can connect their work with specific individuals to broader social programmes in ways that do not stigmatize. They can map, and then reverse the processes even within education itself, by which some people or groups become socially and educationally excluded.

If education is to be successful in its wider mission, it needs:

- acceptance by a range of services of the emphasis to be given to educational outcomes, overcoming, for example, the tension between social services and education in respect of the education of children in care
- to focus intervention on key points of transition, such as leaving school
- agreement on a realistic set of performance indicators which reflect broader goals than academic attainment, for example including the community use of resources and the development of co-operative practices
- good quality professionals who draw on different skills and values and who are not precious about their particular service
- sufficient funding, for Standard Spending Assessments, which can often resemble voodoo economics, should reflect the additional educational needs of disadvantaged areas. Too many initiatives and projects receive only short-term funding and cannot be sustained in disadvantaged communities.

Many schools will also need the curriculum to pay more attention to those skills in learning how to learn, in learning how to live, to solve problems, to develop a consequential mentality – 'if I do this, then that will follow'. They will need to re-discover the simple purposes expressed in Chapter 1 of the Education Act (1988) – to promote the spiritual, moral, cultural, mental and physical development of the pupil and society, and to prepare pupils for the opportunities, responsibilities and experiences of adult life. It is important that the forthcoming review of the National Curriculum, dominated last time by subject specialists, should not on this occasion be captured by narrow fundamentalists who eschew such wider goals.

We need to pay a good deal more attention to the place of the peer group in adolescence, to its capacity to shape and reform individual biographies and to sustain or undermine personal commitment to learning. Too much attention in school is paid to whole-class teaching or is focused on individual performance; too little on working with peer groups to develop values and teamwork. Such a role is more common in the less formal settings used by youth work. Youth work practitioners need to focus more sharply on the quality of learning which it is possible to achieve in small, well-tasked groups. In doing so, they alter the hierarchy of esteem within them and enable young people to become more effective educators of their own peers. Young people often turn to each other to find support and clarification and youth workers can strengthen these skills.

But before we are all led off towards the community education rainbow (or is it the sunset?), I'd just like to raise some objections to schools becoming great hypermarkets of community life, drawing all to their steady beacon.

The first objection is that of the disillusioned youngster quoted in the Newsom Report 'it might be made of marble but it's still a bloody school' (Newsom, 1963). I have argued above that schools need to be willing to accept the changes in curriculum and pedagogy that will overcome the lack of marble. Of course, pedagogy has moved on from the Jesuits or Christian Brothers: 'Sure it's like banging your head against a brick wall, said Brother Ryan, banging my head against a brick wall' (Patten, 1996). Even so, educators need to accept that some youngsters will still prefer the youth club or even the bus shelter. They choose these spaces for their learning or recreation, and the skills and commitment of those who volunteer to work with them in such settings need greater acknowledgement. Young people are at the leading edge of the cultural changes which are re-shaping our society, and on their own, schools cannot hope to connect with their interests in music or fashion, or even their acceptance of diverse life styles.

The second is that, in too much of the practice of community education, the needs and interests of the less biddable adolescent can easily be overlooked through institutional attention to more straightforward client groups. The playgroup, or one of Maeve Binchy's evening classes in Italian, somehow just seem more attractive to the headteacher than appointing another denim-jacketed detached youth worker, especially when she's likely to go on about drug misuse by year 10s in the local park.

An emerging challenge may be the changing role of the community itself. It is not necessary to call to mind the Majoresque image, based on Orwell, 'of old maids cycling to Holy Communion past the long shadows falling on the cricket ground', to suggest that communities have changed. No bad thing, perhaps. Many communities, when stripped of the filter of nostalgia, were typically inward-looking, highly resistant to innovation and they drew much of their solidarity from being hostile to outsiders. The ties that bound the people together were those of isolation, unremitting labour and, frequently, patriarchal domination. There can be no going back to the 'traditional' forms of marriage, family and community. What is emerging in their place, a new study suggests, is the growth of friendship and friend-like relationships threading through life. As well as needing familial or community support, people often need to break out from their constraining ties if they are to cope with a risk-society and exploit fully opportunities from a flexible labour market. Those who have emphasized old-style links based on gender, race or ethnicity as a way of empowering disadvantaged people may unwittingly have added to their troubles by making it more difficult for such closer-knit groups to develop 'bridging' relationships to a wider world. Some recent research suggests that ways out of poverty are provided by networking with people on the edges of communities who have new experiences and access to opportunities. In consequence, should we place as much emphasis on helping young people to build friendship as well as families?

The final difficulty with overstating the role of the school is that expressed by this author when an HMI in the report on Access and Achievement in Urban Education:

> Schools, and other educational institutions, can do more to improve their own effectiveness, to plan to ensure that pupils have the curriculum to which they are entitled and can build on the learning they have gained. But most schools in these disadvantaged areas do not have within themselves the capacity for sustainable renewal. The rising tide of national educational change is not lifting these boats. Beyond the school gate are underlying social issues such as poverty, unemployment, poor housing, inadequate health care and the frequent break-up of families. Education by itself can only do so much to enable individuals to reach beyond the limiting contours of their personal and social circumstances and succeed.

> (HMI, 1993)

Such doubts, echoing those expressed years ago by Basil Bernstein (1970), were given added bite by the recent study from Centre for Education Reform which suggested that social class, parental interest and peer group pressure were the main factors in determining numeracy or literacy (Robinson, 1997). A further difficulty is that the British labour market is still biased towards low-paid jobs requiring low levels of educational achievement. The demand for skills in the workforce has increased, but around two-thirds of employment in Britain is concentrated among the six lower occupational groups. Only 13 per cent of these jobs require reading skills of Grade C GCSE and above, and only 3 per cent need numeracy skills at GCSE Grade D and above. The study's author, Peter Robinson, calculates that only 37 per cent of jobs demand literacy at Grade C GCSE and above, but already 50 per cent of pupils attain this level. It may take 40 years before the share of employment in the managerial, professional and technical occupations expands to meet the available supply. Such realities make it hard to convince the young of the long-term pay-off from education.

This is not to downplay the role of schooling, to suggest that it makes no difference, or that raising our country's level of skill is irrelevant, but to acknowledge the powerful place of economic and other social policies. One way in which education can help towards equality is by creating a better social mix in schools. It is also important to remember that training people for economic outcomes, for jobs, is only one facet of the educational purpose.

This calls for changes in the daily practice of education in all its settings. It means reshaping young people's expectations about their present and about their accomplishments; it means seeing them as a resource to be developed, not a problem to be managed; it means offering them visible victories and narratives of success, and it means reaching out to develop the imagination through drama and the other arts. For what is success for young people? It is not just a matter of securing a good education, decent housing, a proper job, important though these things are, but counting for something in society and being at ease with themselves.

In disadvantaged localities, no single service can hope to deal with the multi-faceted issues which bear upon young people's lives. Policies need to be better aligned and responses co-ordinated. Not least, services need to be shaped by the views of young people themselves and encouragement given to creating more youth-friendly communities. Such activity could usefully find expression within a three-year development plan, jointly prepared across major local services and the subsequent commissioning of specific initiatives across departmental and institutional boundaries. Data on the well being of young people should be collated and reported systematically. Such activity would begin to treat young people in the round and develop services – including those of schools – more attuned to their needs.

The interplay between social policy and the role of the individual educator is intriguingly captured in *Primary Colors*, the semi-fictional account of Clinton's race for the US Presidency in 1992. The Clinton character visited an innovative reading programme in Harlem and re-joined his wife in New Hampshire. They explored their respective preferences for charismatic teaching and well-constructed social programmes: 'You can't teach inspiration. What you do is come up with a curriculum' is counterpointed by the argument that 'if you can reward teachers for creativity they make their own program' (Anonymous, 1994).

The story's narrator adds his view that the reason for the success in Harlem was:

> the hunger is there. If everyone wanted to read, or whatever, as much as those folks did today, social policy would be a walk in the park. But you both know that's not where the problem is. It's creating the hunger for nutritious things when all they know is junk food.

(Ibid.)

The great enduring mission for educators, whatever their setting, is to create that hunger, and to play some part – blending charisma and curriculum in pointing the ways to its satisfaction.

References

Anonymous (1994) *Primary Colors*, Chatto & Windus, London

Aspire Consultants (1996) *Disaffection & Non-Participation in Education, Training and Employment by Individuals Aged 18-20*, TEC Network, London

Bernstein, B (1970) Education cannot compensate for society, *New Society*, February 1980

Brookfield, C and F B (1905) *Mrs Brookfield and Her Circle*, Pitman, London

Etzioni, A (1995) *The Spirit of Community: Rights, responsibilities and the communitarian agenda*, Collins, London

Goleman, D (1996) *Emotional Intelligence*, Bloomsbury, London

HM Inspectorate (1993) *Access and Achievement in Urban Education*, HMSO, London

Newsom, J (1963) *Half Our Future*, The Newsom Report, HMSO, London

Pahl and Spencer (1997) Friends and neighbours, *New Statesman*, September 1997

Patten, B (1996) The Minister for Exams, in Patten, B, *Armada*, HarperCollins, London

Power, A and Tunstall, R (1997) *Riots and Violent Disturbances in Thirteen Areas of Britain*, York Publishing Services, York

Robinson, P (1997) *Literacy, Numeracy and Economic Performance*, Centre for Education Reform, London

Rutter, M (1991) Pathways from childhood to adult life: The role of schooling, *Pastoral Care*, **9**, (3), September 1991, pp. 3–10

PART VI
Conclusion

12

The Future

Comprehensive Education for Democracy

Bob O'Hagan

The development of comprehensive education

At least as far as schools are concerned, the justifications advanced by governments for recent changes in education policy have been based in large measure on a series of myths, as we have shown. Introduced during the Thatcher years, particularly the second half of the 1980s, the Major administration subsequently pursued them with similar vigour. To the dismay of many professionals, the election of a Labour government did not result in the removal of these myths in determining the policy agenda. Moreover, although most schools, managers and teachers initially criticized and even sought to resist and undermine these changes and the ideology they reflect, many of the myths have taken root within the educational community.

This is not to decry all of the changes. Comprehensive schools have never remained static, nor has the comprehensive movement, and it cannot be argued that by the early 1980s comprehensives had reached their apogee. Policy had only made substantial progress up to that time in the very limited meaning of comprehensive schools, that they provide for all children to be educated within the same establishment. By then grammar and secondary modern schools had a rarity value in many parts of England, and had all but disappeared from Wales and Scotland.

This was only a very limited and tentative victory for the comprehensive reformers. Hargreaves (1982) was moved to observe:

> You will perhaps be familiar with the argument that the trouble with Christianity as a religion is that it has failed, and also familiar with the clever retort

197

that the only trouble with Christianity is that it has never really been tried. I often feel much the same about the comprehensive school. In pessimistic moments I side with those critics who believe it has failed, but when I see some of the marvellous things which are being achieved within comprehensive schools I visit, I then believe that we have not really tried it. And to say that is not to hurl gratuitous insults at the teachers in comprehensive schools, nor is it to denigrate the ideals towards which comprehensive schools are striving. It is, rather, to acknowledge that we are only part of the way there. That is because most of us vastly underestimated the difficulties of creating a comprehensive school, which was so very much more than simply educating all pupils under one roof.

In terms of what went on in comprehensives, there appeared to be a long way still to go. Benn and Chitty (1996, Chapter 6) demonstrated that, although streaming by ability had all but disappeared from comprehensives in the 25 years following the early comprehensive drive (Benn and Simon, 1970), in most cases it had been replaced by other forms of division, including highly stratified setting arrangements. Ball (1997) commented that 'many so-called comprehensive schools clearly had embedded in their practice the aims, values and assumptions of... "segregated education"'. Almost certainly though, the practice of professionals 'on the ground' had moved on. Virtually a new generation of teachers, trained in cognizance of the comprehensive ideal, now populated classrooms and, importantly, staffrooms. Furthermore, pastoral care as a core service within comprehensives had developed and expanded dramatically. With the active support and encouragement of local authorities and government, schools now sought systematically to help children displaying a wide range of personal, academic and social difficulties to be able to cope with the demands of the curriculum. The 'pastoral curriculum' had been born, through initiatives in personal and social education as well as careers guidance. In general, comprehensive schools had become aware of their social responsibilities as well as their academic ones.

Heads, teachers and advisers, well versed in the new demands of comprehensive schooling and mixed-ability teaching, had been introducing their own 'professionally-driven' changes. There were many examples of innovations and experiments at the classroom or institutional level that were setting the agenda for policy-makers to follow, through intermediary institutions like the Schools Council.

Many comprehensive schools had developed excellent practices. However, with the agenda for change being driven from below, and national government responding rather than leading, problems emerged. After all, many schools described as comprehensive still dealt with intakes that remained either well above or well below the national average. Not surprisingly, they encountered fewer of the problems faced by others serving more mixed areas, and in general they were slower to adapt from the traditional styles of grammars and secondary moderns, respectively. Moreover, the private sector remained strong, at least in England, and grew considerably in and around the cities, especially London.

Those serving more deprived areas, often encouraged by their local education authorities, saw the social function of the comprehensive as their primary goal. There can be little doubt that teachers in these schools, like those in the secondary moderns before them, often betrayed low expectations of their children's achievements in terms of academic success. In these schools, subjects, courses and work that could motivate students tangentially, by association rather than intrinsically, sometimes replaced challenging and demanding tasks.

While some comprehensives, especially those serving more disadvantaged areas, fell short of the comprehensive ideal because of their low expectations and student achievements, others associated comprehensive education with a simplistic notion of equality. In its worst form, this notion sought to limit the learning opportunities for those from more advantaged backgrounds if such opportunities allowed them to advance more rapidly than their less advantaged peers. Homework might not be set at all, for fear that it would allow those with helpful parents and lots of reference books at home to benefit unequally. Recognizing that repeated failure usually lowers motivation, they tended to avoid setting demanding tasks and ignored the fact that for many students, failure can be a spur to greater efforts and involvement. In these cases, a version of equality could be achieved, but at the cost of catering to the lowest common denominator.

A third weakness of comprehensives by the early 1980s was the prominence given in some cases to a goal of social engineering. Some saw comprehensives as a means of reducing conflict and division, and of combating the ravages of a class-ridden society. In these schools, individual and group differences were considered anti-social, the cause of envy and aggression. In its most extreme form, for example, it led to calls to abandon competition altogether in school sports.

Whether these weaknesses laid the ground for, or even caused, the subsequent backlash against comprehensive development will be a matter for historians to decide. Undoubtedly, the comprehensive vision was not yet fully articulated. It had become clear that the politicians' claim that comprehensive education would mean 'a grammar school education for all,' was a myth. The premise was wrong.[1] But there was not yet a clearly articulated alternative meaning for what comprehensive education could offer, and too much attention had been attached to denigrating purely academic or intellectual achievement – the development of children's mental faculties and powers – as an acceptable goal. The pendulum had swung too much towards promoting the social function of comprehensives as their main *raison d'être*.

In any event, the public criticism of comprehensives by Prime Minister Callaghan in his 1976 Ruskin College speech became sharper with the election of Margaret Thatcher's Conservative government three years later. Above all, her administration sought to wrest control of the policy agenda from the professionals both in schools and local authorities, and to ensure that government should take the helm in determining the shape and purposes of education.

Despite her public criticism of the social engineering purposes assumed by many supporters of comprehensives, far from distancing education from political intervention, her administration could not resist the temptation to use education to promote its own particular vision of society. During the first half of the 1980s, under the influence of Education Secretary Keith Joseph and Manpower Services Commission Chairman (later Employment Secretary) David Young, she sought to fashion education as a servant of industry. Schools should provide the labour force required for a modern economy. Many commentators have ignored the way in which these early Thatcher years actually promoted a more inclusive – comprehensive even – vision for education. It was during this period that the (New) Technical and Vocational Education Initiative, the GCSE and the post-16 vocational precursor for schools, the Certificate in Pre-Vocational Education, were introduced. Each of these was aimed inclusively at every state school, whether grammar, comprehensive or secondary modern. In addition, they were designed to reduce the purely academic nature of more traditional courses for 14–18 year olds, while propelling more practical, skill-based activities into the range of acceptable status-bearing qualifications. These were, in fact, precisely the sort of positive, forward-looking changes advocated for older students by Ken Spours in Chapter 8.

However, the departure of Keith Joseph and the arrival of Kenneth Baker as Education Secretary coincided with an ideological shift in the Conservatives' vision of education. Henceforward, it would still retain its social engineering role, but the previous inclusive, academic–vocational bridging aspect of policy changes was dismissed in favour of much more traditional, divisive curricular purposes with the accent on preserving academic privilege. Socially, it aimed to promote individual and social behaviour that both reflected and supported the efficient operation of the commercial marketplace through notions of individual and social competition (Ball, 1997).

The Major administration declared its allegiance to its more recent Thatcher inheritance. However, the arrival of New Labour appears to mark both continuity and discontinuity. While there are some signs of adherence to a market-driven model, the Blair–Blunkett policies appear to owe more to the Joseph–Young years than to Kenneth Baker and his Conservative successors. Once again, education has a clear social engineering purpose, but it is above all to provide a labour force fit for a modern economy. The New

Labour government has declared itself opposed to creeping selection and in support of an inclusive education system. Yet it is clearly unwilling to relinquish its leading role in determining the shape and purpose of education, or to devolve significant power to local government, and still less to the professional educators. Taking these policies together, it appears to owe much more to the earlier Thatcher years than to the later ones.

Successive governments have justified these radical breaks with the preceding comprehensive consensus by reference to philosophies, or ideologies, that are based on a sequence of myths, as we have seen throughout this volume. The comprehensive ideal, if it is to provide a realistic alternative once again, must not betray the same fallacious underpinning. This rules out a call to return to past forms of the comprehensive school or college.

The democratic foundations of comprehensive education

What will be the features of a future comprehensive system, when the age of myth has passed? Above all, the enduring characteristic of the comprehensive education system is its commitment to democratic principles. More than anything, the comprehensive ideal is a democratic ideal. The democratic, and indeed the comprehensive, tradition in education stretches back to the nineteenth century, as Benn and Chitty showed in Chapter 1. The nineteenth century was much preoccupied with developing political democracy, in the wake of the French and American Revolutions. And it is in the watchwords of the French Revolution that we may find the key purposes of democratic organization: Liberty, Equality and Fraternity. In modern-day language, these three can be termed Freedom, Fairness and Friendship.

I now wish to explore the meaning of each of these three purposes in relation to the comprehensive school. It is worth bearing in mind that, like the other purposes we have already considered, democratic education contains an element of social engineering. It not only describes a distinctive aspect of the nature of learning (education *in* democracy) and a distinctive pedagogical stance (education *through* democracy), but also a distinctive additional goal or outcome (education *for* democracy). The concept of democracy thus provides a frame of reference or orientation to education.

Liberty, or freedom

First, comprehensive education has a vision of emancipation. Pring (1997, p. 83) emphasizes this:

'Emancipation' is a useful metaphor, for education is to be contrasted with the kind of enslavement associated with ignorance and with the lack of those mental powers, without which one is so easily duped and deceived. To be educated, therefore, is at least this – to be in possession of those understandings, knowledge, skills and dispositions whereby one makes sense of the world around one: the physical world to be understood through the sciences and mathematics, the social and political world within which one's life is too often shaped by others, the moral world of ideals and responsibilities, and the aesthetic world of beauty and style through which one finds pleasure and delight. But entry into those different worlds is more than a making sense of that which is inherited from others. It gives access to the ideas, and thus the tools, through which the learner's own distinctive personal development might actively take place.

Education has the potential to free people from the confinement of their circumstances. Without knowledge, skills and understanding we are at the mercy of physical and human forces external to us. With a mastery of literacy, numeracy and other forms of communication we can express ourselves, understand and influence others. By acquiring skills we can shape our environment, and through complex understanding of things, people, systems and processes we can begin to take control of our own destinies. Of course, for most of us an important element of this will be our ability to secure employment. However, comprehensive education does not seek to engineer this simply in order to provide an efficient workforce or to improve the competitiveness of the national economy. It is primarily in order to enable our students to transcend the limits of their circumstances, both mentally and materially. The circumstances of our birth, for example the economic and cultural capital of our family and neighbourhood, significantly affect our life-chances, but they need not determine anyone's life-chances, at least in a democratic society. Education offers everyone in society the chance to overcome the circumstances of their birth. In fact, knowledge is not itself power, but it is a vital resource in the struggle to change the balance of power (O'Hagan, 1991).

The formal curriculum, both of the school or college as a whole and for each individual, should nurture imagination, creativity, initiative, action and reflection. It should develop a personal sense of purpose and direction. Students should increasingly take responsibility for their own learning, although teachers should exercise their responsibility to ensure that progress and rigour feature within every student's curriculum. There should be an emphasis on active, problem-solving and – more importantly – problem-posing learning styles for all students. To adapt one of Winston Churchill's phrases, every ordinary student is capable of extraordinary achievement.

Clearly, this is not an argument for everyone's learning experience to be the same. On the contrary, emancipatory comprehensive education will develop every individual's talents as well as tackling their weaknesses. For example, the education of a child displaying great sporting potential, but lacking in literacy and numeracy, is not emancipatory if it ignores these weaknesses. Equally though, the comprehensive school is obliged to nurture and extend that special sporting talent.

> A society based on custom will utilize individual variations only up to a limit of conformity with usage; uniformity is the chief ideal within each class. A progressive society counts individual variations as precious since it finds in them the means of its own growth. Hence a democratic society must, in consistency with its ideal, allow for intellectual freedom and the play of diverse gifts and interests in its educational measures.

> (Dewey, 1916: p. 305)

In Chapter 6, Michael Armstrong showed, with the use of a primary school narrative, how the National Curriculum and its associated assessment criteria tend to mould naturally creative expression towards a mediocre uniformity, the antithesis of democratic education for freedom.

As well as promoting freedom for the individual as an outcome, the democratic comprehensive has as its purpose education *through* freedom. Such a school is organized in a way that allows freedom of expression and choice. This is not the same as libertarian education, or educational licence. We are concerned here with democratic education, which has two other dimensions as well as freedom, so this is very far from an argument for licence. As in all democracies, the dimensions of fairness and friendship circumscribe aspects of freedom, so that individual rights for students within the comprehensive imply corresponding duties. Within a democracy, individual responsibility and accountability counterbalance the right to personal freedom. Young people, as emerging personalities developing a personal moral code, cannot be held accountable for their actions in quite the same way that adults can be. However, through their behaviour codes and disciplinary procedures, all schools do demand a large measure of accountability in any case – more, in most cases, than is implied by the degree of freedom they allow to their students. Comprehensive schools, more than other types of school, should enable students to develop the qualities needed to command personal freedom through their own policies, practices, procedures and relationships.

This dimension urges against custom, routine and regimentation and in favour of articulate self-expression, individuality and choice for students in an environment where by tradition, the teachers set most of the rules. Enabling students to play a fully democratic part in rule-setting and school self-evaluation is but one way in which they can express a commitment to the principle of liberty. Moreover, it enables them to practise the values and skills of citizenship, as advocated particularly by Tim Brighouse in Chapter 9 and Tom Wylie in Chapter 11.

The comprehensive school bears a particular responsibility for developing every individual. It must also provide opportunities for students to make real choices about their own education. It must balance the twin needs of covering the basic knowledge and skills needed by everyone – the minimum curriculum – and developing and promoting personal excellence in all its forms. Inevitably, this means setting the highest expectations for all students, and enabling competition between individuals and teams, without making competition its mainspring.

Equality, or fairness

The principle of liberty or freedom finds expression most prominently through the arrangement of the formal curriculum, including both the whole school curriculum and each individual's curriculum. The principle of equality or fairness is more often evident in the operation of what is called the 'hidden curriculum'. As I have already argued, it is not a matter of providing equal outcomes; clearly, this would contradict the principle of freedom. Nevertheless, the fruits of society are not distributed equally, and democratic education has a part to play, however small, in redressing such inequalities. Children arrive at school with different abilities, and few today would argue that education need only allow each to take what they can from the opportunities 'equally' available to all. Comprehensive schools must be prepared to allocate resources unequally in order to promote fairness. All schools are obliged to do so in any case to assist those with special educational needs. Most have also gone through a stage in the 1980s of targeting attention on girls as an underprivileged group and now find themselves doing the opposite to promote boys' achievement. If all students are to become freer through schooling, comprehensives must organize themselves to enable all young people to take advantage of the learning opportunities provided.

Whatever the 'mission statement' or formal school aims, whether a school promotes fairness can be felt through its pores, its atmosphere and ethos. Fairness is not characterized by impartiality. It is partial on behalf of the disadvantaged and those who suffer unfair treatment. It is not undiscriminating; it helps young people to develop sophisticated powers of discrimination, although it seeks to establish a pervasive climate in which expressions of prejudice and unfair discrimination are challenged by all members of the community.

Such a climate will help young people to appreciate the rights of everyone to positive discrimination, to extra resources and attention at some stage, and that for some this will continue to be necessary. Young people commonly have a keen sense of natural justice, and have a sophisticated appreciation that upholding equality does not mean dealing with everyone in exactly the same way.

Democracy is not just a matter of counting votes either. Such a simplistic notion can lead to the tyranny of the majority. Democratic education also requires protection of minorities, and of the individual. While they have an obligation to widen the franchise to include students in decision-making processes, comprehensive schools must also operate within a charter or constitutional framework that prevents individuals and groups being treated unfairly by the majority.

Fraternity, or friendship

The principle of fraternity, or friendship reflects a commitment to fostering supportive relationships between individuals and between groups, strengthening bonds of commonality and solidarity within the local, national and international communities. Over the last century, and during the past few decades in particular, social life has become more segmented. Life consists much less of common, shared experiences. Whereas in the past, people within a neighbourhood experienced family life, school, work and leisure to a large degree in common, whether in cities or villages, nowadays they are involved in activities that are more diverse and divergent. The inhabitants of a street are unlikely to share a common workplace, to take part in the same leisure activities or even to have the same family structure. There is much more movement to a variety of locations during the course of a day. The corner shop, pub, working men's club or church is unlikely to be an all-embracing meeting place for the community, where discourse cements the sharing of experience. For some, the football ground, the primary school gate or the community centre provides a venue for these shared experiences, but even these are much diminished in comparison. This is not to say that life is lived in a more isolated way, although the need for groups like the Samaritans might suggest this is also the case. Rather, we are members of many more groups and our existence moves in a wide network of looser relationships. Our membership of these groups is more likely to be the result of a personal choice, reflecting the complex set of interests and passions that we each have. The shift from an organic to a more functional solidarity has been inexorable.

The school, particularly the comprehensive school, whether primary or secondary, remains a dominant shared experience for children, second only to the family in most cases. Yet outside of the school, young people share in activities with different groups for different purposes here too.

There are, after all, countless organized activities, as well as looser clubs and societies competing for their leisure time.

Thus, while our waking lives are still predominantly spent in social activities of one kind or another, these activities are ever more diverse, and the number of relationships we enter into is ever increasing. If schools are to help prepare young people for such an existence, it means that they must teach cohorts that do not display homogeneity. Furthermore, it means that they must help young people to deal effectively with an almost bewildering variety of relationships.

Indeed, it demands even more of the comprehensive school, which is the most heterogeneous type of school. The pastoral curriculum in particular should promote human relations that are caring and tolerant of individual differences and that respect the needs, rights and beliefs of others. Since young people will associate with many people who do not share the same, or even similar, experiences, they must be encouraged through teaching to develop empathy for others and a repertoire for effective communication. They also need to acquire an awareness of cultural variation and to value the distinctive contributions different groups have made and continue to make to our cultural heritage. Collectively, our cultural heritage has diverse roots. They come together to make up a single cultural heritage though. The Anglo-Saxons, the Normans, the Huguenots, the Irish, the Afro-Caribbeans, the Indians, the Chinese and so on have all made a contribution to contemporary British culture which is different from the contributions they have made to any other cultural heritage. This fact makes British culture, or any other culture for that matter, unique. Those who now identify with Britain share that common culture.

In truth, democratic education has to be inclusive. Caroline Benn and Clyde Chitty pointed to the central importance of the comprehensive school and the comprehensive system in this endeavour in Chapter 1. The segregationist and ultimately divisive nature of non-comprehensive systems prevents the successful achievement of these objectives.

AH Halsey based his 1978 Reith Lectures on the *social principle of fraternity* as a solution to growing social conflict. Critical to this would be increasing awareness of a shared common culture – human feelings, needs, aspirations and understandings. Divided schooling would hinder the development of such shared understanding and a common culture (Halsey, 1978). The task of democratic education following the principle of fraternity is to help young people towards that shared understanding.

The dimension of friendship points not only to the need to develop young people's interpersonal skills though. Recognizing the dysfunctional aspects of more heterogeneous groups and the inherent danger of disintegration, it points to another aspect of social engineering – the building of a unity that does not arise from common experience or interests. Such integration requires a functional solidarity – something more than a social contract – that binds the loose network of individuals and groups together. This sort of solidarity has to be created within the institution of the school, but also taking account of the neighbourhood, regional, national and international levels of community.

Reinforcing Caroline Benn and Clyde Chitty, Michael Fielding has shown in Chapter 4 how policies pursued in recent years have operated in the opposite direction, destroying rather than building community. Further, he has shown how they have taken dangerous root in the language and practices of many schools, including comprehensives. Equally, the pressures of the National Curriculum have led many schools to reduce the time they devote to teaching interpersonal skills and to promoting solidarity at these various levels.

It will be clear that the comprehensive school that seeks to become an insulated safe haven for its pupils within a turbulent world is tilting against the historical wind as well as undermining fraternity. Colin Fletcher's chapter argued cogently for comprehensives to welcome parents, not just as helpers, supporters and vicarious consumers, but as equal partners. This is not simply a matter of helping parents to participate in the school's agenda but for schools to accept parents' interests and needs and to devote some of their energies to realizing them.

More than any other of the three principles underpinning democracy, fraternity calls for a community dimension to schooling. A school undermines fraternity if it tries to insulate its curriculum from the home, as if students enter a capsule as they enter the school, to be taught by predominantly white European, middle-class teachers who live some distance away. Supplementing the National Curriculum and school curriculum with a home–community curriculum of the sort described by Tim Brighouse in Chapter 9 will enable the school to promote and even embody part of that common culture. Tom Wylie's chapter exemplified the directions the comprehensive school must take if it is to develop neighbourhood solidarity, a key element of fraternity.

Combining freedom, fairness and friendship

The association of the three demands Liberty, Equality and Fraternity began as a rallying cry for democrats in the French Revolution. Although for many it was discredited by the subsequent actions of the Revolution's victorious leaders, the linking of these three dimensions remains a powerful tool for evaluating democratic intent. Any one of the three dimensions, taken alone, contains anti-democratic elements. It is only by triangulating the different perspectives that one can bring the complexity of the democratic ideal into focus. Fielding (1989) asserts:

> Adherence to the principle of liberty ensures the freedom to speak and to act. The principle of equality guarantees not only the hand of reciprocity, but also the psychological confidence which both supports and conditions that freedom so that it does not become dominating or condescending. Fraternity is a kind of caring – one which is neither restrictive nor possessive of any of the parties to the relationship.

Tensions exist between the elements. The pure pursuit of liberty pays scant regard to equality or friendship. The single-minded enforcement of equality limits personal freedom and tests friendship, while placing fraternal ties above other values will almost certainly deny wider freedom and equality. Each dimension tempers the other two without over-riding or obscuring them. In combination, we see the positive democratic elements of each.

To some extent, the most destructive of the modern educational myths have arisen from an ideology in which individual liberty has had a paramount position. More than anything of course, this has been the Thatcher legacy, its weaknesses not only evident in education. The comprehensive ideal balances the three principles, and there can be little doubt that proponents at every stage of its history have appreciated the importance of personal freedom alongside the others. Indeed, it was perhaps more than anything else, outrage at the denial of freedom to so many, virtually guaranteed by their second-class secondary modern school, that has spurred successive supporters of comprehensive reorganizations. Nevertheless, particular governments, local authorities and schools have failed to realize the ideal, giving one or another of the three principles undue importance or even paramount status. In some cases, the pursuit of equality has denied some students a truly liberating education and generated unnecessary division and conflict. In others, an almost exclusive emphasis on social and moral education and personal relations has denied some students access to intellectual stimulation and failed to address problems of inequality adequately. And in the wake of policy changes in the past decade, the pressure towards individual achievement and personal choice has been at the cost of fairness and collective solidarity.

Implications within the comprehensive school

The challenge for comprehensive school managers is to create an organization that balances these dimensions for the whole school as well as for each of its students. As Stephen Ball has shown in Chapter 5, the New

Managerialism is particularly unbalanced in this regard. Caroline Benn and Clyde Chitty pointed out how so-called parental choice of school – linked to performance tables, limited school capacity and funding driven by pupil numbers – has actually resulted in a greater tendency for schools to choose their pupils. This is unfair, it undermines the comprehensive principle and it has led to greater polarization. However, making schools more comprehensive in future will make them even more heterogeneous than I have argued they have become already. This is the conundrum for school managers. Ensuring that all students enjoy a liberating education by developing their various talents (and, more complex still, recognizing that the individual's talents and potential change over time) while guaranteeing fairness and friendship is very demanding for a single, heterogeneous institution. Comprehensive schools are inherently large, for reasons of economies of scale, and providing each student with almost a unique curricular provision to meet their particular needs, interests and talents is unlikely to be easy.

It is not realistic to expect teachers to take a heterogeneous group and provide a fully individualized learning experience that is rigorous. Most teachers can and do teach classes in a differentiated way, but they organize the work, broadly speaking, according to three sub-groups: the average, above average and below average. For most teachers, this is true whether they are teaching a mixed ability or a severely streamed or setted class, in a comprehensive or a selective school. Few lack the ability to do this, and many can differentiate the work almost to the level of the individual for the duration of a lesson or two. Of course, individualized learning of this sort is a standard method to the special needs teacher who is charged with tiny numbers of pupils at one time. For the class teacher, though, I do not believe such a high level of differentiation is possible for an extended period with the class sizes typical of the modern school.

There are alternative ways of achieving greater differentiation for the heterogeneous class, and thereby meeting the challenge of freedom without sacrificing fairness or friendship. One of these is through differentiated homework tasks. Where a good deal of the differentiation that is possible within the classroom is achieved through outcome rather than task, homework provides greater opportunities to achieve differentiation by task. Thus, the most talented students in the class can be set particularly demanding tasks, and those with least aptitude quite different homework. While normal class teaching addresses triple-tranche differentiation, differentiated homework can enable at least two more tranches to be added. Particularly where homework tasks are planned by the teacher in advance, the educational route or experience for students through any one course is considerably more differentiated.

It is possible for teachers to provide more differentiated learning without making it unmanageable for the professional. There is a parallel task for the school's managers: to individualize the curriculum in a way that is practicable in a large comprehensive.

Differentiated homework is only one of the manageable ways to achieve more heterogeneity in the routes through schooling. Extra-curricular activities such as clubs provide opportunities to develop particular student interests. In recent years, many schools have extended the range by adding voluntary activities for academic subjects such as maths, science and languages to the traditional arts and sports clubs. Form teachers and personal tutors commonly provide individual guidance and counselling to every student, often on a regular, structured and intensive basis. Where the tutors are skilled and trained, the educational experience of each student is likely to be different, of course. Many schools supplement this with intensive mentoring, either by their own staff or by outside volunteers, and others assign tutors or mentors for particular subjects.

Tim Brighouse has offered a useful checklist of other forms of provision that can link the work of schools in their 15 per cent of waking time with the diverse worlds of the other 85 per cent. They represent a potential home–community curriculum entitlement, but they also afford further opportunities for supporting and building on the diversity of needs and talents. They include residentials, holiday learning, public performances and sporting events.

In these and other ways, comprehensive schools and colleges can provide increasingly individualized educational experiences for an ever more heterogeneous student population within the concept of entitlement. In principle, this is achieved in a manageable way by analysing and tracking students' needs, interests and aptitudes across a broad range of dimensions. It is manageable to provide a limited number of alternative arrangements or experiences for each of the dimensions, and within such a matrix to multiply exponentially the number of ways in which these arrangements can be combined. Many thousands of combinations can cater for the diversity of student needs by providing only tens of different schemes for example.

At the same time, however, the school does not sacrifice equality or fairness, provided all students benefit similarly, and no group is unfairly advantaged when the whole of their curriculum is taken into account. All students should be entitled to proportionately more resources and attention for some part or parts of their educational life, and those who are most in need can be sure of more favourable treatment throughout their schooling.

If a comprehensive school is to practise democracy, then the dimensions of freedom, fairness and friendship provide a sort of 'moral constitution' which constrains the formulation of policies and procedures. Provided they do not offend against the balance of these three, policies and procedures should be arrived at democratically. This does mean involvement of students and teachers at important stages in the policy-making process. Where, for the sake of efficiency, certain individuals and groups have freedom of responsibility, with it must go accountability. Accountability is one of the ways in which equality tempers freedom and prevents excesses. Thus, for example, while the Head Teacher is inevitably accountable to governors and other outside organizations, including parents following Colin Fletcher's argument, in a democratic school, she or he will also be accountable to staff and to students. A comprehensive school should not lack the formal mechanisms of representative democracy.

Implications for comprehensive schools

Comprehensive schools should be accountable for their adherence to democratic principles. School governors have an important role 'on the spot' but they are essentially part of the school's own organization. On the other hand, central government, even through its appointed quangos, is too remote to offer a mechanism of accountability. As Maurice Kogan has argued in Chapter 3, their knowledge is 'cold'. He has elaborated the case for teachers and schools to enjoy more professional freedom but this too must be tempered by accountability which he represents as a 'corporatist bargain'.

If schools are to be democratically accountable for their democratic organization and outcomes, some sort of representative local authority is needed, and in Chapter 2, Valerie Hannon outlined what form such an organization might take in future. Such a body – let us call it the Local Education Authority for simplicity's sake – will also have an obligation to promote freedom, fairness and friendship among the schools in its area. They should be accountable to it and it should be accountable to them.

Freedom

The LEA should help to liberate *schools*, by developing their talents and helping them to tackle their weaknesses, just as the school should with its *pupils*. Like pupils, comprehensive schools should be expected to display heterogeneity. Diversity should be encouraged and innovation welcomed. However, the reason for this is not in order to provide a 'genuine choice for parents'; as Benn and Chitty have shown in Chapter 1, this is not the outcome anyway. Rather, its purposes are to allow the talents and interests of teachers to flourish and to allow the school to reflect local factors that distinguish it from others. If schools are accountable in some measure to parents and students, then we should expect schools to have distinctive features. LEAs should encourage and provide support for such individual freedom. As Maurice Kogan and Valerie Hannon have suggested, less government interference should mean more not less accountability for schools and should be accompanied by a consequently greater, if different, role for local government. Michael Armstrong's arguments in Chapter 6 against the tyranny of mediocrity attendant upon the detailed national curriculum, and Bob Moon's critique of the standardized test's inevitable 'bell curve' provide good grounds for less government specification of detail. LEAs should not take their place and impose their own tyrannies but as Valerie Hannon explained, they can help to moderate the greater freedom that would then be available to schools.

Fairness

Accountability of schools to LEAs is necessary to ensure fairness, for as I have argued, accountability is a means by which fairness tempers freedom. The educational market has signally failed to provide a forum for school accountability and, by polarizing school intakes, has failed to generate school improvement. LEAs are uniquely placed to promote fairness between schools, to divert additional resources when needed and to discriminate positively when needed. All schools need help from time to time, and most importantly, some body representative of the whole community must arbitrate between schools in conflict. Similarly, government has to unlock the sort of curriculum gridlock occasioned by the intransigence of academic qualifications. In Chapter 8, Ken Spours articulated a vision, and the stages towards it, for the unification of the academic and the vocational.

Friendship

Almost everyone with more than a passing involvement in schools longs for co-operation to replace competition. Taking the parallel of the 'common culture' described above, one of the most notable features of the present arrangement of schools is that even so-called comprehensives do not share a 'common educational culture'. Michael Fielding and Stephen Ball referred to the dysfunctions of competition and separate 'corporate cultures' that separate professionals from one another. If schools have opposing visions and are unable to co-operate, then one of the responsibilities of a LEA should be to bring sympathy and harmony by establishing and expressing a collective vision. LEAs can provide a moral lead for the schools they represent.

In essence, comprehensive schools are the educational arm of a democratic society. If, as I fervently hope, these modern educational myths are exposed and quickly consigned to history, then the comprehensive school will be able to continue its historic mission: to bring freedom, fairness and friendship through a form of community education to generations to come.

Note

1. Paradoxically, Pring (1997) makes the opposite remark, that too much emphasis among the early comprehensives on re-creating the traditional academic curriculum had 'created that earlier comprehensive ideal, namely, a "grammar school education for all" which, inappropriate for many, resulted in so much alienation from formal education'.

References

Ball, S (1997) Markets, equity and values in education, in R Pring and G Walford (eds) *Affirming the Comprehensive Ideal*, pp. 69–82, Falmer, London

Benn, C and Chitty, C (1996) *Thirty Years On: Is Comprehensive Education Alive And Well Or Struggling To Survive?*, David Fulton, London

Benn, C and Simon, B (1970) *Half Way There*, Penguin, Harmondsworth

Dewey, J (1916) *Democracy And Education*, Free Press Edition (1996), Collier-Macmillan, London

Fielding, M (1989) The fraternal foundations of democracy: towards emancipatory practice in school-based INSET, in C Harber and R Meighan (eds) *The Democratic School: Educational Management and the Practice of Democracy*, pp. 133–45, Education Now, Ticknall

Halsey, AH (1978) Change in British society, Reith Lectures, quoted in R Pring and G Walford (eds) *Affirming the Comprehensive School*, p. 87, Falmer, London

Hargreaves, D (1982) 'Making schools comprehensive: some alternative proposals, in C Harber, R Meighan and B Roberts (eds) *Alternative Educational Futures*, pp. 27–39, Holt, Rinehart & Winston, London

O'Hagan, B (1991) Fallacy: knowledge is power, in B O'Hagan (ed.) *The Charnwood Papers: Fallacies in Community Education*, pp. 107–22, Education Now, Ticknall

Pring, R (1997) Educating persons, in R Pring and G Walford (eds) *Affirming the Comprehensive Ideal*, pp. 83–96, Falmer, London

Index

VISIT KOGAN PAGE
ON-LINE

http://www.kogan-page.co.uk

For comprehensive information on Kogan Page titles, visit our website.

Features include

- complete catalogue listings, including book reviews and descriptions

- special monthly promotions

- information on NEW titles and BESTSELLING titles

- a secure shopping basket facility for on-line ordering

PLUS everything you need to know about
KOGAN PAGE